THE VIETNAM WAR

WITHDRAWN

THE VIETNAM WAR

Edited by

Peter Lowe
Reader in History
University of Manchester

First published 1998 by
MACMILLAN PRESS LTD
Houndmills, Basingstoke, Hampshire RG21 6XS
and London
Companies and representatives throughout the world

ISBN 0–333–65830–2 hardcover
ISBN 0–333–65831–0 paperback

A catalogue record for this book is available from the British Library.

This book is printed on paper suitable for recycling and made from
fully managed and sustained forest sources.

10   9   8   7   6   5   4   3   2   1
07   06   05   04   03   02   01   00   99   98

Printed in Hong Kong

CONTENTS

v

Acknowledgements

I am most grateful to Professor Brian Pullan for inviting me to edit the first volume in a new series, associated with the Department of History in the University of Manchester, of which he is the general editor. I have been greatly encouraged by the enthusiasm and vigour revealed by the contributors to this volume. They have responded carefully and effectively to produce lucid, concise surveys of the principal issues relating to the country or theme examined in their essays. The outcome is a trenchant analysis of developments determining the course of the conflict in Vietnam. Professor Stein Tønnesson gave me helpful advice at an early stage of planning which was much appreciated. I have received additional encouragement and guidance from the staff of Macmillan, particularly from Jonathan Reeve. I am grateful to Keith Povey for his considerable assistance as copy-editor. Finally, I wish to thank Jean Davenport for her customary efficiency in assisting with typing.

The editor and publishers wish to thank the following for permission to use copyright material:

Oxford University Press for reuse of material from Chen Jian 'China and the first Indo-China War 1950–1954' (March 1993) and 'China's Involvement in the Vietnam War, 1964–1969' (July 1995), both published in *The China Quarterly*.

PETER LOWE

ABBREVIATIONS

AATV	Australian Army Training Team, Vietnam
ALP	Australian Labor Party
ANZAM	Australia, New Zealand and Malay Agreement
ANZUS	Australia, New Zealand, United States Agreement
ARVN	Army of the Republic of Vietnam (South Vietnam)
BRIAM	British Advisory Mission
CCP	Chinese Communist Party
CCDS	Central Committee Directorate for the South
CIA	Central Intelligence Agency
CMAG	Chinese Military Advisory Group
COSVN	Central Office for South Vietnam
CPSU	Communist Party of the Soviet Union
DLP	Democratic Labor Party
DRV	Democratic Republic of Vietnam (North Vietnam)
FBI	Federal Bureau of Investigation
GVN	Government of South Vietnam
ICC	International Control Commission
ICP	Indochinese Communist Party
LBJ	Lyndon Baines Johnson
MACV	Military Assistance Command, Vietnam
NATO	North Atlantic Treaty Organization
NLF	National Liberation Front
NSC	National Security Council
NVA	North Vietnamese Army
PAVN	People's Army of Vietnam (North Vietnam)
PLA	People's Liberation Army (China)
PLAVN	People's Liberation Army (North Vietnam)
PRC	People's Republic of China
PRG	People's Revolutionary Government
RAN	Royal Australian Navy

ROTC	Reserve Officers Training Corps
RVN	Republic of Vietnam (South Vietnam)
SANE	Committee for a Sane Nuclear Policy
SDS	Students for a Democratic Society
SEATO	South East Asia Treaty Organization
SWP	Socialists Workers Party
UN	United Nations
US	United States
VWP	Vietnamese Workers Party

NOTES ON THE CONTRIBUTORS

David L. Anderson is Professor of History and Chair of the Department of History and Political Science at the University of Indianapolis. His books include *Trapped by Success: the Eisenhower Administration and Vietnam* (1991), *Shadow on the White House: Presidents and the Vietnam War* (1993), and *Facing My Lai: Moving beyond the Massacre* (1998).

Carl Bridge is Professor of Australian Studies and Head of the Sir Robert Menzies Centre for Australian Studies, University of London. His recent works include two edited books, *Munich to Vietnam* (Melbourne, 1991) and *Manning Clark* (Melbourne, 1994).

Chen Jian is an Associate Professor of History at Southern Ilinois University and was a senior fellow at the United States Institute of Peace for the 1996–7 academic year. He has taught previously at East China Normal University, Tibetan Nationality College, and the State University of New York at Geneseo. Among his publications are *China's Road to the Korean War* (1994) and *Chinese Communist Foreign Policy and the cold war in Asia* (co-editor, 1996).

Ilya V. Gaiduk is a research fellow at the Institute of World History in Moscow, specializing in Soviet–American relations. He has been a fellow of the cold war International History Project at the Woodrow Wilson Center for Scholars in Washington, DC and of the Norwegian Nobel Institute. He is the author of *The Soviet Union and the Vietnam War* (1996).

Ngo Vinh Long is Associate Professor of Asian Studies at the University of Maine, teaching courses on China, Japan, South Asia, South-East Asia, and the United States' relations with Asian countries. He serves as a coordinator of several research projects on social and economic issues in Vietnam. His publications include *Before the Revolution: The Vietnamese Peasants under the French* (1973, 1991), *Vietnamese Women in Society and Revolution* (1974) and *Coming to Terms: The United States, Indochina and the War* (co-editor, 1991).

Peter Lowe is Reader in History at the University of Manchester. Among his publications are *Containing the cold war in East Asia: British Policies towards Japan, China and Korea, 1948–1953* (1997) and *The Origins of the Korean War,* second edition (1997).

Alastair Parker studied Modern History at Christ Church, Oxford. After serving as a lecturer in the University of Manchester, he became a Fellow of Queen's College, Oxford in 1957. His recent publications include *Struggle for Survival: the History of the Second World War* (1989) and *Chamberlain and Appeasement* (1993).

Anthony Short was formerly Reader in International Relations and Warden of Dunbar Hall in the University of Aberdeen. Among his publications are *The Communist Insurrection in Malaya, 1948–1960* (1975) and *The Origins of the Vietnam War* (1989).

Nguyen Vu Tung is a graduate of the Fletcher School of Law and Diplomacy, Tufts University. He is a researcher at the Institute of International Relations, Hanoi, and is the author of a number of articles on political and security developments in contemporary South-East Asia.

Tom Wells earned a PhD in Sociology from the University of California, Berkeley, and has taught at the University of San Francisco, San Jose State University and Mills College. He is the author of *The War Within: America's Battle over Vietnam* (1994, paperback, 1996). He is currently writing a biography of Daniel Ellsberg.

INTRODUCTION

Peter Lowe

The conflict in Vietnam was one of the most traumatic and long-lasting struggles, pursued within the broad context of the cold war, since the conclusion of the Second World War. For the peoples of Vietnam – to which Cambodia and Laos may be added for much of the period – a generation of suffering, injury and death arising from the bitter strife between occidental forces and indigenous movements ended in April 1975 with the collapse of the brittle anti-communist regimes in South Vietnam, Cambodia and Laos. The close of an era dominated by French and American endeavours to contain communist–nationalist movements ironically did not herald the dawn of an era of peace. Cambodia lurched into the grotesque period of dominance by the Khmer Rouge, which witnessed the worst record of mass murder and torture seen since the death camps operated by Nazi Germany, resulting in the demise of at least two million people. The unified Vietnam became embroiled in conflict with China in 1978–9. Slowly Vietnam has started to rebuild its society and economy in the later 1980s and 1990s. The legacy of the Vietnam War lives on for Vietnamese and for Americans. For the former the struggle to rebuild a divided and shattered country from an extremely low base has provided immense challenges for a ruling party wishing to emulate the Chinese Communist Party (CCP) in maintaining its authority while stimulating rapid economic growth. For Americans memories of the war in Vietnam remind them of the divisions within American society that the conflict engendered. It is only in the mid-1990s that the United States developed diplomatic relations with Vietnam; however, the fact that this development has occurred emphasizes that the divisions are beginning to recede.

1

Where does the Vietnam War stand within the history of the world since 1945? The cold war was primarily European in its origins and impact. It was dominated by the United States and the Soviet Union in its formative stages: Harry Truman, Joseph Stalin and their successors regarded Europe as the most vital region, hence the importance of Berlin as a potential flashpoint and the associated deep anxiety of the Soviet leadership over the future of Central and Eastern Europe. However, the triumph of Mao Zedong's party in the Chinese civil war (1946–9) marked the extension of the cold war to Asia in a major way, accentuating the alarm caused previously by the communist movements in Malaya and Indo-China. For American policy-makers, the cold war was perceived in global terms: this characterized a highly significant American policy decision, contained in document 'NSC-68' (National Security Council policy paper), approved by President Truman in April 1950. For the wider American public anti-communism was identified with McCarthyism, a crude, simplistic approach to combating communist foes through all-out action that included concentrating on the exposure of alleged traitors within. The outbreak of the Korean War in June 1950 constituted a vital development in the events that led to American intervention in Vietnam. When the war started, the North Korean regime of Kim Il Sung was perceived by many in the West as a satellite state controlled by the Soviet Union. Evidence that has come to light since the end of the cold war has demonstrated the degree of Stalin's interest in Korea, but this interest was encouraged sedulously by Kim, who was spurred on by a passionate zeal to secure the unification of Korea on a basis that would combine communism and nationalism. Owing to a curious blunder by Stalin – still not explained fully – the absence of a Soviet delegate from the United Nations (UN) Security Council enabled the United States to secure UN military action in Korea in order to defeat the North Korean offensive. In the wider sense, the most vital action in Korea came in October–November 1950 with the massive military intervention by China. This appeared to confirm the dire forebodings of the vocal Republican Party critics of Truman and Dean Acheson, men such as Senators Robert A. Taft, William Knowland, Richard Nixon and Joseph McCarthy and Congressman Walter Judd. There was a serious danger that the Korean War could escalate into an atomic conflict: this was avoided because of the fundamental common sense shown by Harry Truman and Dwight Eisenhower, itself in part the product of firm representations from other members of the UN supporting the United

States in Korea. Victory in Korea proved to be impossible for either side to achieve and eventually, when each wearied of the fighting and of the interminable propaganda exchanges at Panmunjom, an armistice was signed in July 1953. But there was no political settlement in Korea, which was still divided by two bitterly antagonistic regimes. The situation in the Korean peninsula remained fraught thereafter and included the threat of renewed fighting during the instability following Kim Il Sung's death in 1994.

The Korean War included a savage struggle between American and Chinese forces. For twenty years thereafter China was seen as a grave menace by American leaders and officials. The cold war now embraced Asia fully as much as Europe, and this explained the determination of American leaders to implement an active policy of containing communism in Asia. In Vietnam this predated the Korean War: the United States recognized Bao Dai as head of state as part of the French attempt to depict the situation in Indo-China in a manner that might appeal more to conservative nationalism within Vietnam, as well as to foreign powers. In May 1950 the United States committed itself to large-scale economic assistance for France, which led to American underwriting of the bulk of the cost of the French campaigns. The surrender of the French fortress of Dien Bien Phu and the summoning of the Geneva conference in 1954 signalled the bankruptcy of French and American policies. These developments are considered by Anthony Short in his stimulating chapter examining how the United States blundered into the Vietnam War in the 1960s. Short is particularly adept at suggesting points when history might have taken a different turn had a certain development or a key personality had an impact of a contrasting nature. In 1954–5 John Foster Dulles helped in creating the South East Asia Treaty Organization (SEATO) as a means of fostering greater cooperation against communism in an area where the dominoes might start toppling in an ominous fashion. However, SEATO was never more than a pale imitation of the North Atlantic Treaty Organization (NATO), because it was impossible to generate in Asia the degree of cohesion evinced in Europe.

The purpose of this volume is to focus upon the perspectives, policies and approaches of countries or states that either were central to the struggle in Vietnam or else illustrate reasons why particular states did not become involved deeply or at all in fighting, as they had become involved in Korea. Naturally the two competing Vietnamese states must be the principal focus for initial discussion, once we have reflected on the broad questions raised by Anthony Short in his chapter. Ho Chi Minh achieved internal legitimacy for the Viet Minh in the summer of 1945, in the dying weeks of the war in Asia and the Pacific, and he is the most intriguing personality discussed in this volume. A fervent nationalist, committed deeply to the unification of his country, Ho was also a long-committed communist, a founder member of the French Communist Party in 1920 and a Comintern agent. He was ruthless and tenacious, yet he possessed much appeal in Vietnam and outside. He symbolized the indomitable qualities of the opponents of foreign intervention. In August–September 1945 Ho seized the initiative amid the eclipse of the French administration and the encouragement given by the Japanese to the destruction of Western imperialism in Asia. He proclaimed the formation of a new regime, a step then acquiesced in by Emperor Bao Dai. Ho lacked the strength to maintain his government, but he had acquired internal legitimacy in Vietnam in the eyes of many, which he did not forfeit thereafter. Ho sought foreign recognition, but this took much longer to secure. Ho was always conscious of the need to pursue the aim of external legitimacy. In 1950 he gained the unsurprising recognition of the Soviet Union, China and the satellite states. In the 1960s Ho became a hero to many in the West who were not communist but who respected his valiant struggle to ensure the survival of North Vietnam, itself signifying the resistance of a small state to the intimidation and aggression of a powerful country.

Nguyen Vu Tung has produced a lucid analysis of the strategies applied by North Vietnam between 1954 and 1975, including consideration of developments from 1945. This incorporates a discussion of the diverse approaches to consolidating the regime within the North, attitudes towards the newly established regime in the South, and relations with the Soviet Union and China. Dr Tung is based in Hanoi and his essay is important for utilizing sources illustrating the evolving views within the Communist Party and the army. Errors were made in the North in the implementation of the land reform and in exploiting opportunities for swiftly undermining the regime in Saigon. Ho and his colleagues were irate at the decision of the Soviet Union and China to accept the division of Vietnam in the Geneva conference. North Vietnam was reluctant to encourage premature rebellion against the South Vietnamese state in case the United States intervened militarily. That there was considerable tension in the relationship between communists from the North and South emerges in part in Dr Tung's essay, and is emphasized more strongly in the following essay by Professor Ngo Vinh Long. Pressure from Southerners for decisive action in the South, plus the rottenness and corruption of Ngo Dinh Diem's administration, convinced North Vietnam's leaders that they must encourage action and this developed from 1959. Tung underlines the fierce resolution that inspired North Vietnam's approach during the military escalation in the 1960s and the ferocious American bombing of the North.

Ngo Vinh Long has written a vigorous and fascinating account of the failure of South Vietnam to evolve into a viable state. The division of a country can produce viable states, at least in the short-to-medium term. Korea is an example. Most, if not all, Koreans were opposed to the division of their country in 1945, but the rival regimes sponsored by the United States and the Soviet Union achieved viability. Admittedly, South Korea only became viable as a consequence of the Korean War and because of the economic and military support forthcoming from the United States. North Korea became viable more swiftly, although relying heavily on support from the Soviet Union; it remained viable until the economic decline developed from the early 1970s, exacerbated by the bizarre nature of Kim Il Sung's regime. South Vietnam could not develop into a self-sustaining state, for the reasons explained by Professor Long: Ngo Dinh Diem did not possess the qualities required for successful leadership and the South Vietnam army possessed the brutality without the redeeming features that enabled army leaders in South Korea to advance the economy successfully. South Vietnam was kept going by massive American aid and by inept decisions taken on occasion in Hanoi. Long portrays interestingly the attempts by North Vietnam's leaders to conceal dissent and mistakes, which included discriminating against the military hero Vo Nguyen Giap.

David Anderson provides a very lucid discussion of the immense tragedy of the disastrous decisions that led the White House, the State Department and the Pentagon into the quagmire. American leaders were imprisoned within the crusade to contain communism launched by Harry Truman in 1947, extended in NSC-68 in 1950 and reiterated glowingly by John F. Kennedy in 1961. Lyndon Johnson had grappled with the inheritance: as Anderson remarks, LBJ lacked knowledge and confidence in handling foreign issues. A supreme 'wheeler-dealer' and an outstanding Senate majority leader in the 1950s, Johnson viewed international issues simplistically and did not wish to risk being castigated by Republicans for the 'loss' of Vietnam as Truman had been condemned for the 'loss' of China. Robert McNamara has written graphically in his memoirs of the anguished debates and erroneous decisions in which he played a leading part as secretary for defence. Vietnam destroyed the Johnson administration, notwithstanding the boldness and courage with which Johnson pursued civil rights and social reform. It was left, appropriately in some respects, to Richard M. Nixon to take the decisions that pointed to the extrication of American forces. One of the most bitter critics of the Truman administration over China and Korea, *c.* 1949–53, Nixon approved a basic change in American foreign policy in Asia in 1971–2 so that the United States at last moved towards *rapprochement* with China. Nixon's unelected successor, Gerald Ford, was compelled to accept the most humiliating reverse experienced by the United States in war, symbolized by the desperate scenes accompanying the fall of the Saigon regime in April 1975.

An important contributory factor to the failure of American policy in Vietnam was the growth of an anti-war movement in the United States. Tom Wells writes vividly of the mixture of emotions and political viewpoints (or the absence of the latter) that produced extensive vociferous demonstrations against military intervention. A huge demonstration assembled in New York in April 1967, with over 300 000 participating, the biggest protest in American history to this time. As Dr Wells indicates, the fortunes of anti-war protestors fluctuated, but there is no doubt that they affected deeply the attitudes and approaches of the Johnson and Nixon administrations. The pressures of coping with the intractable problems in Vietnam and with anti-war demonstrations drove the two political foes more closely together in 1967–70, as LBJ and Nixon deplored leaks from the bureaucracy or Congress and the tenacity of those assailing their policies. Anti-war demonstrations in the United States encouraged similar protests elsewhere, as discussed by Carl Bridge and Alastair Parker in their chapters.

Ilya V. Gaiduk clarifies the role of the Soviet Union in his chapter. Soviet leaders viewed Vietnam warily: it was necessary to express solidarity with North Vietnam and to condemn American imperialism, but Russia must not be drawn into military action. Russian policy was influenced by the emerging split with China, initially concealed but then appearing in all its acidity during the 1960s. The Soviet leadership learned from the misjudgments made by Stalin over Korea in 1950 and was averse to taking risks. In one sense it suited Soviet leaders that the

United States should become embroiled deeply in military action in Asia, just as it suited the United States subsequently when the Soviet Union was embroiled in Afghanistan. But the Soviet Union did not want the war to escalate further, since it would then be far more difficult to avoid Soviet counter-action, if only to prevent Chinese influence becoming too powerful in Hanoi. While Soviet leaders were conscious of the perils of being drawn too deeply into intervention in Vietnam, they moved to exploit the opportunities for maximizing Soviet influence in Hanoi at the expense of China; in addition, they manoeuvred to increase Soviet influence in South East Asia so as to diminish American and Chinese impact.

Chen Jian places Chinese policy in perspective and emphasizes the significance of Chinese aid for Vietnam over a period of twenty years, beginning with the arrival of Chinese communist forces on the Vietnamese border in 1949–50 and declining once the Sino-American rapprochement developed from 1971. Chinese policy in the 1950s was determined by the repercussions of the Korean War and American support for Taiwan. Mao was alienated particularly by the latter. However, the Sino-Soviet rift preoccupied the Chinese leadership, as did the disastrous consequences of the 'Great Leap Forward' and of the terrible famine that killed so many Chinese. China was then consumed with the civil war within the CCP which accompanied the Cultural Revolution. North Vietnam's leaders had no intention of becoming unduly dependent upon China or the Soviet Union, but the exigencies they faced compelled them to rely substantially on Chinese assistance. Professor Chen underlines the speed with which Sino-Vietnamese relations unravelled, to culminate in a short war in 1979 which revealed embarrassing deficiencies in the PLA.

Carl Bridge contributes a lively assessment of the Australian role in Vietnam. Australian politics was dominated in the 1950s and 1960s by conservative forces comprising the Liberal and Country Parties, a coalition skilfully directed by Robert Menzies. The ANZUS alliance, dating from 1951, meant that Australia and New Zealand needed to cherish their relationship with the United States (in contrast to the dissension that developed in the 1980s, particularly between New Zealand and the United States): thus both countries provided forces for Vietnam. Professor Bridge quotes an Australian officer's comparison of the perceived efficiency of his own troops with the cavalier conduct of their American opposite numbers. The beginnings of Australian demonstrations over Vietnam coincided with a decline in the grip of conservative political forces, a revival in the fortunes of the Labor Party and a revolt against the reactionary social and sexual attitudes that had prevailed hitherto.

Alastair Parker places the Vietnam conflict in the wider perspective of international relations, with particular reference to Anglo-American exchanges. American leaders wanted British assistance in Vietnam, but there was no possibility of this occurring. Dr Parker provides a fascinating summary of the relationship between Harold Wilson's Labour government and Lyndon Johnson's Democratic administration. Wilson liked to boast of his warm relations with LBJ, but the reality was that Johnson regarded Wilson with a combination of exasperation and contempt. The state of the British economy rendered it unwise to antagonize Washington, but it was impossible for a Labour government to contemplate sending troops to Asia, as Attlee's Labour government had done in 1950. The left wing of the Labour party was unhappy with the pro-American line pursued by Harold Wilson, Michael Stewart and George Brown, and British demonstrations against the war developed significantly in the later 1960s. Reactions in Western Europe, not least from President de Gaulle in France, emphasized the large divergence from the American relationship with its allies that had prevailed during the Korean conflict. Britain's role on the sidelines revealed the extent of British decline and the positive aspects of this in preventing British lives being lost in a futile struggle.

Robert McNamara, in his reflective and frequently self-critical memoirs, summarizes succinctly the lack of understanding shown by policymakers in Washington:

> but the president, I and others among his civilian advisers must share the burden of responsibility for consenting to fight a guerrilla war with conventional military tactics against a foe willing to absorb enormous casualties in a country without the political stability necessary to conduct effective military and pacification operations. It could not be done, and it was not done.[1]

The essays in this volume comprise a balanced, integrated investigation of the origins and character of the Vietnam War between 1954 and 1975. New evidence has been incorporated in each aspect surveyed, and the outcome is a fresh examination which provides an illuminating introduction to one of the most traumatic and haunting struggles of the twentieth century.

1

ORIGINS AND ALTERNATIVES: COMMENTS, COUNTER-FACTS AND COMMITMENTS

Anthony Short

Would Ho Chi Minh have been a good newscaster? Would things have been different if he had gone to San Francisco in the summer of 1944 to broadcast the news in Vietnamese? As David Marr says, one cannot help but wonder;[1] and one cannot help but wonder also what other events might have turned out differently; and whether, in or out of the event, the course of modern Vietnamese history could have been changed. Whether, in conception, the Vietnam War was a tragedy because it had to happen as it did. Or whether it was a tragedy because it might have been averted.

Suppose, anyway, that the US Office of War Information in China had been able to get Ho a visa and had persuaded him to go to the United States where he might, in turn, have persuaded many more Americans of the justice of the Vietminh cause. Would it have made much difference to what happened? Or, to take another example from Marr, suppose de Gaulle had found time in July 1945 to see and to listen to Jean Sainteny. Would Sainteny have managed to dispel the idea that the Vietnamese would be overjoyed to see the French return? And, in any event, would it in any way have changed French policy and determination to return as soon as possible? In the turmoil of French restoration, who was listening to Leon Pignon's sensational message from China a couple of weeks before the Japanese surrender? Collaboration with the Viet Minh, he said, was still possible if France could bring itself to proclaim 'Independence': 'no other word can replace it'.[2]

Post-match analysis of the American defeat in Vietnam now suggests that lots of people in American administrations had their doubts at some time or other whether the USA would succeed in its purposes. Not only McNamara, the 'justified sinner',[3] but perhaps even Kennedy and Johnson as well. In setting the stage for the French war in Vietnam there were Frenchmen, too, such as Sainteny, head of de Gaulle's intelligence mission in Kunming, Laurentie, head of the political affairs section at the colonial ministry in Paris, as well as Pignon, one of de Gaulle's political advisers, who were sounding the alarm, even before the August Revolution of 1945, or, at least, telling it like it was. Vietnam had been transformed. It would not necessarily welcome the returning French and would certainly not welcome the return of pre-war French colonial attitudes. To all this, apparently, de Gaulle was oblivious. Or perhaps he was distracted. Whatever it was, in order to gain even a modicum of support the declaration of the Provisional Government in Paris, made in the emotional aftermath of the Japanese coup of March 1945, was totally inadequate. Whether or not they could be convinced that they were now fighting for a common cause, the peoples of Indo-China could only look forward to an Indo-Chinese Federation whose government was to be appropriate to the development of its resources; and the people of Vietnam were not even mentioned by name. The French would return to the pre-war status quo. Annam had an emperor (shortly to abdicate). Tonkin was a protectorate. Cochin-China was, and was obviously intended to remain, a French colony.

Was there before, during or after the dramatic unfolding of events as the Second World War came to an end, any hope of compromise, any chance that the war in Vietnam could have been averted?

One engaging act – two scenes – sees the arrival of de Gaulle. In Saigon he tells the cheering crowds, mostly *colons*, 'Je vous ai compris.' End of story. No war. Happy reconciliation of Vietnamese patriotism and France's glorious traditions of freedom and revolution! Except, of course, that it was utterly inconceivable. The revolutionary, and ruthless, de Gaulle who cut the Algerian knot in 1962 might well have had the prestige in 1945 to transform French policy towards Vietnam, and one wonders what he and Ho would have made of each other: the irrepressible patriots and the supreme opportunists. Rather more, certainly, than Leclerc made of the presumptuous Giap; but it was on the issue of prestige – France's prestige rather than that of the General, even if de Gaulle seemed to believe they were the same – that France was unable to pronounce the one word that might have prevented war.

That, perhaps, was a matter of will: but if it was, it was the *volonté générale*. Who in their right mind in France in the summer of 1945 would have been prepared to call it a day in Vietnam? Then there were the various matters of fact, starting with the bad luck which terminated the French presence in Vietnam, no matter how shameful it might have been as Japanese acolytes, less than six months before the war ended. The fact that the French flag continued to fly for so long induced unreal expectations and pretence. Perhaps it would have been better had there been a clear-cut defeat and a clean break as there had been for the British in Singapore in February 1942. For the French it was more like a greenstick fracture when the Japanese arrived in 1940; serious, but not so dramatic as to prompt a radical review of policy, intentions and capability. Yes, they were increasingly wary of American intentions and influence – less so than the Dutch, but not so much inclined as the Foreign Office 'to contemplate the abandonment of claims to lost colonies in deference to American opinion'[4] – and increasingly frustrated by the restrictions placed by Wedemeyer and Jiang on SEAC interest and activities in Indo-China. If Stein Tønnesson's source is correct then the French must have been elated to hear that the Allied combined chiefs of staff meeting in London on the eve of the Japanese surrender had decided to give Mountbatten responsibility for all of Indo-China: it was to be treated in the same way as Hong Kong. And cruelly disappointed to find instead that the whole of Indo-China north of the 16th parallel would surrender to and thus be occupied by Jiang's Chinese armies.[5] But suppose, for a moment, that the French *had* had a free run under Mountbatten: even that the Americans had given wholehearted assistance to those French forces who were still engaging the Japanese after the coup. Would it have made any difference: and was it even conceivable? Roosevelt's opposition, until the last weeks of his life, to the French return to Indo-China is well known. What is less well known is the conjecture that it might have been Roosevelt himself who deliberately provoked the Japanese coup in the first place. Should Admiral Halsey's massive raid on the coast of Vietnam in January 1945 be taken at face value? That is, that he was simply intent on destroying a Japanese battle fleet? Or had the operation, as Tønnesson suggests, 'been transformed into a deception operation masterminded by the President himself'? Tønnesson *thinks* this was indeed the case, although he admits he does not *know*. Apart from the circumstantial evidence, his causal connection runs like this: (1) the Japanese would not have expected an imminent US invasion had it not been for Admiral Halsey's raid; (2) had they not expected an imminent US invasion the Japanese would not have removed the French colonial administration; (3) had this not happened, the August Revolution itself would not have taken place.

Whether or not this was Roosevelt's intention, it certainly seems to have been the effect; and would have been a godsend to Roosevelt's anti-colonial policies.

> If the Japanese attacked and defeated the French colonial army, then Indochina would become a territory ruled directly by the enemy. As such it would be liberated later on by Sino-American forces. The morally and politically difficult operation of eliminating the French colonial regime would then be left to the Japanese, and the United States would never be involved.[6]

In any event, according to Tønnesson, American 'Ultra' intelligence had deciphered the whole text of the ultimatum which the Japanese commander in Indo-China was to deliver to the French when the coup was launched a week later. Like the more famous occasion when part of the Japanese ultimatum to the US had been decoded in 1941 – and which had no material effect on American preparedness at Pearl Harbor nor, indeed, anywhere else – if the French forces had known that a Japanese attack was imminent no doubt their dispositions would have been different. But one can hardly doubt that the outcome would have been the same. As it was, the first condition for dramatic change had been met. French power, French government and, no matter how attenuated, French sovereignty had been removed from Vietnam. Six months later the second condition was also in place: the emperor of Annam, the only other source of more or less legitimate authority in Vietnam, abdicated whatever power he had left.

The Vietnamese revolution of 1945 has been dealt with most recently and in great detail by both Tønnesson and Marr. The overwhelming impression – something which is implicit as well as explicit – is that nature, in Vietnam as elsewhere, abhors a vacuum. Be that as it may, the sudden and largely unexpected Japanese surrender imploded upon the political structure of the Dutch East Indies and Malaya as well as upon Vietnam. In Indonesia, after a similar hiatus, resistance to the Dutch return took on a nationalist form and dimension. In Malaya, with the British forces poised for invasion, the opportunity for a communist-led resistance, such as it was, was comparatively circumscribed.

In any event, the Malayan People's Anti-Japanese Army were reckoned by the British to be at least temporarily accredited allies and when, three years later, they became the Malayan People's Anti-British Army they had then to overturn a colonial administration which had been restored and probably accepted by a substantial part of the population. The revolutionary moment in Malaya in 1945 had passed. Both in Malaya and Vietnam, however, there had been demands from within the Communist Party for instant insurrection so as to confront the returning colonial power with a *fait accompli*. One may speculate about the outcome had they been heeded in Vietnam. Would the Vietminh have been prepared to take on the Japanese army? Could they have succeeded? Would the Japanese have been prepared to lay down their arms, to allow a native government – recognized in Indonesia and Annam, unrecognized in Tonkin and Cochin-China – to create maximum embarrassment and hindrance to colonial restoration? Suppose, even, that the Japanese had been prepared to defend the flimsy regime of Bao Dai? Or that circumstances had allowed Ngo Dinh Diem to come to the aid of the imperial party? Would any of this have diverted the course of pent-up Vietnamese nationalism once it had been released at the moment of great opportunity: a moment which happens only once in a thousand years? And could the djinn, once escaped, have been put back in the bottle?

When it occurred, in August 1945, the event seems on the surface to have been as much demonstration as revolution. Not many shots were fired even if, in that sinister expression, enemies of the people were killed in hundreds and probably thousands. It was perhaps just as well for the Vietminh that they did not destroy themselves by attacking the Japanese army. Once the Chinese armies appeared in Tonkin, in even greater strength, a process of mutual accommodation began which, when it ended eighteen months later, allowed the Vietminh to confront the French, on their return, with the reasonable facsimile of a working administration. It could, conceivably, have gone on working on two conditions. First, that the delineation of sovereignty allowed for ultimate Vietnamese rather than French authority; second, that the French did not attempt to detach Cochin-China, the southern and most valuable part of the country, and did not treat it in name and in fact as a French colony.

The Vietnamese revolution in a sense was still on hold. Like the future ambiguities of the Geneva settlement of 1954, the March 1946 agreement looked promising: but there was at least a latent contradiction in terms. How could the Democratic Republic of Vietnam – in effect the Democratic Republic of Tonkin – be a free state, with its own government and parliament, if it was circumscribed by the Indo-China Federation – *and* by the French Union? A referendum, which was promised, might be expected to unite the constituent parts of Vietnam; but there was absolutely no guarantee that even a Democratic Republic of Tonkin would be independent, let alone a Democratic Republic which included Annam and Cochin-China as well. In the original proposals for the French Union, it was to be based on free consent. By the time the Viet Minh delegation arrived in France to continue their negotiations on exactly what the preliminary agreement meant, the draft French constitution had been rejected, and with it the principle of free consent as the basis of the French Union. Elections to the French Constituent Assembly had seen heavy losses for the socialists – who, more than the communists at this time, might have been expected to be sympathetic to the cause of Vietnamese independence – and the winners, the Catholic MRP, were prepared to concede practically nothing. Was it the structures in place and the forces in play which prevented a settlement? Or did it come down to individuals?

After the Fontainebleau conference of July–August 1946 – a qualified fiasco – the principal French negotiator, Max André, put it down to the intransigence of the Vietminh delegates. Because these were led by Vo Nguyen Giap and Pham Van Dong, he had a point. Equally, one could say that on every occasion when agreement could conceivably have been reached, the French had the wrong man in the wrong place: d'Argenlieu in place in Vietnam doing his best to wreck any settlement, André unable to concede anything which would diminish the reality or the image of the French imperial presence and, like Bidault, almost as much as de Gaulle, convinced of the continuing necessity for the greatness of France. Would anyone else have made a difference? Leclerc, for example, who twice, reputedly on de Gaulle's advice, turned down Indo-China appointments? Ho Chi Minh himself, had he been present at Fontainebleau, might have presented the more acceptable face of Vietnamese nationalism: even if, after the event, one finds it hard to agree with Sainteny that Ho wanted to keep Vietnam within the French Union. Whatever Ho's intentions, and whether one stresses the communist or nationalist nature of his ambitions, one doubts whether they could have been limited to Tonkin, or whether he could have overcome the bad faith of the French who wanted to impose that limit on him and, if necessary, to destroy his power in Tonkin itself.

The French bombardment of Haiphong in November 1946, like the Dutch 'police actions' in Indonesia, was an act of war. Whether six thousand or one thousand people were killed it would today be recognized as an atrocity. The scale was exceptional; but the series went back to the massacre and mutilation of French women and children in Saigon in September 1945 and had been going on intermittently ever since then. Whether or not the French high command needed to have Haiphong as a bridgehead for the evacuation or reinforcement of Tonkin as a whole, and whether they and the Vietminh mistook each other's intentions, a critical stage in the Vietnamese revolution had been reached. From the Vietminh point of view, if the revolution was to succeed, it had to be defended. The bombardment of Haiphong, like the cannonade of Valmy, was the turning point. The French had shown their unremitting hostility to the independence the Viet Minh may have thought they had achieved in August 1945. Now it was time to put achievement to the test. For the Viet Minh, for Giap in particular, and for Moutet, the minister for french overseas territories, once the fighting had begun, a military decision was necessary. Perhaps at the last moment the war might have been averted, or at least the battle would not have begun in Hanoi. On 16 December 1946, less than a month after the bombardment of Haiphong, Léon Blum had once again become socialist prime minister of France. A week earlier he had written of the need for a genuine agreement with the Viet Minh based on independence and friendship. These were dangerous signs of accommodation, at least as far as some people in Saigon were concerned, and a conciliatory response from Ho Chi Minh was inexplicably – or perhaps explicably – delayed. Blum's intentions were genuine, Ho's perhaps less so, but for historians and for those who would have it otherwise, averting war at this stage is a straw-clutching exercise. Neither side trusted the other. One side, perhaps both, considered that war would at least put an end to uncertainty.

It is, of course, conceivable that somebody jumped the gun: that the irreconcilables or the *enragés* among the Viet Minh made sure that there would be no peaceful solution: and this is one of the possibilities Tønnesson explores in an earlier work with the resonant subtitle 'Sicilian Vespers'.[7] The same argument, incidentally, may apply to Malaya in June 1948, when the killing of three British planters prompted the colonial government to declare a state of emergency and outlaw the Malayan Communist Party. But in both countries, Malaya and Vietnam, the communist parties had, in effect, announced publicly, in their newspapers, that a war was about to take place. In Malaya, the party newspaper had declared 'For the sake of our lives we must fight our way out through struggle.'[8] In Vietnam, it was announced that the moment of peril had arrived: all compatriots were to hold themselves ready to rise as soon as the government issued the order.[9]

The Viet Minh attack began, in conditions of some treachery, on the night of 19 December 1946; it may, however, be seen as an act born of weakness rather than strength. For the Viet Minh the moment of peril had indeed arrived. With formidable French power deployed in Hanoi at least, a simple invitation to battle could have had disastrous consequences. That it did not was because it was now as much a revolution as a war: and in these circumstances the prudent observer might have concluded that all bets on the result were off. For an imperial power such as France, the prospect of a seven-year war might not perhaps have been too daunting, even if it was hardly envisaged, provided it was a low-key operation. After all, the French pacification of Morocco had taken twenty years, and apart from one or two awkward moments the experience had not upset the stability of France. Vietnam in the nineteenth century had sometimes seemed more intractable; but after 1945, with France restored at home and abroad, until a Soviet threat had taken shape and a resurgent Germany had become an alarming possibility, she was free to deploy her regular military forces, French and colonial, as well as the usual but German-augmented ranks of the Foreign Legion: which should or might have been more than enough to cope with tribal insurrection. Unlike Malaya, conscript soldiers of the colonial power never served in Vietnam; but it is unlikely that they would have made much difference to the outcome of the war. On a parallel with the Greek Civil War, however, what might well have made all the difference would have been the closing of the frontier with China: if, for example, the Guomindang forces had not lost so quickly to their communist adversaries or, less conceivably, had not lost at all.

As it was, from 1950 onwards the contiguous presence of the Chinese People's Republic meant that France was engaging not one but two communist powers. While this had compensations, at least as far as American perceptions of the struggle were concerned, it led to a significant shift in the balance of forces – to the point where one would doubt whether, from then on, victory was ever within the French grasp. It was, nonetheless, a 'see-saw' war. French successes in 1947, disasters in 1950. In 1951, in a somewhat premature attempt to reach a military decision, Giap committed more than twenty battalions in mass attacks not-far from Hanoi, and in this and subsequent engagements suffered heavy losses in more or less conventional battles. Apart from their air power, the French now had the advantage of an exceptional commander: General de Lattre de Tassigny: 'Le Roi Jean'. Might such a resourceful general be able to secure victory with the forces he already had? Would more resources be needed? Would France be willing to supply them? And how do you define victory anyway?

Belated French (and not always successful) efforts to raise battalions in a Vietnamese national army were rather like making bricks without straw: a national army, but where was the national sovereignty they were asked to defend? It was essentially a French war; and it was the manifestation of French power which, ultimately, kept in place the Emperor Bao Dai as the doubly dubious symbol of Vietnamese independence. Hardly anyone thought much of him; and practically until the end of the war the French could not bring themselves to relinquish enough power to make Vietnamese independence fact rather than fiction. Vietnamese nationalism, on the other hand, was at least as much centred on the Vietminh, even if it was inextricably mixed with communism. From time to time the French seemed to be looking for alternatives to Bao Dai, but in the end no one turned up. In the meantime, with the French increasingly on the defensive, it is hardly surprising how French thoughts turned to a negotiated settlement. What is rather more surprising is how many Frenchmen, like the Americans who followed them, were convinced that negotiation might have been successful in the absence of significant military gains or a manifest increase in Vietnamese political support or affiliation. De Lattre's victories were ephemeral. He himself died of cancer scarcely more than a year after he had arrived in Saigon. With him disappeared the hope of some dramatic victory which could, conceivably, have persuaded the Vietminh that they would be unable to dislodge the French in the foreseeable future. And as Kissinger was subsequently to discover, the regular armies lose if they do not win. The guerrilla wins if he does not lose. To which one might add: the guerrilla also wins if he not only transcends his limitations but also succeeds in an astonishing act of role reversal.

The battle of Dien Bien Phu was the decisive engagement in France's Vietnam war. It was also one of the decisive battles of the twentieth century. Whatever its origins, in the event it was a set-piece battle in which the manpower and firepower of erstwhile guerrillas overwhelmed and destroyed a French force of 13 000 men in France's greatest colonial defeat since Montcalm died on the Heights of Abraham. Was it, however, a battle which the French really wanted to fight, and could the result conceivably have been different? The answer to both these questions involves, and serves to introduce, the United States. Their major contribution to French costs – money and material but not, significantly, men – is comparatively well known. Rather more speculative is whether it was at the prompting and insistence of the US that General Navarre prepared his 'aggressive new concept for the conduct of operations in Indo-China',[10] and in doing so virtually sealed France's fate as well as his own.

Before the Truman administration demitted office in January 1953 it had identified South-East Asia in general and Vietnam in particular as vital to American national interests and had been persuaded, or persuaded itself, that the war in Vietnam and the war in Korea were virtually one. In one major respect the US leaders were at a disadvantage in Vietnam: they had to rely on French forces for the success of American policies; and, overall, they did not rate either French plans or performance highly. The new Eisenhower administration shared these misgivings, but it was typical of a new, buoyant if impatient, mood that Admiral Radford, C-in-C Pacific, should have insisted that in the critical Tonkin Delta 'two good American divisions with the normal aggressive spirit could clean up the situation in ten months'. Forecasts such as this, or the even more extraordinary assertion that an extra 10000 French African troops might wind up the war in six months, defied the evidence as well as probability. Of the 7000 villages in the Delta, 5000 were reckoned to be in the hands of the Vietminh. Bao Dai, whether for rhetorical effect or not, told Adlai Stevenson that half his country was in enemy hands; and with the French prepared to pull out, or at least to try and reach a negotiated settlement, the last thing they wanted, one would have thought, was a plan which was 'to break the back of the Vietminh in twenty-four months'. But this was what Dulles had called for, what Eisenhower had demanded and what Letourneau, accompanying Prime Minister Mayer to Washington in March 1953, had offered to deliver. For the previous four years Letourneau, more than anyone else, had been responsible for France's Indo-China policy. The concentration of power – as high commissioner in Indo-China and, at the same time, as a French cabinet minister – was extraordinary; but so was Letourneau's experience and so, one might have imagined, was his understanding of the realities of the problem. If anyone deserved to be heard by Eisenhower and Dulles and the

American military, it was him; and if anyone led the Americans on in the belief that victory lay just around the corner, it was him also. Putting previous acrimony and misunderstandings on one side, it promised to be a triumph of Franco-American cooperation. The French would create 54 new 'light' battalions of the Vietnamese army. The US would pay. In fact, the US would be expected to pay for the training, arming and equipping of 135 000 additional Vietnamese troops, but these were numbers which would tilt the balance. Together with other Franco-Vietnamese units they would somehow 'clean up' the enemy centres of resistance in south and central Vietnam; the more heavily armed Franco-Vietnamese regular units would then take on their Viet Minh counterparts in the North; and 'it is estimated that these latter forces will be brought to a decisive battle during the first half of 1955'.[11]

It was a shockingly optimistic and wildly improbably forecast. It might also be seen as a last desperate attempt to pull something out of the hat before nemesis arrived in the shape of a devastating parliamentary report, which was to cost Letourneau his job and lead to the fall of the Mayer government two months later. Conceivably, a more honest and realistic report in Washington would have led to second thoughts about potentially massive American involvement. As it was, General Collins had considerable doubts: but he also suggested improvements to what the French would do. Among them was the recommendation that they should construct their defence line across, and thus presumably interdict, the Vietminh's supply lines from China. The American Joint Chiefs of Staff, too, wanted big-unit operations: something which would cut the enemy's supply lines in northern Indo-China: and when, finally, Navarre, with notable American encouragement, put his 'aggressive new concept' into practice, Dien Bien Phu was an obvious choice – if it had worked.

It is impossible to see how the French, left to themselves, might have made it work. It represented failure in almost all its forms: planning, logistics, intelligence and anticipation. The exception was courage, of heroic dimensions, on both sides. The other exception to these failures, in hindsight, is what might have been achieved had the United States added its weight to the battle. Some historians have discounted the offer, apparently made by Dulles to Bidault, of two atomic bombs, as well as any intention the US might have had to intervene. Admiral Radford, the irrepressible chairman of the American JCS, may only have been speaking for himself when he talked about squadrons of B-29s and swarms of American carrier-borne fighters and fighter-bombers: but there was a report from a JCS committee which concluded that three tactical atomic bombs, properly employed, would have been sufficient to smash the Vietminh siege of Dien Bien Phu. The present writer believes that the US in fact came extraordinarily close to intervention, but that Britain, Anthony Eden in particular, proved to be an insuperable obstacle. But suppose, for the moment, that nuclear or conventional weapons had incinerated the Vietminh supply points, if not the besieging Vietminh and Chinese anti-aircraft gunners: would this have proved to be such a shock – to the Vietminh, to the Chinese, to the Russians – that they, rather than the French, would have been desperate to call an armistice? And what would have happened then?

For the moment, diplomacy at its highest level seemed about to determine the fate of Vietnam. The Geneva conference had convened and the Vietnam sessions were about to begin. Curiously, as far as the US was concerned, Vietnam did not seem to be all that important: or at least the Vietminh hardly seemed to be regarded as a power in its own right. China, or its shadow, was the principal concern and General Bedell Smith, the principal American negotiator at Geneva, is on record as saying 'It is not inconceivable, given the proper circumstances, that the Communist Chinese might be impelled to pull the rug out from Ho Chi Minh.'[12] Bidault, the beleaguered French foreign minister, was even more hopeful. According to Jean Chauvel, the French ambassador to Switzerland, he envisaged direct talks with the Chinese, and had, unbelievably, his own reasons to believe that, in exchange for equipment which they needed, the Chinese would be willing to offer Ho Chi Minh a chair in politics at Peking University.[13]

In the end it was the Chinese and the Russians who restrained the Viet Minh. Dien Bien Phu had been a débâcle for the French but, even had it not, the political problem would have been unresolved. A year earlier, 'the conclusion of an honourable armistice, the immediate cessation of hostilities and the prompt initiation of political discussion leading to the holding of free elections' had been recommended by Eisenhower. But that was a prescription for Korea, not Vietnam, and there is at least enough rhetorical evidence to suggest that Dulles was utterly opposed to any settlement which would register an advance for communism in South-East Asia. Considering the magnitude of the American investment, his ideological predispositions and the constraints on the Republican Party before it moved out of its

McCarthy period, this was understandable. In practice, however, it meant that Dulles was unlikely to approve of *any* settlement at Geneva; and that the US would not guarantee, even if it recognized the inevitability of, what had been done. In this one may argue, lay the genesis of the American tragedy. An episode of colonial war had been altered and overtaken by the perceptions of the cold war. France, as a colonial power, no longer felt able to continue the struggle. The United States, in its role as defender of the free world, was reluctant to concede defeat. Hence the image of Dulles, sulking like Achilles in his tent, and hence the open question whether there was to be temporary partition and whether Vietnam was, henceforth, to be one state or two.

The concept of nation-building is easier to understand than the conditions for its success. A divided Korea would eventually turn, in the South, into a phenomenally successful economy and dynamic nation state. The strength and attraction of West Germany ultimately overwhelmed its eastern neighbour. Could a similar nation state have been created in South Vietnam? Was it permissible? Would it have been legal? Of these issues feasibility is the more important; but it turns on the convergence of Chinese and American interests. It might have been bluff, or downright deception, but the impression Zhou Enlai gave in the final phase of the Geneva conference in 1954 was that he was expecting a separate state in South Vietnam, and that it would be recognized by China.[14] Legally, in so far as there was anything legal about the unsigned final declaration at Geneva, there was no such presumption. The settlement of Vietnamese political problems was to be effected on the basis of respect for the principles of independence, unity and territorial integrity. There was no mention of partition.

Fruitful contradictions are not normally the stock in trade of non-Marxist politicians: but the way in which Dulles and Ngo Dinh Diem exploited the ambiguities of the Geneva settlement gave South Vietnam a lease as a nominally independent state which lasted twenty years. It could conceivably have been longer still, however. Let us assume that the primary Chinese objective at Geneva was the neutralization of the Indo-China states and the assurance, if not the guarantee, that they would not be host to US bases or what the Chinese called 'aggressive intentions'. Did it not appear likely that they, in turn, would have been prepared to guarantee the division of Vietnam: on condition that the US joined in the guarantee as well? Let us assume also that the Russians, Molotov in particular, who appeared to be comparatively relaxed, were prepared to accede to Chinese interests and that they had no prima facie reason why the Vietminh should be supported in a fight to the finish against the French. Eden's attachment to the Locarno Treaties of 1925 may have been misjudged, but the idea of a 'reciprocal defensive arrangement in which each member gives guarantees', which he suggested to the House of Commons, could have turned the unsigned and unratified 'agreements' of Geneva into a full-blown and perhaps enforceable treaty. This is exactly the prospect which appalled Dulles, the Republican Party and practically the entire House of Representatives. For Dulles, carrying the weight of so much Republican historical and emotional baggage, it was a simple issue: 'We could not get ourselves into the "Yalta business" of guaranteeing Soviet conquests.' The United States, he insisted, was in no way honour-bound to guarantee the Geneva settlement. Even the declaration that the US would not disrupt it by force was to be unilateral; in no circumstances would the US become co-signatory with the communists to anything.

Then, of course, there was the matter of Vietnam itself. Even if the authority, such as it was, of the government in Saigon no longer pertained in half the country, was that government, in principle at least, independent? And was it party to the agreement that had been reached? The answer to the first question is more or less. To the second, definitely and ostentatiously not. It may be a moot point whether in 1954 'Vietnam', headed by Emperor Bao Dai, was a sovereign state before 20 July, when the Geneva settlement was made, or after 30 July, when the French finally conceded the realities of independence. Whichever is the case, the agreement had already been denounced by the new Vietnamese prime minister, of whom the US embassy in Paris had reported that 'on balance we were favourably impressed

> but only in the realisation that we are prepared to accept the seemingly ridiculous prospect that this Yogi-like mystic could assume the charge he is apparently about to undertake only because the standard set by his predecessors is so low.[15]

For the next nine years the fortunes of South Vietnam and Ngo Dinh Diem were inextricable. So, it might be said, was the connection between Diem and the US. Perhaps appointed by Bao Dai in the first place because it was thought he would have American approval and support, Diem looked like an authentic nationalist. In the hopeful forecast of that grey eminence, Colonel Lansdale, the original 'Quiet American', he might even have become the father of his country. In spite of the comparison to George Washington, by comparison with Ho Chi Minh Diem would have been unlikely to win a popularity contest in Vietnam as a whole. But if there was to be at least a temporary state in South Vietnam, Diem was the alternative nationalist: anti-communist, anti-French, Catholic and decidedly pro-American. Even if nationwide elections had taken place in 1956, which the Geneva texts seemed to imply, was there a chance that, with the support of the million or so Catholics who were leaving the North, not to mention those for whom the communist version of nationalism was less appealing, he might have won a free election in the South? Or was the US about to make a fatal mistake in entrusting Diem with both South Vietnam's future and its own?

In the later years of the American commitment to Vietnam, one is struck by the dominance of the Defense Department over the State Department: the confidence and apparent capability of McNamara, the self-abnegation of Rusk. When the commitment began, it was the other way round. Whether Dulles dominated or deferred to Eisenhower, everyone remembers him as the epitome of Republican foreign policy. Hardly anyone remembers Secretary of Defense Wilson, but in retrospect he seems to have been a better judge of the situation. The only sensible course, he said, was for the US to get out of Indo-China completely, and as soon as possible. The situation there was utterly hopeless and, as Wilson put it, 'These people should be left to stew in their own juice. There would be nothing but grief in store if we remained.'

Was anyone listening? To begin with, apparently not. The first requirement, according to Eisenhower, was a Vietnamese force which would support Diem: 'so many millions of dollars to produce the maximum number of Vietnamese military units on which Prime Minister Diem could depend to sustain himself in power'.[16] The original condition which the American Joint Chiefs of Staff laid down for training the new South Vietnamese army – absolutely essential, they said – was that there should be a reasonably strong, stable, civil government in control. This was now discounted, or, rather, the process was reversed: US military assistance would be given in order to produce this government in the first place. It was, moreover, in the nature of a personal commitment, as Eisenhower's letter to Diem revealed, and when Eisenhower sent to Vietnam General J. Lawton Collins, perhaps his best and most trusted corps commander from the Second World War, it was 'to assist in stabilising and strengthening the legal government of Vietnam under the premiership of Ngo Dinh Diem'.

Was Diem capable of bearing the burden of American expectations which rested upon him? Dulles told Mendès-France in November 1954 that Diem was 'our last and only hope', but he had also told Collins that his chances of success were only one in ten. Collins's reporting from Vietnam was not altogether consistent, but by early December 1954 it looked as if his mission of support for Diem had failed. If, said Collins, Diem had not demonstrated by about 1 January 1955 that he was capable of governing, then America and France would have to consider alternatives. When Collins returned to Washington in April 1955, the admiral who took notes on the debriefing observed that the State Department was reluctant to face the fact that they must admit failure in US policy, and would obviously attempt to retain Diem in some capacity. Collins' indictment of Diem was comprehensive, to the point where the State Department had reluctantly to agree to his removal; or, rather, in a remarkable prefiguration of what was to come years later, in his final months, Diem was now to be told that, because of his inability to create a broadly based coalition government and because of Vietnamese resistance, the American government was no longer in a position to attempt to prevent his removal from office.

One may speculate on the outcome had this happened. Could the US, or the Vietnamese for that matter, have found anyone as intransigent as Diem? One suspects that, left to themselves, the government in South Vietnam would have been little more than a caretaker administration; that elections would probably have taken place in 1956; and that neither the Emperor Bao Dai, nor any of his appointees, would have been any more of a rallying point for alternative nationalism than they had been over the previous ten years. On the other hand, one can by no means be certain that the US at this point would have been prepared to walk away and to relinquish what was becoming their proprietorial interest in South Vietnam. They might not have been prepared to go as far as their chargé in Saigon had suggested before the Geneva agreement had been reached – that Bao Dai should be removed in a French–American coup – but there was a wider appreciation of his argument: 'bankers have a right to organize a receivership'.[17] In the event, however, in April 1955, it was Bao Dai who was on the point of removing Diem. Collins, as he left Saigon, had told Diem that this was likely to happen, and that it was unlikely that he could be saved.

Whether out of confidence or desperation, Diem now launched his attack on the Binh Xuyen, the gangsters who controlled the Saigon police and his formidable political rivals, and his victory ensured an eleventh-hour reprieve in Washington. At last he seemed to have shown an unsuspected ability for decisive government; instructions for his removal were cancelled, and at this point one can say the bargain was struck between Diem and the US. Their purposes – to halt Vietnamese communism at the 17th parallel – coincided, and in the words of Senator John F. Kennedy the US had become the god-parents of 'little Vietnam'. What this meant, in effect, was that South Vietnam also became an American dependency. Had it been successful, and had the 17th parallel been accepted by all the great powers at Geneva, it might have settled down to an indefinite existence as a sovereign state. For a while it looked as if this could happen. Indeed, in September 1956, two months after elections might have taken place to unite Vietnam, probably under Ho Chi Minh, the State Department was told by General O'Daniel, now acting in a civilian capacity as chairman of the American Friends of Vietnam, that 'Free Vietnam', as he called it, was entirely pacified and secure and that Diem's govern-ment was growing increasingly popular.

In a way, O'Daniel was right. 1956 was Diem's year of triumph – almost. Certainly the numbers of his most implacable political oppo-nents had been drastically reduced. By the summer of 1956, in one province, a senior Vietminh member estimated that 90 per cent of the communist party's cells had been destroyed. Party membership throughout the South, which Duiker reckons had stood at about 5000 in mid-1957, is thought to have fallen to a third of that level by the end of the year. Many members had been picked off like sitting ducks, apparently waiting and hoping for the elections that might have brought them to power, reluctant to abandon the peaceful struggle until it was too late. How extraordinary, then, that Diem and his government, with massive support from the US, were unable to take a leaf out of the Vietminh book and seize the moment of great oppor-tunity. How much more effort, conversely, must it have taken the party in the South, hanging on the ropes, to continue to survive, let alone emerge as a serious threat to an implacable government.

Equivalence such as this, however, is probably both misleading and unfair. Assuming it is usually much harder to create and maintain the stability of a government over the long run than to overturn it, the success of the Diem regime depended as much, probably more, on how and whether it created 'legitimacy' as on its ability to destroy its opponents. In retrospect, it seems to have been a hopeless case; but if one looks first at the government side of the equation one wonders whether different factors or different permutations might have produced a different result. Land reform is reckoned to have been largely ineffective. Together with the appointment, rather than the election, of the heads of village councils, it did nothing to create a rural constituency which was supported by and might in turn have supported the government. The resettlement programme was pretty much of a disaster; at least compared with the New Villages in Malaya, which dried out the guerrillas' 'fishpond' to the point where they became visible. The Vietnamese army was trained by the US to fight a Korean-type war against the invasion of conventional forces from the North and was largely ignored as a force in support of civil power in the South. Diem, in turn, ignored or at least neglected the Buddhist susceptibilities of his fellow-countrymen and preferred to rely on fellow Catholics he felt he could trust. Ultimately, however, he depended on the US; and the more he depended on them the less convincing was his projection as an authentic nationalist leader.

Could any of this have been changed and, if so, by whom? Given his obsessive character, probably not by Diem himself. In retrospect, the cavalcade of ambitious soldiers – and an airman – who followed contains no obvious candidates: although, again, to be fair it must be said that they took over in dramatically deteriorating circumstances. Given, also, the dominance of Diem and a political style which was described as 'heavy-handed' (State Department) or, at least, 'stern' (Defense Department) one can perhaps see why no one of the calibre of Magsaysay (President of the Philippines, 1953–7) emerged as at least a potential leader, and why the US found it difficult to change the direction of Diem's policies. Perhaps it would have been impossible anyway; but it is worth looking at the contrasting inputs from America's civil and military representatives in South Vietnam both before and after US policy reached one of its nodal points – the change-over from the Eisenhower to the Kennedy presidency. Quite early on in his posting, Ambassador Reinhardt had identified the problem: Diem himself. Rather late in the day his successor, Ambassador Durbrow, balked at assuring Diem that 'we will back him at all times, under all circumstances and forever'. In between, however, there was General Williams, who headed the American Military Assistance Advisory Group, and who was at least equal in importance to either ambassador.

In a recent book, *Masters of War*, Professor Robert Buzzanco seeks to absolve significant numbers – and members – of the US military leadership of any enthusiasm for the Vietnam War – those he calls the 'dissenters' and 'doubters'. At the same time, he recognizes the exception of the 'ever sanguine' General Williams who was, he says, 'as optimistic and deaf to criticism as his predecessor, O'Daniel, had been'.[18] General Williams did not like negative reporting from his subordinates, understandably in that it would reflect upon the effectiveness of his mission. His confidence in Diem may also be understandable if eventually misplaced, but Williams failed on at least two counts. First, he did not see, or would not admit, that things were getting worse and that his reports therefore distorted reality. Second, by creating a Vietnamese army of seven regular divisions he might have been able to fight a Korean-type war, but it was an army which would be practically useless when confronted with mounting insurgency. What is more remarkable, perhaps, is how local military optimism persisted in the face of mounting evidence. In April 1959, the deputy chief of MAAG claimed that the internal security of South Vietnam was nearly complete; but in less than twelve months the American Counterinsurgency Plan, bearing the impress of General McGarr, General Williams's successor, discerned a trend which was 'adverse to the stability and effectiveness of President Diem's government'.

The plan reached Washington in January 1961, just before President Kennedy's inauguration. In spite of 'the steady expansion of guerrilla warfare by the Vietnamese communists', the US government reckoned that the government of Vietnam had the basic potential to cope with the Viet Cong guerrilla threat, but only if the necessary corrective measures were taken and adequate forces were provided. In fact, both 'corrective measures' and 'adequate powers' would have to be provided by the US. Conceivably, had the onus rested on the outgoing Eisenhower administration, yet another required increment of American support would have lent some weight to Ambassador Durbrow's speculation: that it might be time to look for Diem's replacement; but, as in 1955, in November 1960 Diem's ability to withstand a rather half- hearted coup attempt once again postponed his sell-by date.

Whatever the quality of reporting from Vietnam, nothing much seemed to dent official confidence in Washington – to the point where a Senate subcommittee, reassured by Durbrow, announced that MAAG could be phased out in the foreseeable future – and when the situation showed signs of a dramatic change it was seen in terms of geopolitical rather than local factors – in a word, Laos. But even if the intervention of Russian transport aircraft in the Laotian civil war had not occurred, even if Kennedy had not been warned by Eisenhower that, *in extremis*, the US should be prepared for unilateral intervention (there are different accounts of the meeting), on a much loftier level there was the apparent global challenge: on the one hand, the rhetoric of the Kennedy inauguration: the US prepared to pay any price, bear any burden to ensure the survival and success of liberty, and, on the other, the almost simultaneous announcement by Khrushchev of world-wide communist support for just wars of national liberation.

Although it looks as if Khrushchev was not in fact pledging direct support for either a just war in the South or reunification with North Vietnam, in all four of the contemporary but inherited crises – Laos, Vietnam, Cuba and the Congo – Kennedy wanted to get moving. We must, he said, be better off in three months than we are now. Perhaps he and his administration were in too much of a hurry. Certainly there was no reappraisal, agonizing or otherwise, of what the US might have got itself into: even if on closer, more leisurely, and academic inspection the terms of the Counterinsurgency Plan, which Kennedy approved ten days after his inauguration, were more suited to an imperial than to an allied power. First, Diem's government was to be induced 'to adopt and vigorously prosecute' the American 'Country Team' plans to defeat communist insurgency:[19] such plans as Diem might have had were presumably inadequate or irrelevant. An Emergency Operations Control System was to be established: to involve planning, programming, budgeting and 'extraordinary action starting at highest levels of government and extending to the lowest political sub-division [defined as the village] to establish and maintain internal security'. That, plus an overhaul of the country's intelligence, communications, border and coastal patrol systems, would have been a big enough undertaking; but what was quite extraordinary was the political (designated 'psychological') role which the US assigned to itself. Much of it might be called public relations – improving communications between government and people, attracting popular loyalty, persuading people that the government was acting in their interests – but the most ambitious of all the Plan's objectives was to 'foster a spirit of national unity and purpose among all elements of the Vietnamese society'.[20] Was this really the job of the United States? If a Vietnamese government could not do it, could anyone else? Was South Vietnam really alliance-worthy? Was anyone in the new American administration worried about taking on an imperial role: or was it even recognized as such? Did anyone realize that they had reached the watershed?

Presumably not. It looked like a necessary increment. The cost was modest: $40 million. And it seems there was an accompanying memorandum which promised that, if the Plan were put into effect, the war could be won in eighteen months. As the author of the magisterial Senate Foreign Relations Committee study puts it, 'Thus, the expansion of the US role in Vietnam provided for by the counterinsurgency plan was approved by the President quickly, firmly and without change.'[21] To which one may add 'and without much reflection, either'. Many years later, Deputy Secretary of Defense Gilpatric said of the Vietnam Task Force, which he chaired, that they had a basic lack of understanding of almost everything about the peoples of Indo-China or how the Vietnamese would react to US involvement and plans to make them more effective. 'We were', he said, 'kidding ourselves into thinking that we were making well-informed decisions.'[22] McNamara, in his recent book *In Retrospect*, goes much further in cataloguing the mistakes and misjudgments of American policy; but one wonders whether anything other than experience could have overcome the innocence and confidence with which, he says, they approached Vietnam in the early days of the Kennedy administration.[23] From then on, until the ambivalent but salutary lesson of the Tet offensive in 1968, there was always enough hope that the US could not lose. Even if that was not quite the same as saying that they were going to win. But then, of course, that was the heroic view of their opponents as well: so this leaves all sorts of conjectures on both sides. Suppose Le Duan had not been a Southerner: might North Vietnam have settled down to socialism in one country and resentful coexistence with the South? Suppose Kennedy had not been shot: what would he have done next? And suppose a sceptical Congress had rejected the Tonkin Gulf resolution? Would any of this have made any difference? Or were both sides condemned to ordeal by battle?

2

COPING WITH THE UNITED STATES: HANOI'S SEARCH FOR AN EFFECTIVE STRATEGY

Nguyen Vu Tung

Introduction

During the twenty years since the end of the Vietnamese War against the United States, fundamental changes have occurred in Vietnam, especially after Vietnam adopted a policy of renovation and the cold war came to an end. These developments, together with recent historical research on the war and access to formerly secret documents, have bettered conditions for more comprehensive studies of a war which, in the history of both the US and Vietnam was long, severe and traumatic. Still, the legacy and the memory of the suffering of several generations of Vietnamese people continue to influence their thinking about the history of the war. It has therefore been difficult to develop an unbiased assessment in Vietnam of relations with the US, which, in the eyes of many Vietnamese people, was always hostile to their nationalist aspirations.

This essay is an attempt to develop a scholarly Vietnamese approach to the study of the war. It examines the reasons why the Democratic Republic of Vietnam (DRV) came to consider the US an enemy and decided to fight it. It also examines specific strategies and policies adopted by Hanoi to win the war, including those related to political, military and diplomatic fields. To examine how Hanoi's policies developed in the complicated contexts of triangular relations between the United States, the Soviet Union (USSR) and the People's Republic of China (PRC), and the triangular relations involving the PRC, the Soviet Union and the DRV, however, is not the aim of this essay: these perspectives are explored in other contributions to this volume.

The US as an Enemy: Developments in the DRV's Perception

For obvious reasons, it is always unwise for a small country to consider a great power as an enemy and especially to go to war against such a power. A country like Vietnam, which has had to confront many great powers through its history, should do its utmost to avoid having enemies among the great powers and notably to have to fight them. But great powers have historically acted upon strategies based on their global geopolitical and economic interests – strategies that have sought to carve out spheres of influence – and by doing so, at times, they have underestimated the smaller country's aspirations and will for independence. This, it seems, is what happened between the United States and Vietnam in the years between 1945 and 1975. A relationship that could have remained peaceful, if not friendly, developed into an all-out war.

US policy towards Vietnam developed through a number of stages. In 1945, the US assisted the Vietminh in building an intelligence network and a guerrilla army against Japanese troops in Indochina. In the period from 1946 to 1949, the US adopted a policy towards Vietnam, that was more or less pro-French, but still neutral, because US leaders needed French support to confront the Soviet Union in Europe, and because the DRV leadership was communist, but Washington still held on to an anti-colonial position. In 1949 and 1950, prior to the Korean War, American policy towards Vietnam was driven by two considerations. On the one hand, by accepting the French 'Bao Dai formula', the US tried to prevent communism from expanding into South-East Asia. On the other hand, it began to take the PRC into account, trying to reach a *modus vivendi* with it regarding Far Eastern issues, including the Franco-Vietnamese war. But after the Korean War broke out, and especially after the PRC intervened in that war, the US grew hostile to the DRV because of a perceived need to defend the 'free world' against further communist aggression everywhere in the context of an intensified cold war and the prevailing anti-communist mood of the US; the American historian Townsend Hoopes has talked of 'a religious obsession that went beyond the rational requirement of US national security'.[1] Moreover, the US considered communism as a monolith, failing to detect national and traditional contradictions within and among the communist countries and viewing the Vietnamese national liberation movement as part of a scheme of Soviet and Chinese expansion in Asia. Therefore, US geopolitical and economic interests globally, in a curious combination with blind anti-communism, involving oversimplifications and misjudgements, were the main driving forces behind its policies toward Vietnam. To put it differently, US hostility toward the DRV did not stem from national animosity or a collision of national interests between the two countries but from a collision of world-views and alliance patterns. Apart from this, after the Second World War, US policy-makers seemed to be suffering from 'a victory syndrome', seeing the US as exceptional and invincible. Thus decisive intervention in a poor country like Vietnam could not but be successful.[2]

To regard the United States as its number one enemy did not come naturally for the DRV. It was a matter of historical development. In the early days of the DRV, Ho Chi Minh tried to win US recognition. Truman did not respond to his overtures. Discrete direct contacts did, however, take place in 1946 and 1947 between representatives of the two countries in Bangkok and Hanoi. With a view to gaining American support for their anti-colonial resistance, or at least a moderating US influence on France, the Vietnamese representatives involved in these contacts discussed the possibilities of Vietnamese–American cooperation and held out possibilities of trade, investment and tourism, while avoiding criticism of the United States.[3] Internally circulated documents from the same period, however, reveal that some already considered the US an enemy of the Vietnamese revolution. This was an assessment that probably stemmed from the disappointment felt by Vietminh leaders with the consistent lack of US response to their appeals. But it was also the result of communist ideology. The DRV's policies were based mainly on the Vietnamese search for recognized nationhood. Under the leadership of a communist party, the movement for national unity and independence blended nationalism with communist ideology.

In January 1948, an enlarged Central Committee Plenum of the Indochinese Communist Party (ICP) adopted an analysis of the world situation, which included the following observation: 'The anti-democratic, democratic, imperialist and anti-imperialist forces have been gathering in two camps, i.e. the "democratic and anti-imperialist camp" and the "imperialist and anti-democratic" one whose leader is the United States.' The plenum also predicted that the US would sooner or later intervene in Indochina.[4] Given this stated vision, the DRV policies aimed at winning American support, as well as support from the non-socialist, nationalist countries in South-East Asia, including Thailand and Burma, were tactical in scope and purpose. Despite Ho Chi Minh's initial reservations, the diplomatic recognition extended by the PRC, the USSR and other socialist countries in early 1950 was considered, both officially and privately, a real victory for the DRV. Their importance was confirmed with the victory of the late 1950 border campaign, conducted with Chinese assistance[5] – a campaign that drove away French forces from much of the border area and effectively linked up Viet Minh-controlled areas with China, and further, thus facilitating support also from the Soviet Union and Eastern Europe.

While fighting in the jungle, however, the Viet Minh leaders lacked the ability to analyse clearly and thoroughly their relationship with the communist countries. They had no comprehensive explanation for the failure of the Soviet Union to support Vietnam in the period from 1945 to 1949; for why the French Communist Party had not supported the ICP-led resistance in the beginning; or for the background to the breakdown of relations between Tito and Stalin; the failure of the Greek Communist Party; or later, the outbreak of the Korean War. Believing like the Americans that communism was monolithic, the Vietnamese communist leaders were loyal to their ideology.

The simple logic of the cold war, therefore, led Vietnamese leaders from 1948 through 1950 to view the US as an enemy, and this in fact explains why they did not pursue contacts with the US during this period. With the change in US policy in the year of 1950, when Washington stated its intention to support France actively, and with the ensuing growth of America's involvement in Vietnam, their view of the US seemed to be confirmed. The political Report of the Second National Congress of the Vietnamese Workers Party (VWP) in February 1951 is a further testimony to a by then firm belief:

> Vietnam is a part of the world democratic camp. It is at present a bastion against imperialism, against the anti-democratic camp headed by the US.[6]

After assessing US policy and activities to aim for direct intervention in Vietnam, the Resolution of September 1954 of the VWP Central Committee Plenum reached the following conclusion: 'US imperialism is the number one and most dangerous enemy.'[7]

Despite such ideological views, the Vietnamese leaders had considered the possibility of a middle course – trying to be neutral, or non-aligned, in the emerging cold war. In 1950, they not only had reservations about mutual Sino-Vietnamese recognition, but also about Mao's eagerness to support the Viet Minh, as this could make Vietnam a flashpoint for cold war confrontation.[8] In addition, because of their lack of information and well-thought-out analysis of the dynamics of international relations, Vietnamese leaders could not take full advantage of America's possible willingness to accept an 'Asian Titoism'. Even had they been far-sighted enough to do this, however, their goal would have been difficult to achieve, because Vietnam was a small country by comparison with China, to which the concept of 'Asian Titoism' had been applied,[9] and since events, particularly after the outbreak of the Korean War, tended to strengthen the US commitment to containing communism, whatever its local flavour, even in peripheral areas of the world.[10]

Having initially regarded the US, for the most part, as an ideological enemy and an albeit lukewarm supporter of France, the DRV leaders came to see America as the main enemy of their struggle for national independence. As the United States gradually replaced France, bolstered a pro-American regime in South Vietnam, and thus prolonged the partition of the country, the US became the most direct obstacle to the national liberation movement of Vietnam. More than anything else, this was the reason the US became the DRV's enemy. Regardless of ideology, the Vietnamese leaders were opposed to any form of foreign domination. Moreover, after 1945 and the August Revolution, the Vietnamese people were ardent in their defence of the national independence they had won, for the first time in Vietnamese modern history. Even Bao Dai and the South Vietnamese regime that succeeded him aimed for complete national independence from France.

Once perceiving the US as their number one enemy, the DRV leaders had to confront a powerful superpower if they were to win the national independence and unification they claimed were Vietnam's destiny. Their determination was very high. So, too, they would learn, was the price that the Vietnamese people would pay for that dedication.

From Peaceful Unification to Political and Armed Struggle

On 20 July 1954, the Geneva accords were signed. The accords provided for the temporary division of Vietnam along the 17th parallel pending a nationwide election to be held within the summer of 1956. The five-year interlude between the Geneva accords of 1954 and the political impasse that led to a renewal of active warfare in the South of Vietnam saw the US becoming the main supporter of the South Vietnamese regime. The cold war context and the US obsession with global credibility made it a hostage to developments in South Vietnam. Washington may have found the relative stability in the South after 1954 encouraging (although it was based on brutal suppression of all kinds of opposition), but by 1959 US policy-makers were faced with dissension within the Saigon regime itself, emerging friction between themselves and Diem, and with Hanoi's decision to launch both armed and political struggle in the South.

At the outset, the DRV policy strictly followed the Geneva accords. Dubbed the policy of 'peaceful reunification' or 'struggle by peaceful means', the DRV's intentions at the time to adhere to the accords were clear from several party documents. The VWP Central Committee Plenum resolutions adopted in March and August 1955 are a case in point:

> The specific enemies of our entire people at present are US imperialism, French colonialism, and the Ngo Dinh Diem clique. US imperialists are the principal and most dangerous enemy.
>
> Our policy is to achieve reunification on the basis of independence and democracy through peaceful means.
>
> Our immediate objectives are peace, reunification, independence and democracy.
>
> Our key slogan is to strengthen peace, and to realise reunification.[11]

In 1955 the DRV launched a political struggle in Vietnam, which lasted for two years and involved massive rallies, demonstrations and collections of signatures. The DRV campaign demanded that the Diem government implement the Geneva accords and condemned Diem's terror campaign against patriots and those who took part in the anti-French resistance in the south of Vietnam. The DRV government itself repeatedly sent letters, memoranda and proposals to Diem's

government requesting consultations and general elections, and reject-
ing any idea of holding separate elections in the South.

Many times the DRV used its diplomatic channels and its media to
criticize the US for its interference in the internal affairs of Vietnam
and for sabotaging the Geneva accords. The US was attacked for giving
South Vietnam protocol-nation status in the South-East Asian Treaty
Organization (SEATO), for sending US military personnel and weapons
to South Vietnam and for allowing the CIA to sponsor 'paramilitary
operations' and 'political–psychological warfare' in North Vietnam.
The DRV also tried to engage the Geneva machinery by appealing
to the co- chairman of the Geneva conference – the United Kingdom
and the USSR – and the members of the International Control Commission (ICC) to urge Diem to respect the accords. At the same time,
the leaders in Hanoi were conducting a substantial international
campaign with the aim of winning world public opinion for the reunification of the country.[12]

None of these moves, however, evoked a positive response from
Diem's government, but then, Diem's US-backed policies were aimed
at dividing permanently the two parts of Vietnam – at least as long as
North Vietnam had a communist regime. Diem's position, therefore,
effectively prevented implementation of the provisions of political settlement called for by the Geneva accords. While the DRV's policy of
peaceful reunification was supportive of the schedule laid out in the
accords, the deadlines for consultations and elections passed without
either one taking place. On 17 May 1958 the DRV delegation to the
ICC had to leave Saigon.

The DRV nonetheless stuck to its policy, insisting on the political
struggle for reunification through elections. In September 1956 a VWP
Politburo Resolution regarding the matter was issued:

> Our people's task of national liberation has not been completed;
> our struggle for national salvation is still going on, regardless of the
> armistice. The means of struggle, however, should be changed.
> We should complete the course of national liberation in a new
> way... Realisation of reunification means that the two sides agree
> to hold elections to elect a coalition government, and it does not
> mean either side will coerce or annex the other. As the Geneva accords
> are an internationally legal basis, we should actively strive for
> the implementation of the accords in order to strengthen peace, realise
> reunification.[13]

Why, at this time, the Democratic Republic of Vietnam pursued the course of *peaceful* reunification could be explained by Vietnamese choices and beliefs, together with internal and external influences.

To begin with, it was the choice that Hanoi leaders made between the task of reconstructing the North and the task of liberating the South. Both tasks were considered 'strategic',[14] but the task of reconstructing the backward and war-torn society and economy of the North was given priority.

The DRV's adherence to the policy of reunification by peaceful means also reflected the common belief, in both the DRV's leadership and its people, in the legality and practicality of the Geneva accords. By contrast to the bilateral agreements that the DRV had signed with France in 1946, which France could break without any international reactions, the Geneva accords were international and multilateral accords, arrived at through great-power diplomacy. The commitment of the Soviet Union, the People's Republic of China, France and Britain to the accords, the establishment of the International Control Committee and the smooth implementation of the military provisions in 1954 made Hanoi believe that the rest of the agreement could be respected as well. The bitterness and puzzlement felt among the cadres in 1956, especially those who had regrouped from the South to the North, when the scheduled elections were not held, testifies to this belief.

Apart from this belief, as researchers in Hanoi have argued, the influence of a 'post-war psyche' on some of the DRV's leadership and people is also discernible. After more than nine years of fighting and hardship, the mood favoured peace rather than renewed struggle. This mood inclined many to limit themselves to a political struggle for reunification through peaceful means. The inclination was also to believe that, when the elections were held, the electorate in the South would massively support the DRV platform for unification of North and South. Even the terror of Diem's government against the revolutionary forces in the South seemed bearable if victory could be achieved through non-violent means.

Finally, the DRV policy of peaceful reunification was influenced by the Soviet Union and the PRC, who were both at this time seeking a global peaceful environment. In February 1956 the Twentieth Congress of the Communist Party of the Soviet Union (CPSU) adopted the policy of peaceful coexistence, based on the principle and belief that the transition from capitalism to socialism could take place by legal, non-violent means, that revolution was no longer necessary and that communism would conquer the world through peaceful competition, and that international conflicts could be solved through peaceful means. Acting on the new policy, Khrushchev initiated the process of Soviet-American détente with his visit to the USA in 1957.[15] The PRC also wished to enjoy a peaceful international environment to focus on its economic Great Leap Forward Plan. It actively implemented the policy of peaceful coexistence, using principles in accordance with the spirit of the 1955 Bandung conference of non-aligned countries. The DRV's policy of reunification by peaceful means differed little from these Soviet and Chinese policies.

For all these reasons, the policy of peaceful reunification was adopted. Yet, the policy failed to achieve its goals because Diem and the US decided to ignore the pledge to hold elections. This deprived the DRV of any peaceful means to achieve reunification, and at the same time Hanoi's policy precluded any effective action by the revolutionary forces in the South to counter Diem's policy of bloody terror. Thus the communist and progressive movement in the South was depleted. During Diem's repressive campaign from 1955 to 1959, according to the Vietnamese historian Nguyen Khac Vien, massacres, tortures, deportation, mass imprisonment and terror raids took more victims in South Vietnam than the whole war from 1945 to 1954.[16] As Nguyen Huu Tho, who, though not a communist himself, later became the chairman of the National Liberation Front, described it, they were 'victims of circumstances when, on the one hand, the Government of Vietnam (GVNO – the Saigon regime) was brutally chasing them, and on the other hand, the Party's resolutions were strictly tightening their hand.'[17]

At some point in 1956, a certain difference of attitude developed among the party leaders over the policy. Le Duan, who remained in the South after 1954 as General Secretary of the Vietnamese Workers Party (VWP) Central Committee Directorate for the South (CCDS), and several other leaders in Hanoi, particularly those regrouped from the South, were pressing hard for the renewal of armed struggle while the general line remained to support political struggle alone. The party leadership was forced to consider the option of armed struggle. When Le Duan completed his theoretical work, 'The Path of the South Vietnamese Revolution', in August 1956, he concluded:

In order to oppose the US–Diem regime, apart from the part of revolution, the people in the south do not have any other alternative.

It is necessary to continue the national democratic revolution in South Vietnam, and it is necessary to use force to overthrow the feudalist-imperialist regime in order to establish a revolutionary democratic coalition and create the conditions for the peaceful reunification of the Fatherland.[18]

When Le Duan became a member of the VWP Politburo in 1957, the policy of armed struggle gained a strong voice within the Hanoi leadership. At the same time VWP cadres in the South – simply in order to survive – shifted, incrementally but surely, to armed struggle, contrary to the party's instructions. Moreover, they continued pressuring the leadership in Hanoi to change its policy.

After the cease-fire took effect in July 1954, the VWP kept its cadres in the South, ordering them to 'skilfully hide forces and combine legitimate and underground activities to preserve the revolutionary forces'[19] and to be the core of the political struggle in the South. Weapons were ordered to be hidden away, and the Viet Minh War Zones during the Resistance ceased to exist. Facing the 'Denounce Communism' campaign and struggling for their survival, many party cadres spontaneously either joined the remnants of the military forces of the Cao Dai and Hoa Hao sects or led people in their localities to fight back. Some of them were reportedly disciplined for going against the party's policy of peaceful reunification.[20] These spontaneous armed undertakings, however, helped the VWP leaders in the South create a strong case for revising current party policy. In 1956, the CCDS held several meetings to re-evaluate the situation, the result of which was a proposal for policy changes that would allow a 'mainly limited and typically self- defending kind of armed struggle'. In December the Second Conference of the CCDS, chaired by Le Duan, came to a decision:

> The revolution in the south has to use people's forces with a view to completing the general uprisings. Due to the needs of revolution, there have to be, to some extent, armed forces to support the political struggle and to eventually topple the US—Diem regime... [We must] actively build armed forces, build military bases in mountainous areas.[21]

The Third Conference of the CCDS, held in mid-1958 and chaired by Nguyen Van Linh, adopted another resolution, expanding upon the cause for armed struggle:

In order to encourage the people's political movement and partly to solve the difficulties caused by the lack of equipment and weapons necessary for the armed forces to be built, the Conference has decided to open a number of active armed struggles.[22]

Later that year, the Fourth CCDS Conference, also chaired by Nguyen Van Linh, unanimously approved petitioning the VWP Central Committee for a change in the party's policy of struggle by peaceful means.[23]

The petition was accepted ultimately by the VWP Central Committee, and on 13 January 1959 the 15th VWP Central Committee Plenum was held in Hanoi to review developments and reorient policy in the South. The final text of the 15th Plenum was completed and adopted in May 1959, and the '15th Resolution', as it was dubbed, made a new policy official:

The basic revolutionary path of the south is through uprisings to seize power into people's hands...According to the specific situation and present requirements of revolution, this path is to use the people's power as a basic force while combining it with the armed forces in order to overthrow the feudalist–imperialist oppressive regime and establish the people's government.[24]

In the final analysis, Hanoi's ambivalence and debate over policy and the means to achieve reunification ended with the 15th Resolution. Military organization in the North designed to support armed struggle in the South quickly followed. On 19 May 1959 the Military Land Transportation Directorate coded 'Unit 559' was organized, followed in July 1959 by the Sea Transportation Directorate coded 'Unit 759'. They were given the task of building transportation routes so that military personnel and equipment could be brought to the South. The 338th Division, which included the Southern regrouped soldiers, started its special training programmes designed to make the soldiers ready for return to the Southern military theatres. By the end of 1959 500 armed force officers and several thousands of combat and engineering troops with about 19 tons of equipment, completed a southerly march along a route that later became widely known as the Ho Chi Minh Trail.[25] The strategic shift from 'political struggle only' to a combination of armed and political struggle resulted mainly from three precipitating factors: the Southern Vietnamese spontaneous armed struggle against Diem's atrocities; the

CCDS decision to adopt armed struggle, thus creating both a *'fait accompli'* in the South and a strong argument for those favouring a general change of policy; and the pressure from Le Duan and his supporters in Hanoi. The policy debate ended when Le Duan became General Secretary of the VWP in September 1960. Researchers in Hanoi share the view that Ho Chi Minh himself nominated Le Duan to the post of party chief, since he believed strongly that Le Duan, who understood conditions in the South and was most determined to liberate the South, could fulfil his desire for national reunification.[26]

An Application of the Neutrality Formula

The new decade opened with a new phase of intensive guerrilla war in the South. The 'simultaneous uprisings' movement, a product of Hanoi's decision to combine political with armed struggle, and the internal dissension within the Saigon regime pushed the government in the South into a profound political crisis. A state of war between the United States and Vietnam, however indirect, emerged in the form of 'the special war' in the years from 1960 to 1964. US President John F. Kennedy changed US cold war strategy, replacing Eisenhower's 'massive retaliation' with 'flexible response'. The latter required that the US expand and modernize its conventional military forces to 'help those emerging nations that became the battleground in which the forces of freedom and Communism compete' and to develop an effective response to any communist advance, including guerrilla warfare.[27] On 28 January 1961, Kennedy approved the Basic Counterinsurgency Plan for Vietnam (CIP). The CIP was designed to increase the size of Saigon's army – referred to as the Army of the Republic of Vietnam (ARVN) – with additional assistance from the US to counter guerrilla warfare tactics. After the death of Diem and especially under President Lyndon B. Johnson, the US increased its commitment to the South Vietnamese regime and sent rapidly increasing numbers of military 'advisers'.

Hanoi's departure from its policy of 'consolidating the North and keeping in mind the South' was evident at the Third National Congress of the Vietnamese Workers' Party, which convened in Hanoi in September 1960. The Political Report of the Congress was even more resolute:

> In the present stage, the Vietnamese Revolution has two strategic tasks: first, to carry out the socialist revolution in North Vietnam; second, to liberate South Vietnam from the ruling yoke of the US imperialists and their henchmen in order to achieve national unity and complete independence and freedom throughout the country. These two strategic tasks are closely related to each other and spur each other forward... The common task of the Vietnamese Revolution at present is: To strengthen the unity of all the people; to struggle resolutely to maintain peace; to accelerate the socialist revolution in the North while at the same time stepping up the National People's Democratic Revolution in the South.[28]

The lessons of the August Revolution, which brought about Vietnamese independence through political mass organization supported by armed units, reverberated in the document: the struggle in South Vietnam was again considered one for national independence. In strict accordance with this new policy, the National Liberation Front (NLF) – a popular front in the South as a formal body, in the name of which the people in the South could be rallied and international support could be sought – was founded in December 1960. All south-based military units were reorganized and merged into the People's Liberation Armed Forces (PLAF) in February 1961. At the same time Hanoi increased its support to the forces in the South by sending more troops and war material.

This was indeed different from the policy of the previous years, when the DRV had been willing to deal with the Saigon regime, just urging it to abide by the Geneva accords. Now the DRV's objectives were to overthrow the Saigon regime, establish a coalition government that would adopt a policy of neutrality and ask the US to withdraw its military forces. This would lead eventually to national reunification. The policy has since been described by Hanoi scholars as 'defeating Nguy[29] and then driving away the Americans'. Armed struggle was not considered as possessing a more decisive character than political struggle, and, as armed struggle achieved political success, the new national coalition government could then ask the US to leave Vietnam.

The question arises: why, during this period, did Hanoi adopt the policy of 'defeating the US policy of aggression by overthrowing its henchmen's government and creating an independent and neutral one in South Vietnam'?[30] It was clear that the leadership in Hanoi did not want to confront the US directly and militarily. In his letter to COSVN

(the Party's Central Office for South Vietnam) chief Nguyen Van Linh
in July 1962, Le Duan warned of the risk:

> That the US must be defeated is unquestionable, but we have to
> carefully and accurately calculate to what extent the US would be
> defeated and to what extent we would win. If we yield to American
> intimidation, our course of revolution cannot progress. But if we try
> excessively hard, especially in the armed struggle, which the correla-
> tion of forces does not permit, it will lead to [US] reactions whose
> extent we are unable to measure.[31]

Hanoi's strategy, then, while based on the 'decisive characteristics of the
armed struggle', put emphasis on the condition of South Vietnam's
neutrality, considering neutrality an 'appropriate requirement that any
normal democratic regime should have' and an 'appropriate suitable
policy that could reflect the extent to which we could win and the
enemy could be defeated'.[32]

Hanoi's support for a neutral government in Saigon was designed to
widen the gap between factions in the ruling circles in Saigon and rally
more of the South's population, making political points and further
isolating those who still opposed neutrality. It was also designed to put
the US in a politically vulnerable position: no longer pro-American, an
officially neutral government could ask the US to withdraw its forces.

For international relations, the policy of a neutral government in
Saigon was of significance to the DRV. It could not only ensure a 'quick
and decisive victory' in the South and avoid great losses, both human
and material, but could also lessen the DRV's dependence on socialist
countries, especially the Soviet Union and the PRC.[33] Furthermore, it
could win the sympathy and support of socialist countries, nationalist
countries and the forces of peace in the world, convincing them that
the Vietnamese struggle was limited to the goal of national liberation
and that the struggle was part of the world's struggle for peace. Well
considered by leaders in Hanoi, the policy was in step with the international political context of peaceful coexistence.

The form of neutrality in Laos had also been considered relevant to
South Vietnam. The Pathet Lao, or Patriotic Front, which included the
People's Revolutionary Party in the early 1960s, had shifted from a
policy of political struggle to one that combined both political and
armed struggles. The political and military pressure exerted by the
Pathet Lao subsequently led to the establishment of several neutral

governments in Vientiane and finally led to the June 1962 Geneva accords that internationally recognized Laos as a peaceful and neutral country with a coalition government in which the Pathet Lao participated.[34] This was precisely what Hanoi wished to achieve in South Vietnam: with regard to Saigon, a neutral and coalition government in the South would enable the NLF to participate and later to control it *de facto*. With regard to Washington, the presence of a neutral coalition government would enable Hanoi to ask and pave the way for the US to withdraw forces from Vietnam. In a May 1965 letter to Nguyen Chi Thanh, who then was the head of COSVN, Le Duan explained his plan:

> We would control that government: the lower levels would be completely in our control; at the central levels, we would control the key ministries, i.e. defence, home and foreign affairs ministries. At the same time, the government should publicly avoid connections with the NLF and the North and focus on negotiation with the NLF on the cessation of hostilities, asking the US to withdraw its troops and reconvening the Geneva conference on Vietnam to ensure peace and neutrality in South Vietnam.[35]

In all, the goals of the multifaceted strategy adopted by Hanoi were to use political, military and diplomatic pressure to effect the establishment of a neutral coalition government in South Vietnam, whose policies would prevent a direct American intervention and, moreover, create the conditions for the withdrawal of US military forces – not a strategy intended to prolong the war in South Vietnam.

The Hanoi leaders calculated that if they could 'defeat Nguy totally before the US could act, the possibility for the US to turn the special war into a limited war would be minimised'.[36] Their calculations, however, proved unrealistic, for President Johnson opted for direct intervention – giving his approval to his advisers' recommendations to bomb North Vietnam and send combat troops to save the Saigon regime.

Encouraged by the widening Sino-Soviet rift, but concerned that the Saigon regime seemed on the verge of collapse, the Johnson administration hoped that an aerial war against North Vietnam and the sending of American ground troops to South Vietnam could save the situation. The American intervention was generally motivated by US anti-communism in the context of the cold war and, more specifically, by US concern about the credibility of its global commitment to counterinsurgency. Johnson's decisiveness was also a result of what American critics of the war would later call 'arrogance of power'.[37] At a time when the world socialist bloc seemed to be dissolving, the US intervention in Vietnam was hardly necessary from the general perspective of US cold war strategy. It caused a long-lasting rift in Vietnamese–US relations that worked against the interests of both countries. From 1965 a state of war existed between the United States and the Democratic Republic of Vietnam.

Seeking for the Most Suitable Strategic Choice

For several years after Johnson's decision to intervene directly, the US and the DRV were locked in a full-scale, destructive and costly war. Americans refer to the high-intensity conflict as 'the Vietnam War'; the DRV and the NLF called it the 'Anti-American War of Resistance for National Salvation'. Hanoi's three-pronged strategy to confront the American challenge on military, political and diplomatic fronts was focused on forcing the US to withdraw its troops completely and halting its hostile actions against the DRV, so that the NLF could be free to challenge and remove the Saigon regime, with support from the DRV. With the Tet offensive in early 1968, the leadership in Hanoi believed it had found an effective strategy for winning the war.

The new US commitment in Vietnam brought war to the entire Vietnamese territory – the worst scenario Hanoi had envisaged, and the one it had tried to avoid. Washington continued sending ground troops to South Vietnam, increasing the total number from 75 000 in 1964 to 184 000 in late 1965 and 480 000 in late 1967 to 540 000 in late 1968.[38] In late 1965 American ground troops had begun fighting in the South. In 1966, US bombing raids occurred in South Vietnam along the Ho Chi Minh Trail and in North Vietnam, where the targets included not only military outposts, but also populated areas and sites of economic importance. Hanoi was now face to face with the world's number one economic and military superpower and a power that had never been defeated in war. The Vietnam War caused enormous losses and destruction. It also evoked a strong sense of heroic nationalism among the Vietnamese. Hanoi could rally support for the just cause of national unification and liberation.[39] US military force could not destroy this generally held aspiration. The more the war intensified and expanded, the broader the patriotic sentiment of the Vietnamese, and the greater was the willingness to accept sacrifices.

Yet it was not solely nationalist determination that encouraged Hanoi in its belief that the war could be won. Hanoi had carefully assessed the weaknesses of the US strategy and its own strengths, and come to the conclusion that:

> The US is weak both militarily and politically, and the revolutionary war in South Vietnam is strong both politically and militarily. South Vietnam is not a life-and-death issue for the United States. The US has to face other issues in other places in the world, playing its role of a global gendarme. That is why the US cannot use all its forces to fight in Vietnam. Besides, the US is thousands of miles away from Vietnam. The largest war effort that the US can mobilise, therefore, is weakened to a great extent. This looks like the US can only use an arm to fight in Vietnam. Moreover, this arm is cut off from the body and is not supported by the whole body's force. Contrarily, the Vietnamese revolutionaries are fighting with all their force and potentially, in their own country and with the rising trend of world revolution against imperialism. Our forces are, therefore, politically and militarily strong and are based on very solid ground.[40]

With that conclusion, Hanoi's task was to seek an effective strategy through a series of important choices in its conduct of the war.

The first important choice was to aim for a protracted war with guerrilla tactics in the military field and mobilization of international support in the diplomatic field. Hanoi did not expect to defeat the US militarily (although it may have hoped to do so). Facing a mighty power like the US, the Vietnamese leadership calculated only that its strategy would effectively 'defeat the will of aggression' of the US. Once accomplished, this would lead the US to seek a negotiated settlement leading to withdrawal. From time to time Hanoi revealed its strategic goal of the fighting. In a letter to the COSVN in November 1965, following a Politburo meeting to assess the situation after the US had intervened, VWP General Secretary Le Duan wrote:

> To whatever extent and scope the present war will develop, the revolutionary forces in the south, actively supported by the north, can and must defeat the US . . . [We will fight the war] in which the

US imperialists cannot exercise all of their forces and eventually will have to accept a 'limited defeat' in order to avoid greater and more bitter defeats with unforeseeable consequences.[41]

This strategy, therefore, clearly aimed at confining the war within Vietnamese territory and seeking a stalemate rather than military success over the US, creating a 'no win' situation for the US and forcing the US to seek a negotiated settlement of the war in order to defend its greater interests. Le Duan, therefore, could write with a strong sense of confidence that: 'We believe that the United States cannot fight us for a long period of time; a protracted resistance will surely bring us final victory.'[42]

It is worth noting that Hanoi's leaders were prepared to fight a protracted war, yet they made every effort to gain a quick military victory. This strategic thinking was first revealed in Le Duan's letter to the COSVN in November 1965, in which he pointed out the task of 'seizing the moment, making great efforts in achieving a decisive victory in a relatively short time', when the enemies were 'facing grave crisis'.[43] Hanoi was convinced by late 1966 that the moment had come for planning a decisive victory. In his letter of 1 February 1967 to the VWP Saigon Committee, Le Duan issued a directive regarding the next steps: 'The immediate tasks now are to quickly build up our forces and be ready for the moment of General Offensive–General Uprisings.'[44] In December 1967, the VWP Central Committee adopted its resolution about Vietnam's moment of opportunity:

> We are facing a great strategic prospect and opportunity: the US is in a state of strategic deadlock...The situation allows us to shift our revolution into a new stage, that of decisive victory through [the immediate goals of] a general offensive and General Uprising.

Hanoi was motivated to reach its highest goal – a quick military victory over both the US and the Saigon forces in South Vietnam through its general offensive and the Saigon regime through the general uprising. And it tried to motivate its compatriots in the South as regards tactics. In January 1968 Le Duan wrote to the COSVN:

> The US strategy is now in a dilemma. if we compare its political and military objectives with the present political, social and economic situation in the US, what becomes clear is that the US war efforts

in Vietnam have reached their highest peak. This situation allows us to shift the revolutionary war to the stage of decisive victory. There is now a strategic opportunity to launch a general offensive and general uprisings...The nature of the immediate task is that we try to change the course of war, further shaking the will of aggression of the US, forcing the US to change its war strategy and de-escalate its war efforts.[45]

After several deceptive moves militarily and diplomatically, on New Year's Eve of the lunar calendar, 30 January 1968, the general offensive and general uprisings, or the Tet offensive, began.[46] The VWP Central Committee Resolution of December 1967 had set the objectives for a decisive victory through the general offensive and general uprisings:

To break down the bulk of the puppet troops, topple the puppet administration at all levels, and take power into the hands of the people.
To destroy the major part of the US forces and their war material and render them unable to fulfil their political and military duties in Vietnam.
On this basis, to break the US will of aggression, force it to accept defeat in the south, and put an end to all acts of war against the north. With this, we will achieve the immediate objectives of our revolution – independence, democracy, peace and neutrality for the south – and we can proceed to national reunification.[47]

Judging from the outcome of the Tet offensive, Hanoi did not achieve these objectives and some would say it was because they were not well based. Tran Van Tra, for example, has pointed to three reasons. First, the balance of forces was not favourable to the DRV and the NLF. By no means could they defeat the US and Saigon forces, which had five times more troops, had absolute advantage in naval and air forces, and could mobilize force strength from other military bases in the South Pacific region. Second, failing to defeat the US and Saigon forces meant Saigon's administrative power at all levels could not be toppled. So, the general offensive was bound to fail, and then no general uprisings could take place. The general uprising in Hué was an exception, but the NLF administrative power only lasted 25 days. Lastly, the armed forces in South Vietnam had a very short period of time to prepare. Three months of preparation were not enough to acquire supplementary troops and ammunition, and to study the field of military operation – the urban areas unfamiliar to the armed forces, in which the majority of population had not been mobilized.[48]

In a veiled acknowledgement of the failure of the general offensive and general uprisings, Le Duan commented in late 1969: 'The Tet is a *bombarder* that galvanised the political factors.'[49] He was referring to new opportunities brought about by Tet. While the DRV had failed to 'totally defeat the US militarily', many in Vietnam believed that the military and diplomatic pressure by Hanoi had, nonetheless, forced the US to change its policy in Vietnam, thus 'defeating the US will of aggression', and changing the course of war as Hanoi had earlier anticipated.[50] The Tet offensive occurred just as dissent in the US over Vietnam had been catapulted by the opening exchanges of the 1968 presidential election campaign, from a debate within inner official circles to a national public one heated by the mass media. The impact of the Tet offensive on public opinion therefore influenced the administration in a manner favourable to the DRV.

Already by mid-March Johnson had rejected Westmoreland's proposal to increase the troops in South Vietnam from 525 000 to 732 000 and he replaced the defence secretary Robert McNamara with Clark Clifford and General Westmoreland with General Creighton Abrams. Abrams was then authorized to implement his plan of 'Vietnamizing the war'.[51] On 25 March 1968 Johnson met with the group of former officials known as the Wise Men and was advised to disengage from Vietnam, withdraw American troops, and seek a negotiated settlement.[52]

In Hanoi's analysis, Johnson's decisions for limited bombing of North Vietnam and gradual disengagement were the first sign of US intentions to de-escalate its war effort. Johnson's announcement confirmed leaders in Hanoi in their belief that they had chosen an effective strategy of combining military, political and diplomatic struggles. After Johnson's statement, Hanoi saw an opportunity to 'draw the US to the negotiating table' and decided to respond. On 3 April 1968, Hanoi released an official statement of the DRV's government:

> It is obvious that the US government has not seriously and adequately met the legitimate demand of the government of the Democratic Republic of Vietnam, of progressive American opinion, and world opinion. However, for its part, the government of the Democratic Republic of Vietnam declares its readiness to appoint a representative

to contact a US representative for the purpose of ascertaining with the American side the unconditional cessation of the US bombing raids and all other acts of war against the Democratic Republic of Vietnam so that talks may start.[53]

Johnson's announcement regarding 'limited bombing' did not totally satisfy the DRV. In its earlier position statement by the DRV foreign minister Nguyen Duy Trinh in 1967, the DRV had demanded 'the unconditional and total stop of bombing'. By 3 April 1968, however, Hanoi decided to open contact with the US. Several reasons have been offered to explain Hanoi's decision. As Hanoi calculated, if it insisted on asking Washington for a total and unconditional halt to the bombing of North Vietnam before talks could begin then it would miss the chance to 'draw the US to the negotiation table' because world public opinion might blame Hanoi for its lack of interest in seeking a way out of the war. The 'hawks' in Washington would, therefore, have more easy excuses in demanding an increase in the war effort. In addition, if Hanoi agreed to open talks with Washington then it would have to talk under US terms, as bombing was still continuing over parts of North Vietnam. So, Hanoi decided to show its 'readiness to contact' Washington 'for the purpose of ascertaining with the American side the unconditional cessation of US bombing raids and all other acts of war against the DRV'. In this way, evaluating Hanoi's 'diplomatic offensive' as a success meant that by not turning down Washington's proposal, and by offering the US the possibility of a face-saving solution, talks would be opened. It meant, too, that by opening talks, Hanoi could continue to win world public opinion for its cause and begin to exercise its tactic of 'fighting while talking'.[54] On 2 May 1968, the DRV and the US agreed that Paris would be the place for the two sides to begin talks. As far as Hanoi was concerned, however, its participation in the talks would not involve discussions of a political solution to the war unless the US agreed unconditionally to stop bombing the North.

During the remainder of 1968, Hanoi conducted its second and third rounds of general offensive and general uprisings, commencing in April and August – the Tet offensive having been the first. Hanoi believed that it was its military pressure that had forced the US to the negotiating table when, on 13 May, Johnson decided to send American representatives to Paris to begin the talks.[55] Many lives were lost in these offensives, and the criticism has been made that the price was too high. The North Vietnamese troops (PAVN) and the PLAF suffered more than 111 306 casualties in the second and third rounds of 1968.[56] In addition, the NLF-affiliated organizations and sympathizers in the countryside were exposed during the general uprisings. In the following years, they were oppressed by Saigon and US forces. But scholars of DRV diplomacy during the war have argued that even if the offensives in 1968 were costly, they were of strategic significance, contributing importantly to the process that led Johnson to halt the bombing of North Vietnam unconditionally and start negotiations. On 31 October 1968 Johnson announced that the US would cease all air, naval and artillery bombardment of North Vietnam as of 1 November, and on that date the US and the DRV agreed to open quadripartite talks in Paris between the US, the GVN (Government of South Vietnam), the DRV and the NLF. Hanoi issued its statement 'On the US Government's Unconditional Cessation of Bombing and Bombardment of North Vietnam' on 2 November, announcing its willingness to join the US in discussions for the purpose of 'finding a political solution to the question of Vietnam'. The DRV government, the statement went on, 'was ready for the quadripartite negotiations'.[57]

The military failure of the general offensives and subsequent failure of the general uprisings pushed Hanoi to the realization that its goals of defeating both the US forces and the Saigon regime simultaneously were unrealistic. But having effected the unconditional cessation of military hostilities against North Vietnam and the opening of negotiations, Hanoi now turned its attention to attaining a US withdrawal through diplomatic and psychological means. On 3 November, Ho Chi Minh made an appeal to the nation: 'So long as a single aggressor remains on our soil, we must continue our fight and wipe him out.'[58] With this, it was clear that Hanoi had defined the enemy of first priority in its strategy for success in the war. Its three-pronged struggle, Hanoi believed, had led to this point in the war, and perseverance would lead to the withdrawal of US forces – and that would next lead to the fall of the Saigon regime. Ho Chi Minh broadcast Hanoi's strategic thinking in his New Year's Greetings to the nation on 1 January 1969:

> Last year we won brilliant successes.
> This year still greater victories will surely be ours on the fronts.
> For the sake of independence and freedom.
> Let us fight till the Americans quit and the puppets are toppled.[59]

Hanoi viewed its experiences since the US direct intervention – its choices and the outcomes – as proof of the efficacy of its strategy. As a tactic for achieving the withdrawal of US troops, then, fighting while negotiating was increasingly seen by Hanoi as not only a way to press onward, but also the one with the best prospects.

The period from 1969 to 1975 was to show how this strategic choice was put into execution. As a result of the offensives in 1968, Hanoi and NLF armed forces were weakened and time was needed for their recovery. Political and diplomatic means were considered more important. Laid out in a cable from the VWP Politburo, the context of Hanoi's approach reached the heads of the DRV's delegation at the Paris peace talks, Le Duc Tho and Xuan Thuy, on 14 January 1969:

> Because we have limited material resources and we don't want to be dependent on any other country, and because the worsening Sino-Soviet relations continue to cause difficulty for us, we are not able to endure great war efforts, to prolong the war and to defeat the US militarily, thus forcing the US to withdraw. We have, therefore, to combine military, political and diplomatic struggles in order to gain victory.[60]

It was noteworthy that in the early 1960s the DRV leadership had attached great importance to the conduct of its foreign relations. Hanoi refined its meaning of the term 'diplomatic struggle', making a distinction between the 'internationally political struggle' to win world public opinion and support for the Vietnamese war effort and the 'diplomatic struggle' to create the conditions for a negotiated settlement of the war.

In November 1966, the VWP Politburo adopted a resolution that in part explained:

> In the meantime, while we are stepping up the political and military struggles at home, [we should] open a new struggle by attacking the enemies by internationally political and diplomatic means. Supporting the political and military struggles, we should take the initiative to carry out the tactics of 'fighting while negotiating' in order to win world public opinion, isolate the American imperialists, cause more difficulties and internal controversy among them and push them into a more defensive posture.[61]

Concerning the internationally political struggle, the VWP Central Committee's 11th and 12th Resolutions, passed in February 1965 and December 1965, called for 'rallying all forces that can be rallied, making more friends, avoiding more enemies, dividing the imperialists, thus best isolating the US'.[62] Vietnamese historians of the war have analysed the reasons Hanoi enjoyed international support. The Vietnam War had become a focal point of world attention and of great importance to the world national liberation, socialist workers' and peace movements. Hanoi saw the war breaking out at a point in history when the national liberation movement was facing a policy crisis, opposing both colonialism and non-colonialism, and when the communist workers' movement was deeply divided. The war, it seemed, served a unifying purpose for consolidating revolutionary forces and precipitated the breakthrough for a resolution of the policy crisis.[63] As the war in Vietnam escalated with great human losses and massive destruction wrought by the fierce hostilities, it touched deep feelings in people throughout the world. An international movement supporting the Vietnam struggle and opposing the US emerged and grew stronger. A clear sign of the developing international support for the Vietnamese came with the proposal by Bertrand Russell in 1966 for the process of an international court on American War Crimes[64] and the Stockholm 1967–72 international conference, which denounced US war efforts in Vietnam and forged a relationship with the American peace movement. Encouraged by Vietnamese tenacity and sustained efforts, world public opinion became more sympathetic and the world movement became more supportive of the Vietnamese people.[65] As Hanoi put it, 'the fate of the small nation of Vietnam is connected to that of the world's people, and the Vietnamese Anti-American War enjoyed a tremendous world support that no other struggle ever enjoyed'; this support constituted the 'strength of our era, which the US had not anticipated before it went to war with Vietnam'.[66] The Soviet Union had also helped Hanoi and the NLF in conducting the international political struggle by mobilizing its large propaganda machine and exerting its influence in the UN and other international organisations, including the World Peace Council.[67]

As a matter of fact, the DRV's internationally political struggle placed an emphasis on the peace movements in the US as Hanoi considered how best to win support from another front that fought in the enemy's rear between 'the war-like imperialists' and the rest of the American people. Ho Chi Minh wrote of this front in his letter to the American people on 21 May 1964:

The Vietnamese people always differentiate the justice-loving American people and the US administrations which have committed numerous crimes against the Vietnamese people for the last 10 years. The Vietnamese people are extremely grateful for the workers', youth, students' and women's organisations as well as progressive scholars, congressmen and priests who have been bravely demonstrating against the policies of aggression by the US governments and supporting the just struggle of patriotic forces in Vietnam... American people, who are also victims of American imperialism, do fiercely fight, together with the Vietnamese people, against the war-like imperialists in your country.[68]

Addressing the 5th Conference of DRV diplomats on 16 March 1966, Ho Chi Minh reminded them of the growing strength and the impact of the American peace movement and revealed the clear purpose of influencing the domestic debate in the US:

At present, the American people's [peace] movement is on the rise. To win the American people's support, therefore, is very important. In your work abroad, greater attention should be paid to exposing the US war crimes of spraying toxic chemicals, bombing schools, churches... which the movement in the US is now also opposing.[69]

In early 1969 a meeting in Jakarta between two groups of American and Vietnamese women opened contacts between Hanoi and representatives of the peace movement in the US. The Johnson Administration discouraged the discussion about the war going on in Vietnam.[70] However, as the election years drew to an end in 1968 and 1972, national discussion on the war in Vietnam became more heated. Hanoi extended invitations to American university professors and reporters to visit North Vietnam, hoping to influence the on-going campus and public debates in the US.[71]

The international political struggle would continue from 1968 to 1972, and Paris now became the main theatre. After the peace talks began in Paris in 1968, the DRV and NLF delegations met regularly with members of American peace organizations, which according to a head of the NLF delegation 'increased the number of American supporters of the Vietnamese Resistance', and made 'the US government frightened'.[72] Henry Kissinger, a chief negotiator with Hanoi during that time, also told of his Vietnamese counterpart

Le Du Tho's tactics, which showed 'how well Hanoi had grasped America's domestic crisis':

> If Le Duc Tho was in Paris for any length of time without being contacted by the United States government, he was certain to drop many hints to journalists or visiting members of the congress about the Nixon Administration's failure to explore Hanoi's demonstrably peaceful intentions. Given the state of America's domestic controversy, such hints were sure to receive wide currency, and he was capable of dropping them even when talks were talking place.[73]

Diplomacy became a major front later. On 26 January 1967, the 13th VWP Central Committee adopted a resolution, directing the diplomatic struggle:

> Military and political struggles in South Vietnam are main factors that not only determine victories in the battlefields, but also those in the diplomatic struggle. We can only gain at the negotiating table what we have achieved in the battlefields. The diplomatic struggle, however, does not simply reflect the military struggle. In the context of the present international situation and the nature of the war with our enemies, the diplomatic struggle also plays an important, positive and active role. Together with the military and political struggles, we, therefore, should also attack our enemies in the diplomatic struggle and combine these three struggles in order to achieve ever greater victories.[74]

Hanoi launched its plan for diplomatic offensives in early 1967. The context, however, was its general offensive and uprisings, and its objectives were to cover up and prepare for intensified military attacks, and to build favourable conditions for negotiations in the later stage. The conditions were different in the aftermath of the 1968 offensives. Direct negotiations were open between Washington and Hanoi, and although Washington was getting deeper bogged down in Vietnam, Hanoi and the NLF could not win the war militarily. Diplomatic struggle, therefore, was intensified initially to open more contacts with the US (especially after there were clearer signs of improved Soviet and Chinese relations with the US) and to ascertain the Americans' will and intentions regarding negotiations. In a later stage, with more troops, and especially with a large quantity of Soviet military aid in sophisticated

and heavy weaponry, the military struggle was stepped up as Hanoi
started to conduct big-unit and high-tech warfare in the South. Following the military Easter offensive in 1972, Hanoi decided to go into
more substantial negotiations to complement its military outcomes and
to utilize further the tactics of 'fighting while negotiating'. Leaders in
Hanoi by this time felt vindicated by reaching a negotiated deal on
their own terms:

> When victory in the military struggle is to a sufficient extent gained,
> we will be able to use the diplomatic struggle to pave the way for the
> US to withdraw from Vietnam with honour and force it to conclude
> the war on our terms.[75]

Some diplomatic historians in Hanoi have recently spoken of Hanoi's
style of diplomatic negotiations in Paris: the ultimate goal was openly
publicized in order to win public opinion and to ascertain further the
intentions of the other side. When the moment arrived, even after a
long period of stalemate, closed-door discussions would soon conclude
an agreement on a more limited gain. Even though the withdrawal of
US military forces was the objective of first priority, Hanoi asked for
both total American withdrawal and the dismantling of Thieu's regime
together. Therefore, little progress was made during the initial phase
from 1968 to 1972. After being certain that the American withdrawal
was irreversible, Hanoi decided to come to more substantial negotiations, and a breakthrough was reached by October 1972. Hanoi now
agreed that the Saigon regime was to be kept intact, and political issues
in South Vietnam were to be solved by the Vietnamese after the US
withdrew forces from Vietnam. The agreement was signed later, however, in January 1973 after the 1972 Christmas bombing that caused
more destruction for North Vietnam. Several historians in Hanoi have
tried to see how the negotiating style of Hanoi, among other things,
contributed to this. They have argued that while Hanoi was trying to
handle the diplomatic struggle, which proved to be something new and
complicated in kind, it was necessary for it not to hurry. Moreover, as
its opponents became more divided at home, Hanoi could wait and
keep its maximum demands. In other words, the protracted warfare
tactics were also applied to the diplomatic struggle. In general, these
tactics worked. At the same time, however, it produced an 'inflexibility
side-effect'. The more Hanoi seemed to be insistent on removal
of Thieu, the more the regime in Saigon became resistant and

the more Washington had to show support for it. In addition, as some pointed out, Hanoi was also too persistent on 'minor issues', that is on the redefinition of the Demilitarized Zone. This led to a suspension of negotiations after the breakthrough was reached in October 1972. Chief negotiators Le Duc Tho and Kissinger returned to Hanoi and Washington for their Christmas 'vacation' and heavy bombing took place in December 1972.[76]

The two sides in Paris agreed, among other things, that the US would withdraw from Vietnam and let the Vietnamese settle the political issues. It was a significant victory for Hanoi, because the first and most important objective of its war strategy had now been achieved. After the withdrawal of American forces, the next task was to topple the Saigon regime. With the agreement reached in Paris, and with new developments in domestic politics in the US, especially after Watergate, the possibility of an American recommitment in Vietnam became more remote. The Paris agreement, on the one hand, required the total withdrawal of American military forces from Vietnam, and, on the other, allowed Hanoi to retain its troops in South Vietnam. The balance of forces, therefore, was clearly in favour of Hanoi and the NLF. Hanoi felt more confident that it would defeat the regime in Saigon, which was now left without substantial American support. In March 1968, the new defence secretary, Clark Clifford, was authorized to implement the plan of 'Vietnamizing the war',[77] which later became known as Nixon's doctrine of Vietnamization. In 1970, Le Duc Tho was said to have asked Kissinger how the US expected to prevail with the South Vietnamese army alone when it could not win with the assistance of 500 000 Americans.[78] This confidence was proved correct when in 1974 Hanoi and the NLF launched renewed military general offensives that finally led to the fall of Saigon and national reunification in April 1975.

In short, beginning in 1969, Hanoi's tactics of fighting while negotiating appeared largely successful. The negotiating did not prevent Hanoi from continuing the armed struggle and the fighting, while the fighting in fact led to more substantial talks. Fighting while negotiating deterred the US from re-escalating its war efforts and stimulated conflicts between the US and the Saigon regime as well as among opposing factions in Washington and Saigon. In addition, it enhanced the position of the NLF abroad and at home, winning greater public support in world opinion, even in the US.[79]

Scholars of the war on both sides have noted that fighting while negotiating 'appears to have been borrowed from Mao Zedong's

Chinese revolutionaries, but the technique itself was deeply rooted in Vietnamese history, an approach to war refined over centuries of confrontation with more powerful enemies.'[80] During the course of the war, the DRV received advice from its powerful allies – the Soviets and the Chinese – on various methods of conducting the war. The Hanoi leadership, however, tried to conduct the war independently. As a result, the talks that began in Paris in 1968 were significantly different from those that took place in Geneva in 1954. In the Paris talks the Vietnamese negotiated directly with the Americans, without the interference of their socialist allies. In the end, in January 1973, the DRV arrived at an agreement with the US after it had mounted political and diplomatic, military and psychological pressure for the US to bear, despite the costly efforts and the pressures from the Sino-American rapprochement and improved Soviet-American relations. Vietnamese researchers have later described the DRV's experience this way:

> There were different views of what direction the road of revolution should take. Many disagreed with ours. Some wanted us to carry out mainly the military struggle; some advised us to carry out mainly the diplomatic struggle. The advice supporting military struggle came from advisers intending to enjoy the monopoly of talks with the US, leaving us to do the fighting; the advice supporting the diplomatic struggle was based on an incorrect estimation of American strength. The experience of our struggle showed that only through the combination of all three struggles – the military, political and diplomatic ones – could we bring into full play the strength of our nation and those of our time which enable us to defeat a mighty enemy like the US.[81]

Conclusion

From 1945, United States policies with regard to Vietnam largely and consistently depended on its global geopolitical and economic interests, and also on the state of its relations with the Soviet Union and China in the context of the intensifying cold war. In the 1950s the US committed itself to the South Vietnamese regime in order to stop communism from expanding. When the Sino-Soviet rift developed, which in practical terms meant the dissolution of the world socialist bloc, the idea of a monolithic communism, which had been a premise for the US policy, proved to be invalid. The US, however, still could not withdraw its forces from Vietnam and allow a regime that was communist but independent from both China and the Soviet Union to gain power over the whole country. The US instead intervened in the ground war in South Vietnam and launched an aerial war in North Vietnam to maintain Vietnam's division and defend the general credibility of its global commitments. The animosity that developed between the US and the DRV was thus originally caused by external factors, rather than any national hatred or collision of national interests between the two countries. In other words, thinking in global terms, the US administrations misunderstood and oversimplified the nature of the national independence movement in Vietnam; and, believing in its strength as a superpower, they also underestimated the strength of Vietnamese nationalism. McNamara – one of the main architects of the Vietnam War – has also recently acknowledged this.[82]

National independence, liberation and unification were the highest objectives of the DRV's policies. Yet the Vietnamese national liberation movement was led by a communist party. Vietnamese policies toward the US, therefore, were also influenced by the communist ideology. This, however, did not prevent Vietminh leaders from seeking American assistance to achieve the Vietnamese independence in 1945 and from trying to neutralize the US in the Franco-Vietnamese war. Only after it replaced France to commit itself directly to South Vietnam in 1954 did the US become the main enemy of the DRV.

Even then, however, the DRV leadership did not mean to seek military confrontation with the US. Had elections been organized in accordance with the 1954 Geneva accords, or had a neutral government been established, then this would have proven Hanoi's policy of a merely political struggle successful, and might have given the US a way to withdraw from Vietnam without much loss of honour. In 1968, Henry Kissinger wrote, 'We fought a military war; our opponent fought a political one.'[83] This assessment was partly true. After they were forced to accept the military challenge posed by the US, policymakers in Hanoi tried to work out an effective strategy that, on the one hand, did not seek to defeat the US militarily but psychologically instead – that is, to defeat the 'will of aggression' of the US – and, on the other hand, combined the political, military and diplomatic efforts with a view to seeking a negotiated settlement, thus avoiding greater losses, casualties and destruction. In general, this combined strategy worked, and the war ended as Hanoi had planned. Hanoi's process of strategic choices was, however, going through stages where mistakes were made, which included the pursuance of the policy for peaceful reunification through 1957–8, and the unrealistic targets set for the Tet offensive. Le Duan once said:

> When undertaking our cause of revolution, we can only at best anticipate 70 or 80 percent of what is going to happen. But just do it and we will earn more from reality.[84]

Hanoi's strategy also proved effective in the international arena. While escalating its efforts in Vietnam, the US hoped that the Sino-Soviet rift would weaken support for the DRV. Hanoi, however, managed to gain maximum assistance from both the Soviet Union and China, while at the same time keeping its independence in the conduct of war and diplomacy. Besides, Vietnam's determination demonstrated in the course of the war and its success in winning support from world public opinion led to a tremendous international peace movement. However, judging from the reality that the international communist camp no longer really existed after the Sino-Soviet rift in 1959, which developed into Sino-Soviet enmity following the border clashes in 1969, there was no united action among the socialist countries during the Vietnam War, and Vietnam had to wage the war in the context of the 'great powers' game', involving mainly the United States, the Soviet Union and the People's Republic of China. Against this background, researchers in Hanoi maintain that Vietnam's victory was mainly a triumph of Vietnamese nationalism and for the Vietnamese traditions of fighting mighty foreign invaders for national independence and unification.

Acknowledgements

I wish to express my gratitude to the Norwegian Nobel Institute in Oslo for its support in my research. As a Nobel Fellow in the Institute's research programme on 'The Vietnam War and International Relations in Asia' during winter–spring 1995, I was afforded the offices and resources of the Institute and the excellent library services and generosity of the staff. I am also grateful to the Institute of International Relations in Hanoi for generously giving me research leave in the first half of 1995. For the benefits of their comments and suggestions, I am also thankful to Luu Doan Huynh, Linda Kimball, Geir Lundestad, Dao Huy Ngoc, Mari Olsen, Richard Shultz, Stein Tønnesson and Odd Arne Westad, and other scholars and researchers including my colleagues, Nobel Fellows Ilya Gaiduk, Jeffrey Kimball and Zhang Shuquang.

3

SOUTH VIETNAM
Ngo Vinh Long

The name South Vietnam was first officially used by the United States in August 1954 when it decided to establish a separate state south of the seventeenth parallel in direct contravention of the Geneva agreements.[1] Two of the most fundamental provisions of the agreements were the establishment of the seventeenth parallel as a temporary dividing line between two military regrouping zones, with 'the People's Army of Vietnam forces to the north of the line and the forces of the French Union to the south' (article 1), and the projected reunification of the country through internationally supervised general elections scheduled for July 1956 (article 14 and the final declaration).

In its 'unilateral declaration' of 21 July 1954 the United States had referred to a single Vietnam and promised to abide by all the provisions of the agreements. But, according to the *Pentagon Papers*, 'when, in August, papers were drawn up for the National Security Council, the Geneva Conference was evaluated as a major defeat for United States diplomacy and a potential disaster for United States security interest in the Far East.'[2] Various plans for direct American intervention in Vietnam to remedy the situation, however, were rejected by President Eisenhower, and a 'compromise' that involved the setting up of a 'stable, independent government' in South Vietnam was reached.[3] This later came to be known as the 'Diem Solution', a decision that precipitated the so-called Vietnam War.

From 1955 to 1975 the southern half of Vietnam became the main theatre of this war; and the southern inhabitants – called 'South Vietnamese' by the Americans – became the principal targets of this long and increasingly brutal war. But the responses of the southern population – both rural and urban – in a wide variety of forms to all the means of repression and destruction hurled at them were key factors that shaped decisive outcomes at every stage of that long war. This point deserves central focus in this essay partly because since 1975 it has been intentionally obfuscated in official Vietnamese analyses of the war as well as in US conservative sources, each for their own ideological and political reasons.

As soon as the war ended, North Vietnamese communist leaders began a concerted effort at overemphasizing the roles of Northern forces and leaders and denigrating the achievements of the Southern struggle movements and their revolutionary leaders in order to justify Hanoi's taking the lion's share of state power after the war, short of an all-out *coup d'état*. Many Southern revolutionary leaders were purged, and other non-party political activists became marginalized.[4] Even high officials in the North, such as General Vo Nguyen Giap, who disagreed with the revisionist party line, were not spared.

In an article published on 31 June and 1 July 1975 in the party daily *Nhan Dan* (The People) and the army newspaper *Quan Doi Nhan Dan* (The People's Army), General Giap gave detailed analyses of the reasons for the Vietnamese victory. In it he stressed repeatedly that the key was the 'combined strength of revolutionary war' that included combined military attacks with popular uprisings and military struggle with political struggle as well as the 'return of power to the people' in both the rural and urban areas. The article was immediately withdrawn from circulation and was never again mentioned in any official Vietnamese publication.[5] As late as 1988 Le Duc Tho, who was at that time still considered by many as the most powerful man in Vietnam, stated in a lecture given to the Institute of Military History that there was no such thing as popular uprisings and that the urban opposition in the South had been only a minor irritant to the various Saigon regimes and not much else.[6]

Not long after the suppression of his article General Giap was replaced as defence minister by General Van Tien Dung who authored, with a party ghostwriter named But Thep (Iron Pen), a book whose revision of the historical records and reinterpretations of events leading to the liberation of South Vietnam served to bolster the new party line mentioned above.[7] In 1982 General Tran Van Tra, commander of the People's Liberation Armed Forces of South Vietnam from 1963 to 1975 and deputy commander of the Ho Chi Minh Campaign that liberated the South, published his memoirs of that campaign as a veiled attempt to set the record straight.[8] But high party leaders in Hanoi disapproved of its publication and hence not only was the book abruptly withdrawn from circulation but General Tra was also relieved of all official duties. Likewise, General Giap was subsequently stripped of his positions in both the Politburo and the party Central Committee.

Efforts at revisionism in Vietnam, however, have resulted not only in strained relationships between once fraternal revolutionary leaders and their followers in both the North and the South after the war. Ironically, such rewriting of history has also given much support to the American conservatives in their assertion that 'North Vietnamese aggression' could have been checked and that the war could have been won if the American military had been allowed to 'go all out' against the North. These conservatives have also blamed the 'liberal' American press and the American anti-war movement as being ultimately responsible for the defeatist attitude of the American Congress, whose reduction of aid to the Saigon regime purportedly led to the 'loss' of South Vietnam. This stab-in-the-back theory produced much recrimination in the United States and also served to prevent normalization of relations between Washington and Hanoi for nearly a quarter of a century.

Although in the last few years a trend towards reconciliation in both the United States and Vietnam has increased, and relations between the two countries have improved, there is still a need to discuss developments in the South during the war years objectively and truthfully. To this end, in this chapter I try to focus in on aspects that I think have been misrepresented or glossed over in the various stages of the war from 1955 to 1975.

Generally speaking, the war in the South can be divided roughly into five periods: the first period, from 1955 to 1960, involves spontaneous and widespread resistance to the repression and oppression of the Diem regime that culminated in the 'general uprisings' (*dong khoi*, also translated as 'simultaneous uprisings' and 'spontaneous uprisings' in various English language sources) of 1960 and the formation of the National Liberation Front of South Vietnam (NLF) by the end of that year. The second period, from the beginning of 1961 to mid-1965, saw coordinated struggles under the leadership of the NLF in the countryside and widespread urban opposition led by a variety of religious and political organisations that brought about the fall of the Diem regime and at least half a dozen subsequent Saigon administrations. The third period, from mid-1965 to the end of 1968, was referred to by the

American policy-makers and military leaders as the period of 'the limited war' or 'war of attrition'. But the war during this period was limited only by the availability of resources that the United States could marshal to destroy the South Vietnamese countryside and then the urban areas during and after the 1968 Tet offensive. The fourth period, from the beginning of 1969 to the end of 1972, was variously called the 'talk–fight' period, the 'Vietnamization' period, or the 'Nixon War' period. It was during this period that President Richard Nixon made it 'perfectly clear' every time he appeared on American television that progress at the Paris peace talks depended on the success of his 'Vietnamization' programme. This period involved unprecedented destruction of South Vietnam through increased bombing and through the 'Accelerated Pacification Program'. And the fifth and final period, from after the signing of the Paris agreement in late January 1973 to the fall of the Saigon regime by late April 1975, was known as the 'post-war war' period. In order to prevent the formation of a Tripartite Government of National Reconciliation and Concorde as stipulated by the agreement, the Saigon regime immediately unleashed massive attacks on areas under the control of the Provisional Revolutionary Government (PRG) and, at the same time, carried out merciless repression against the Third Force (which was formally recognized by the agreement as an equal segment with the PRG and Saigon in representing all those not belonging to either camp in the tripartite coalition government). Counterattacks by PRG forces and widespread reactions by most other political and religious groups in the country finally led to the demise of the Saigon regime and the end of the war.

The First Period, 1955–1960

Right after the conclusion of the Geneva accords the United States decided to make the southern half of Vietnam into an 'independent' country under American control by using force to eliminate the revolutionary movement in there. But since the French were the guarantors of the accords and of the stipulated elections to reunify Vietnam in 1956, the United States, in the words of the *Pentagon Papers*, demanded, in August 1954 a 'dramatic transformation of French policy', purportedly in order 'to win the active loyalty and support of the population for a South Vietnamese Government'. Basically, the United States asked France to stay in Vietnam militarily, to get out of Vietnamese economic and political life, but at the same time Washington asked for French support and cooperation in implementing US programmes.[9]

The reason for this curious demand was because the Bao Dai administration, with Ngo Dinh Diem as prime minister, commanded no military forces except for the personal bodyguards. The so-called National Army, which had been severely battered, constituted part of the French Union forces. On 18 August 1954 Secretary of State John Foster Dulles stated in a letter to the defence secretary, Charles Wilson, that 'one of the most efficient means of enabling the Vietnamese Government to become strong' was to build up an army to support it. Dulles added that, 'it would be militarily disastrous to demand the withdrawal of French forces from Vietnam before the creation of a new National Army'.[10]

A crash military programme costing several hundred million dollars annually was approved in October 1954, beginning with the consolidation of all Vietnamese troops in the French Union forces under Vietnamese command. In November the US Joint Chiefs ordered a prompt reassignment of selected personnel and units to maintain 'the security of the legal government in Saigon and other major population centers' execute 'regional security operations in each province' and perform 'territorial pacification missions'.[11]

The aim of these military operations and pacification missions, in direct violation of the terms of the Geneva accords, was to destroy the revolutionary infrastructures in the countryside and to terrorize the population into submitting to the Saigon administration. But after several months of repression the revolutionary infrastructures remained quite strong, thanks to the strong support of the general population, while most of the pro-French religious sections and parties had been liquidated by force of arms or bought off with American dollars. As expressed by Leo Cherne, one of the original promoters of the 'Diem Solution', in the 29 January 1955 issue of *Look* magazine: 'If elections were held today, the overwhelming majority of Vietnamese would vote communist... No more than 18 months remain for us to complete the job of winning over the Vietnamese before they vote. What can we do?'

The first thing to do was to step up the repression and pacification of the rural areas. In mid-1955, soon after the last Viet Minh (short for Viet Nam Doc Lap Dong Minh Hoi or 'League for the Independence of Vietnam') army units had been regrouped to the north, the Diem regime launched a nationwide 'Communist Denunciation Campaign' (Phong trao to cong) in which the population was forced to inform against the revolutionaries and their sympathizers. In May 1956, the Saigon regime officially announced that more than 100 000 former Viet Minh cadres had 'rallied to the government' or surrendered. Tens of thousands of others had been jailed, executed or sent to 're-education camps'. Many of these people had been innocent civilians who had simply voiced their dissatisfaction with Diem's so-called land reform programme, which in effect sent landlords back into the countryside to reclaim lands the revolution had parcelled out to the peasants during the resistance war against the French. And these landlords could collect land rents for as many years back as they could lay claim to.[12]

According to a detailed study by Quynh Cu, a Northern researcher, of the Upper Mekong Delta province of Ben Tre, from the beginning of 1955 to the end of 1956 the Diem regime erected 500 jails in the province's 115 villages. At least 2 519 former Viet Minh cadres had been executed and more than 17 000 of the province's inhabitants had been jailed and subjected to many sadistic forms of torture, which included having the victims' tongues cut, their eyes plucked and their teeth extracted. On average, one out of every 25 residents of the province had been arrested, jailed and tortured during this period. From the end of 1956 to the end of 1958 the Saigon regime conducted almost daily military operations into the province to seize the peasants' land; and close to 79 000 hectares of paddy fields were turned over to landlords. The landlords, in turn, increased land rents from the average of about 10 to 15 *gia* (40 litres or 30 kilograms each) of paddy per hectare of food and hunger resulted; and, in order to survive, many peasant families had to migrate out of the province. And yet the leadership of the party – known as the Vietnam Workers Party (VWP) at that time – in Hanoi strictly forbade party members and their followers in the South to use force to defend themselves.[13]

In a recent overall assessment of the war issued in 1995 by the Central Command for the Overall Assessment of the War of the Politburo of the Vietnamese Communist Party, it is officially stated that 'principally because the party did not come up with any clear-cut policy and appropriate strategy that would allow the population to actively resist the enemy in any effective manner' from 1955 to 1958 'the revolution in the South suffered unprecedented loss'. In the end note to this statement, however, the editors admit that about 90 per cent of all party members had been killed. In the southern region (*Nam bo*, covering practically the same territory as the former French Cochin-China) 70000 party cadres had been killed. Over 90000 other party members and local inhabitants had been arrested, jailed and tortured. About 20000 of these people had become crippled and severely wounded after the torturing. As a result, for example, only one local party cell remained in Bien Hoa province. Only 92 and 162 party members survived in Tien Giang and Ben Tre province respectively. In the central provinces 40 per cent of all provincial party cadres, 60 per cent of all district cadres and 70 per cent of all village cadres had been arrested and killed. In some provinces, only two to three cadres remained. Only in Tri Thien (the provinces of Quang Tri and Thua Thien) did 160 of the former 23400 cadres survive.[14]

Nevertheless, this overall assessment claimed that from 1955 to 1958 'we rallied and organised more than 12 million people to carry out political struggles under various forms and at different levels of intensity'.[15] The fact of the matter was that most of these struggles were started by the local inhabitants and were beyond the control of the party. These struggles, however, had the effect of forcing the party leadership in Hanoi to reassess the situation or risk losing the support of the Southern population completely. In January 1959 the Fifteenth Plenum of the VWP Central Committee was convened under the chairmanship of President Ho Chi Minh and it issued a resolution – called Resolution Fifteen – that authorized the Southern population to use force to defend themselves, but only when absolutely needed.

At an extraordinary conference held in the fall of 1990 at Columbia University, General Tran Van Tra stated that it is correct to interpret Resolution Fifteen as a result of pressure from revolutionaries from the south. But Resolution Fifteen, General Tra added, 'advocated political struggle as the main role and armed struggle as a supplement to the political struggle'.[16] In fact, the 1995 Politburo assessment admits that even before the Fifteenth Plenum and before its resolution could reach the south, 'armed struggles had already exploded in many places'. The assessment states further that: 'By mid-1959, *the South in reality had already been in the middle of the process of uprisings in stages*' [original emphasis].[17]

Quynh Cu, the author of the study on Ben Tre cited above, concludes that from 1957 to 1959:

The revolution in the south entered its darkest months and years. Under the circumstances the southern population could not apply the [party's] policy of 'protracted seize' (*truong ky mai phuc*), the doctrine of waiting things out, but instead HAD to adopt an attack strategy. If at that time the southern population had not defiantly fought for their rights to life and for democracy and, by the end of 1959 and the beginning of 1960, had not started the general uprisings and began a revolutionary war, then the entire revolutionary cause could have faced the danger of being totally squashed. The United States and Diem regime could have [even been encouraged to] carry out their planned attacks against the north. Clearly, there was no other road for the southern population to take but to rise up and attack the enemy continually.[18]

The fierce struggles of the Southern inhabitants, especially of the peasants to defend their land rights, led *Cach Mang Quoc Gia* (Nationalist Revolution, the veritable official organ of the Diem regime) to make the following complaint in the 23 February 1959 issue: 'At present, in the countryside the landowners can no longer collect their land rents because they dare not return to their villages.' This unrest in the countryside was of course blamed on the 'Viet Cong', or literally, 'Vietnamese Communists'. So in the same month, with the help of US and British experts, a pacification programme involving wholesale resettlement of the resident population was forcefully carried out in order to separate so-called loyal from disloyal groups. Because people were taken from their plots of land – on which their houses, paddy fields, ancestral tombs and so on, were located – and moved to totally unsuitable areas, and since it often happened that many 'loyal' families were grouped together with 'suspect' families for no reason other than the fact that they might have relatives who had fought with the Viet Minh against the French, this resettlement technique brought protests even from the ranks of Saigon government officials.[19] In April 1959, more 'sophisticated' relocation sites with barbed wire fences and spiked moats around them were constructed with forced labour and at enormous costs to the peasants and were euphemistically called 'agrovilles'. In many cases, when the houses and fields of those who had been relocated were considered too distant from the newly constructed agrovilles, they were simply burnt down.[20] On 14 July 1959, *Cach Mang Quoc Gia* declared: 'We must let the peasants know that to give shelter to a communist or to follow his advice makes them liable to the death penalty. We must behead them and shoot them as people kill mad dogs.'

The increased repression of the Diem regime presented the Southern population with few alternatives but to take up arms and fight back. Even the 1995 Politburo assessment admits that 'through extremely ingenious and varied forms of uprisings' the Southern population had, from 1950 to 1960, 'caused massive disintegration of the repressive machinery of the puppet regime in the villages and the return of the rights of self-governance to the inhabitants of thousands of villages and hamlets'.[21] Nevertheless, the assessment claims that: 'The great victories of the general uprisings marked the first great leap of the revolution in the south. Clearly Resolution Fifteen was an exemplary success of our Party in terms of advancing the strategy of revolutionary violence and of the arts of leadership in starting the revolutionary war in the south.'[22]

However, General Hoang Van Thai, the highest Northern commander in the South during the war years and deputy defence minister after the war, emphasized in a paper summarizing the results of a conference held in Ben Tre province in mid-July 1982 to assess the war that:

> The resolution of the Fifteenth Plenum only referred to political struggles supplemented by armed support. There was nothing yet about the strategy of 'two legs' [rural and urban struggles] and 'three prongs' [political struggle, military struggle and 'proselytization among enemy troops'] nor the question of 'three pronged coordinated attacks' [an appropriate mix of these three factors in a symbiotic relationship for extending and maintaining revolutionary control]. Only after the uprisings in Ben Tre and other areas and the issuance of the 1961 directive of the Central Committee that slogans like 'attacks and uprisings, uprisings and attacks' and 'two legs and three prongs' slowly came into being in 1962 and 1963. It was not until the ninth plenary session [in November 1963] of the Central Committee that the overall policy and strategy of advancing the revolutionary war in the south was clearly and fully formulated.[23]

Strategically and politically, however, what turned out to be of utmost importance for later years was the decision taken at the Third National Congress of the VWP in September 1960 in Hanoi to create a broad-based coalition capable of rallying the diverse struggle movements in the south. This decision was motivated partly by the realization that the party leadership in Hanoi risked losing control of the Southern revolutionary movement completely unless some kind of strategy for a revolutionary war were adopted. And they thought that the best way to do this was to create a front similar to the Viet Minh Front employed during the war of resistance against the French. As a result, in the next few months Southern revolutionary leaders made contact with most social and political groups in the South and discussed with them the programmes and organizational structures of the forthcoming alliance. On 20 December 1960 representatives from twenty political, social, religious and ethnic groups gathered at a secret location in Tay Ninh province, near the Cambodian border, to form the National Liberation Front of South Vietnam – usually referred to as the National Liberation Front, or simply NLF, in the West. The Front's programme called for the overthrow of the Diem administration, liquidation of all foreign interference, human rights and democratic freedoms, a 'land to the tiller' policy, an independent economy, the establishment of a national coalition government, a foreign policy of peace and neutrality, and a gradual advance toward the peaceful reunification of the country.[24]

The formation of the NLF was significant not only because it provided an umbrella organization for coordinating political and military activities in the south but also because it signalled a willingness by the Hanoi leadership to allow the North to become the 'rear base' for the revolutionary war in the South. In the words of Truong Nhu Tang, a founder of the NLF and Minister of Justice of the Provisional Revolutionary Government (PRG) in later years, on the morning of 21 December 1960, a special broadcast from Hanoi 'reached every corner of the south, announcing the formation of the NLF and offering congratulations from the Workers' Party and the Northern government. It was a time for nourishing the most sublime hope.'[25]

The Second Period, 1961 to Mid-1965

By early 1961, however, the party leadership in the North was still trying to apply the brakes on the struggle in the South. A January 1961 Politburo directive instructed the Southern revolutionaries to pursue a policy of 'special war', which called for small-scale military engagements to be balanced and fine-tuned to the political struggles in various local areas. In February 1961, all the armed units that had been established in the Southern provinces were formally organized into the People's Liberation Armed forces (PLAF). By September 1961 the command of the PLAF was placed under the party's newly-created Central Committee Directorate for the South – called simply COSVN (Central Office of South Vietnam) by the Americans. According to varying US estimates, PLAF strength was around 17000 in late 1961. By late 1962 it grew to between 23000 to 34000 men and women.[26]

Much of the strength and effectiveness of the Southern forces, however, had preceded the creation of the PLAF and COSVN, as can be seen in the case of Long An province which is located immediately south of Saigon.[27] As early as the end of 1959 and the beginning of 1960, through a combination of 'armed propaganda' – involving the use of many tactics to win over Saigon soldiers – and attacks on Saigon military outposts, the revolutionaries had gained control of the province politically and economically. Militarily, the province already had three battalions of regular troops – battalions d506 and d508 operating in the eastern half of the province (later on called Long An owing to administrative redistricting by Saigon) and battalion d504 in the western half (called Kien Tuong after the redistricting). In addition, the province managed to send one platoon each to operate in the Saigon area and the Nha Be River area respectively, as well as one squad to fight in the My Tho district of Dinh Tuong province.

The first important military factor contributing to the development and maintenance of revolutionary control and power in Long An was the building of strong military forces, especially the regular provincial units. In fact, the provincial regular forces were, in 1959, the first to be created and thus had to carry out all the activities that the district units and the village guerrillas were later to perform. By the end of 1961 the province had already managed to train enough district units and village guerrillas who were able to fight on their own at the local levels as well as to coordinate their combat activities with the provincial regular troops. The provincial leadership selected some of the best from its various companies, platoons and squads to lead the district, village and hamlet units. In each district there was an infantry company, a platoon of 'special activities' or commando forces, and a platoon of 'communication troops' (*cong binh*) specializing in attacks along the highways or waterways. They were equipped with sub-machine-guns, machine-guns and other automatic weapons – most of which had been captured from the Saigon forces. In each village there was a platoon of about 25 to 30 guerrillas, and in each hamlet there was a squad of 10 to 15 guerrillas.

This existing strength allowed the NLF and their supporters to resist the onslaught of the American 'counterinsurgency war' after President John F. Kennedy came into office in 1961.

In the fall of 1961 the White House decided to escalate the military war significantly and to pacify the rural areas by driving the peasants into a network of some 16000 so-called 'strategic hamlets' (*ap chien luoc*) out of a total of about 17000 hamlets in all of South Vietnam. In the spring of that year the United States had also begun to use herbicides intentionally to destroy food crops to drive the peasants into Saigon-controlled areas so as to deny the NLF popular support. Over the next eight years one hundred million pounds of herbicides would be dropped on over four million acres of South Vietnam to 'dry up the sea' in an effort to kill the 'revolutionary fish'. By the summer of 1963 the Saigon regime reported that over two-thirds of the population had been forcefully relocated into the fortified strategic hamlets.[28]

The massive relocation and the wholesale destruction of crops created untold suffering and hardship for the people, as well as widespread hunger and starvation. This forced the peasants and NLF forces to fight back by staging many armed struggles against the Diem regime. In January 1963 the war came to a turning point at Ap Bac, 40 miles south-west of Saigon. A small NLF force of about 350 lightly armed guerrillas soundly defeated an ARVN (Army of Vietnam) contingent of 2000 soldiers, supported by American operated helicopter gunships, fighter bombers, armoured personnel carriers and American advisers. The two trump cards of the American military war in South Vietnam, the terrifying helicopter gunships and amphibious tanks, proved to be quite vulnerable.[29]

After Ap Bac, 1963 was marked with severe setbacks for the Saigon army, and the victories of the NLF forces greatly helped the population in their efforts to demolish the strategic hamlets or turned them in to 'combat hamlets' for defending themselves against Saigon's encroachments. In September 1963, Rufus Phillips, special adviser to the President of the United States, reported to him 'estimates of USOM [U.S. Operations Mission to Vietnam] that the Delta was falling under Viet Cong control in areas where pacification was supposedly complete'.[30]

The repeated military and pacification setbacks, plus widespread urban opposition by Buddhist and other groups, convinced Washington that Diem was no longer equal to his task. On 1 November Diem and his brother and chief political confidant, Ngo Dinh Nhu, were murdered in a US-backed coup. After Diem's death, the White House

promptly established a close working relationship with the new government, headed by General Duong Van Minh. The United States
increased its military supplies and aid to Saigon; and in 1964 the
defence secretary, Robert McNamara, came to Saigon to work out
new pacification plans. But the deeply shaken Saigon regime and
army were plunged into an endless crisis: within 20 months since the
fall of Diem, 13 coups, 9 cabinets and 4 charters followed one after
another. The various US services tried in vain to find a formula of
government likely to allow the war to be conducted in an efficient way:
military junta, associated military–civilian government, dictatorship
under one general, rule by veterans or by 'young Turks'.[31] Meanwhile,
in the words of the March 1964 NSAM 288 (National Security Action
Memorandum):

> In 22 of the 43 provinces, the Viet Cong control 50 per cent or more
> of the land area, including 80 per cent of Phuoc Tuy; 90 per cent of
> Bnh Duong; 75 per cent of Hau Nghia; 90 per cent of Long An; 90
> per cent of Kien Tuong; 90 per cent of Dinh Tuong; 90 per cent of
> Kien Hoa; and 85 per cent of An Xuyen... The Viet Cong control
> virtually all facets of peasant life in the southernmost provinces and
> the government troops there are reduced to defending the adminis-
> trative centers.[32]

Also in March 1964, according to the 1995 Politburo assessment, President Ho Chi Minh responded to the situation by convening a so-called
Special Political Conference for all of North Vietnam, with the stated aim
of rallying support for the South, defending the North and fighting for
the eventual reunification of the country. Supply of personnel – mostly
former Southern Viet Minh returnees – and weapons to the South is said
to have increased tenfold in 1964: 17427 persons and 3435 metric tons
of weapons. These newly arrived reinforcements from the North were
integrated into the revolutionary armed forces in the South to form 11
regiments and 15 battalions of main force units.[33] According to General
Tran Van Tra, it often took up to a year to make Northern units operational after they had been integrated into the PLAF.[34] Nevertheless, in
the words of the *Pentagon Papers* historians, by the beginning of 1965 the
increased effectiveness of the NLF had made

> Over a year of US effort to bring about political stability within the
> GVN [Government of Vietnam] seemed to have been fruitlessly

wasted... During May and June [1965] ARVN suffered a series of near catastrophic defeats that were instrumental in deciding the Johnson Administration to act on General [William] Westmoreland's recommendation for a greatly expanded US ground combat role in the war.[35]

The Third Period, Mid-1965 Through 1968

The American military buildup in South Vietnam was quick and massive: over 184,000 men by the end of 1965 around 385,000 by the end of 1966, and some 480,000 by December 1967. The aim, according to General Westmoreland's strategy, was to achieve victory in South Vietnam in three stages: the first stage, which was to last through the end of 1965, was to secure densely populated areas along the coast and halt the downward trend in the war. The second stage was to drive the revolutionary forces out of strategically important areas in the plains and the mountains and cut off the flow of infiltration from the North in the first few months of 1966 with the use of both US and ARVN troops. And the third and final stage was to wipe out all remnants of the insurgency within twelve to eighteen months.[36]

According to the *Pentagon Papers*, in accordance with General Westmoreland's concept of a 'meatgrinder', the United States command found itself 'fighting a war of attrition in South East Asia'.[37] The aim was to kill larger and larger numbers of the enemy through 'search-and-destroy operations' and to force more and more villagers to move into areas controlled by the South Vietnamese government to deprive the NLF of popular support.[38] In congressional testimony in January 1966, the defence secretary, Robert S. McNamara, introduced evidence on the success of air and artillery attacks, including 'the most devastating and frightening' B-52 raids, in forcing the villagers 'to move where they will be safe from attacks... regardless of their attitude to the GNV'. This, McNamara continued, not only disrupted Viet Cong guerrillas' activities but also threatened 'a major deterioration of their economic base'.[39] Again, in November 1966, McNamara explained that it 'has been our task all along' to 'root out the VC infrastructure and establish the GVN presence'.[40] In the hope that hunger would force the rural population to stop supporting the NLF and move over to the US – Saigon controlled areas, by the end of 1966 more than half of the chemicals sprayed were admittedly directed at crops. In February 1967 Donald Hornig, President Johnson's chief scientific adviser, explained to a group of scientists that 'the anticrop programme was aimed chiefly at moving the people'.[41]

'Refugee generation', in act, became a central goal of the US war efforts in Vietnam. In 1966 Robert Komer, who directed the pacification programme – officially called 'The Other War: The War to Win the Hearts and Minds of the People' – stated that refugee generation helped to 'deprive VC of recruiting potential rice growers'.[42] Again, in April 1967 he recommended that the United States must '*step up refugee programs deliberately aimed at depriving the VC of a recruiting base*' [his emphasis].[43] In actuality, by the beginning of 1967, some 40 000 'pacification cadres', about 10 per cent of all US troops and 90 per cent of ARVN regulars, were already being used exclusively for pacification efforts, which included the destruction of villages and wholesale resettlement of the rural population into 'New Life Hamlets' and 'Camps for Refugees Fleeing from Communism' in order to 'secure' them.

The conditions of the refugees were so bad that Saigon newspapers, in spite of the harsh government censorship and the continual government practice of confiscating newspapers and closing their offices, felt compelled to run long articles on the misery endured by these people. *Song* was a Saigon daily specifically created to justify the pacification programme. Its editors and staff were members and leaders of the Rural Development Cadre Teams sponsored and trained by the joint cooperation of the CIA and the USOM. But even *Song* had this to say on 10 December 1967 in a long article entitled 'Looking at the Face of the Two Quang Provinces in War, Hunger, Misery and Corruption':

This is a free area – free for depravity, corruption, irresponsibility, cowardice, obsequiousness, and loss of human dignity. What the devil is dignity when people sit there waiting to be thrown a few hundred piasters and allotted a few dozen kilos of rice a month?

But we seem to like this, and the Americans also like us to perform these kinds of activities so that they can have a lot of big statistics to present to both their houses of Congress. The Americans like to count, count people's heads, count square and cubic meters, and count the money they throw out. They think that the more they can count, the better is the proof of their success, the proof of their humanitarianism, and the proof of their legitimacy in this war... How high a figure has the number of refugees who have to suffer and stay hungry [in the two provinces] reached? Many statistics proudly present the number two million.

The same article hastens to point out that in the province of Quang Tin alone 60 per cent of those who stayed hungry were children from 2 to 14 years of age. The remaining 40 per cent were old men and women. The able-bodied men presumably either were killed or went to fight with the NLF.

The pacification programme created enormous resentment, and consequently resistance, from the Vietnamese so that by mid-1967 US Operation Mission (USOM) data on loyalties of the hamlets reported that only 168 hamlets out of a total of 12 537 in South Vietnam were controlled by the Saigon government. On the other hand, the NLF controlled 3 978. The remainder were listed as 'contested' or partially controlled by both sides.[44] Significantly, the official US 'Hamlet Evaluation System' (HES) admitted in an overall analysis of the 1967 pacification results that to a large extent the NLF dominated the countryside.[45] A Reuters despatch on 11 March 1967 quoted Major John Wilson, the senior US adviser in Long An province as saying:

For every hectare we pacify, we have devoted to this province more men, more dollars and other means that any other province in South Vietnam. Yet, the results of these efforts are meagre . . . In reality, we can control only a very small area, according to the required norms. I would say that we control only 4 per cent in the daytime and only 1 per cent during the night.[46]

Confronted by the deteriorating situation in the Southern countryside, the Johnson administration, according to the *Pentagon Papers*, escalated the air war in the North during 1967 in an effort to get the North to call off Southern attacks in exchange for a bombing halt. This was what LBJ called his 'peace offensive'. It was later dubbed the 'San Antonio Formula' because he presented it in a speech in San Antonio, Texas, on 29 September 1967. When DRV (Democratic Republic of Vietnam) officials resisted such tactics, Johnson denounced them as intransigent and stepped up the bombing.[47]

Meanwhile, to delude the American public into believing that the Saigon regime was not becoming more popular and was therefore worthy of increased support, US leaders helped organize a series of 'democratic elections' to legitimize General Nguyen Van Thieu as president and Air Marshal Nguyen Cao Ky as vice-president. The elections were a cruel farce. Thieu and Ky openly used troops and police to intimidate voters and rivals alike. They even despatched General Nguyen Ngoc Loan, director of the National Police, to force members of the National Assembly to disqualify their most serious opponents. Those who were permitted to run were constantly harassed, detained and treated to the worst kinds of political dirty tricks.

Even with these tactics, with the exclusion of voters in 'insecure' areas as well as those dubbed sympathetic to the NLF, pacifists or neutralists, and with rampant ballot box stuffing by soldiers and police, Thieu and Ky received only 34.8 per cent of the national votes. They lost outright in many larger cities such as Saigon, Danang and Hue.

On 1 October 1967, the day before the National Assembly was scheduled to vote to ratify the elections, combat police blockaded all the streets to it and General Le Nguyen Khang, commander of the Third Military Division, brought his army into Saigon. The following day, General Loan brought his guards into the National Assembly, drew out his pistol, propped up his feet and began drinking beer. The implication was clear. Two hours later, Assembly members voted 58 to 43 to ratify the election. An hour later the body was dissolved. The Johnson administration immediately declared a victory for democracy in South Vietnam and vowed to do all it could to defend the new government.[48]

It was under these circumstances that DRV Politburo members decided to initiate a series of widespread attacks against Southern cities – later on dubbed the 'Tet offensive' of 1968 because it started on Tet, or Vietnamese New Year. This was not a desperate gamble, as many Americans later surmised, but a calculated move to get the United States to de-escalate the air war and start negotiations. According to Tran Bach Dang, who was given the responsibility in August 1967 to draw up the plan for the attacks on Saigon, the idea of a 'general offensive' against urban areas in the south – especially against Saigon, which was the nerve centre of the United States and the Saigon regime – was to create shock waves in the south, and thus force a turning point in the war. But this plan was not new. It had been conceived as a possible plan of action by NLF leaders as early as 1960.

In 1964, a plan of action similar to the 1968 Tet plan was introduced to the Communist Party's Central Committee. At that time there had been sufficient sapper units in the South to carry out the initial attacks, but the regular and regional forces were still not strong enough to deliver the necessary follow up assaults. In addition, the political organizations in and around the cities and towns were considered inadequate for providing the necessary support to sustain the attacks. Moreover, in 1964 communist leaders believed that such a general offensive would have the effect of sucking into Vietnam a huge number of American troops, because the American 'hawks' would be able to argue that the introduction of US forces would help change the situation in the South. The plan was therefore temporarily shelved by the Central Committee. Instead, they directed Southern revolutionaries to lay a better groundwork for such an offensive in the future by building up their military and political forces.

By mid-1967 the Politburo and COSVN ordered that the details of a contingency plan for attacks on Saigon and other cities be worked out. They reasoned that widespread attacks against the urban centres, which were the nerve centres of the United States and Saigon regime, would compel American leaders to pull back most of its forces and firepower to defend the Southern centres, thereby easing their military pressure on the North. They conjectured that by that time the United States had nearly 500 000 troops in the South. They believed that this was nearly the maximum that the United States was capable of sending. Thus, they reasoned that a general offensive would demonstrate to American leaders and citizens that they had no hope of winning and hence would force them into negotiations and troop withdrawals. Representatives from the Politburo, COSVN, the B-2 Military Command, and the Saigon-Giadinh Regional Party Committee held several meetings from July to October to debate the Politburo decision and to discuss details for the offensives.[49] Finally, on 25 October 1967, party Central Committee members issued Resolution Fourteen, ordering a 'general offensive/general uprising' or 'tong cong kich/tong khoi nghia' in the South, mainly against Saigon and the upper Mekong Delta provinces.[50]

The 1968 Tet offensive and its aftermath have been seriously misinterpreted and misrepresented in both official North Vietnamese and US sources. Fortunately, this convergence of official interpretations has recently been effectively countered by scholars on both sides of the Pacific.[51] Briefly, the offensive was composed of three phases, lasting until October of that year. During the first phase, from the end of January until the beginning of March, the NLF strike force achieved dramatic gains. Hundreds of thousands of people provided the NLF forces with the necessary logistical support to enable them to attack almost simultaneously all the major cities, 36 of the 44 provincial capitals and 64 of the 242 district towns. Planned 'uprisings' in the

form of demonstrations or taking over of administrative offices by
civilians were called off, partly because the main force units were
never committed – for unexplained reasons that are still hotly debated
today – to occupy the key target areas that they were supposed to, and
partly because there was no point in doing so when American fire-
power was reducing from 30 per cent to 80 per cent of most cities to
rubble. NLF casualties were also relatively light, partly because not that
many people were used. In Saigon, the main target of the offensive,
only 1000 armed personnel engaged over 11 000 US and ARVN troops
and police for three weeks. Most of the casualties in Hue and Khe Sanh
were North Vietnamese regulars.

NLF troops suffered heavy casualties only after Politburo members
in North Vietnam decided to mount the second and third phases of the
offensive. As a result, revolutionary units were left too long in forward
positions around the urban areas, where they were subjected to hor-
rendous air and artillery strikes. In addition, after the third phase was
mounted, American and ARVN troops 'leapfrogged' over the revolutionary forces who were still massed around the urban areas to attack
them from the rear as well as to take over liberated areas. Caught on
the outskirts of these urban areas, the revolutionary units not only
received heavy casualties in 1968, but also were unable to return to
the countryside in time to provide the necessary protection to NLF
political cadres and sympathetic rural supporters confronted by various
pacification programmes such as the Phoenix Programme and the
Accelerated Pacification Programme. Compounding this, the Vietnamese leadership in Hanoi, in one of its biggest errors of the war, ordered
the remnants of the revolutionary units in the south to retreat to the
border areas of Cambodia and Laos for rebuilding. This was tanta-
mount to surrendering populated areas of the south to the US and
South Vietnamese forces without a fight. When NLF units decided to
return to the villages to help rebuild the revolutionary infrastructures,
they paid a high price for their absence.[52]

Although the Tet Offensive did not overthrow the Saigon government, it was successful in accomplishing its main objective of forcing
the United States to de-escalate the war in the North and to begin
negotiations. On 1 November 1968, President Johnson ordered the
unconditional cessation of the bombing of North Vietnam and
announced a four-party conference with the participation of NLF and
Saigon representatives. This negotiation process would eventually lead
to a peace agreement based on NLF terms in January 1973.

The Fourth Period, 1969–1972

With his promises of bringing about peace, Richard Milhous Nixon got himself elected president of the United States on 5 November 1968 by the narrowest of margins over his Democratic opponent, Vice-President Hubert Horatio Humphrey. Just like Johnson before him, Nixon talked peace in order to make war. Ambassador Averell Harriman, who was still chief US negotiator in Paris in the period between November and Nixon's inauguration on 20 January 1969, later wrote that during that time Nixon manipulated the Nguyen Van Thieu regime deliberately to destroy the chances for a negotiated peace and that, after Nixon took over, Henry Cabot Lodge (who replaced Harriman) succeeded in destroying almost everything that had been achieved. Instead of seeking peace, Nixon put into effect his 'Vietnamization' programme, which he called his 'peace plan'. Harriman denounced Nixon's 'peace plan' in language about as strong as could be expected from a man in his position: 'The Administration's program of Vietnamization of the war is not in my opinion a program for peace, but it is a program for the continuation of the war... Furthermore, the Vietnamization of the war is dependent on an unpopular and repressive government.'[53]

The Vietnamization programme involved the massive buildup of the Saigon forces in an attempt to get Vietnamese to kill other Vietnamese. The Nixon administration was able to carry this out thanks in part to heavy US bombing, which averaged about 100 000 tons a month on South Vietnam in 1969 and 1970. (This is about 20 000 tons more than the total tonnage dropped during the entire Gulf War under the later administration of President George Bush.) An equal amount of high explosives was also delivered by artillery strikes monthly, which in many cases caused more systematic damage than bombardment. The most noticeable results of these air and artillery strikes, according to the 6 April 1971 issue of *Look* magazine, was the destruction of dams, dikes and canals, and mile upon mile of 'rice fields pockmarked with millions of large craters filled with water in which malarial mosquitoes have been breeding in epidemic numbers'. These results, combined with the effects of chemical spraying (which the Pentagon admitted in 1969 was limited only by the ability of the United States to produce it), had by the end of 1970, according to official sources in South Vietnam, destroyed about half of the crops in South Vietnam. About 12 million hectares (30 million acres) of forests and covered hills (six times the total crop land of the south) had been destroyed, and the resulting runoff and erosion during the monsoon seasons caused disastrous floods (which still occur) each year, which destroyed food crops.[54]

By the early 1970s, South Vietnam consequently had to import an average of one million metric tons of rice annually – much of it rice from the United States under the 'Food for Peace' programme – although before the war it had been one of the largest rice exporters in the world. This huge importation of rice was enough to feed 5 million persons, or about a quarter of the population of the South, with 440 pounds of rice each a year. Nevertheless, the heavily censored Saigon daily newspapers frequently reported widespread hunger and starvation, especially in the central provinces, from 1970 on. In districts in the central area many had to eat banana roots, leaves and even cacti to satisfy their hunger. It was almost impossible for the Vietnamese people to survive in the countryside. In these circumstances, by mid-1971 the Nixon administration was able to increase the regular forces of the Saigon army to over 1.1 million men and the local forces to over 4 million out of a total population of about 18 million.[55]

All this was being done not simply to save American lives but also to save American dollars. It cost the United States $38 000 to send an American to Vietnam to fight for one year. But it cost an average of only $400 to support an Asian mercenary – Koreans and Thais included – to fight for a year. Saving American lives and dollars served to persuade the American public that the war was winding down, so that the American people would be more patient with Nixon's conduct of the war. The pressganging of Vietnamese youth into the army also served to deny the NLF fresh supplies of troops. Moreover, Trinh Pho, a Vietnamese officer in the Political Warfare Section of the Saigon army, explained in a long article entitled 'The Mobilization of Soldiers in a New Sweep' in the Saigon magazine *Quan Chung* (5 September 1969) that the main reason for drafting so many people into the army was to keep them under government control.

The Vietnamization programme was opposed by most Vietnamese as soon as Nixon announced it; the first wave of protests was spearheaded by students with wide support among the urban inhabitants. The response of the South Vietnamese government and the US military was increased repression. US military police and Vietnamese combat and service police rounded up hundreds of students and their leaders, detaining them for 'investigations' of possible Viet Cong guerrilla connections; many of the students were tortured during the investigations.

On 25 June 1970 *Tin Sang*, a Catholic daily in Saigon, reported that 124 trade unions representing 100 000 workers in the greater Saigon area called a general strike to give support to the students. Other trade unions, the Disabled Veterans Movement, the An Quang Unified Buddhist Church and several other organizations issued statements praising the strike and pledging their support. The National Student Congress distributed a resolution that included the following points: (1) an immediate end to the war; (2) an immediate and total withdrawal of all US and allied troops from Vietnam and the return of independence to the country; (3) the extension of the university age limit and abandonment of all military training programmes.

President Nguyen Van Thieu was furious. The 16 July 1970 issue of *The New York Times* reported that on 15 July Thieu declared, 'I am ready to smash all movements calling for peace at any price ... We will beat to death the people who demand an immediate peace.' On the same day, the national police chief, Brigadier General Tran Van Hai, told his police chiefs to use 'strong measures, including bayonets and bullets', to smash all demonstrations 'at any price'. Despite these threats, on 25 July 1970 the Women's Movement for the Right to Life came into being. At a meeting attended by 1000 women representatives from all walks of life, the group's president, the Columbia-University-trained lawyer Ngo Ba Thanh, read a four-point manifesto, declaring: (1) the dignity of Vietnamese in general, and the dignity of Vietnamese women in particular, should be respected and protected; (2) women would struggle for peace and the right to life; (3) all US soldiers must be withdrawn from Vietnam as a necessary condition to end the war; and (4) a coalition government should be formed to represent the Vietnamese people. At this meeting women from various parts of the country also testified about the wanton killing, raping and other criminal acts committed by the Americans everywhere. Consequently, hundreds of members of the Women's Movement were arrested and tortured.

Despite this repression, the women's movement grew stronger and stronger and worked closely with all other groups, including the student groups. The close cooperation among various groups led to the organization of the People's Front in Struggle for Peace on 7 October 1970. The majority of civic organizations in Vietnam participated in this group, and on 11 October 1970 the Front issued a ten-point platform headed by a demand 'that the Americans and their allies withdraw completely from Vietnam as the most important precondition for

an end to the war'. From this point on, anti-government activities in the
urban areas in South Vietnam were well coordinated and a strategy for
continual struggle was developed. This invited more repression by the
Thieu government.

In addition to dealing with the ever growing urban opposition, the
Thieu government and the US command also increased pacification of
the rural areas. During the first three years of the Nixon administration,
60 000 'mop up' operations – each involving more than a battalion of
U.S. or allied troops – were directed against the villages. As a result, 1969
and 1970 were the two most difficult years for the Southern revolutionaries. Tens of thousands of NLF fighters were either killed or forced to
desert during this period. In addition, Northern units sent into the
South during 1969 and 1970 could not operate effectively and were
killed in large numbers because they did not have the necessary tactical
grassroots support. The initiative was reclaimed only after the Southern
revolutionaries rebuilt connections between villagers and fighters in
1971 and 1972. This rebuilding process was done mainly through the
tactic of *bam tru* ('clinging to the post', or figuratively, to the people),
although the US and South Vietnamese invasions of Cambodia and Laos
in 1970 and 1971 and the urban struggles during the same years
diverted US and South Vietnamese troops from the rural areas of the
south and thus gave the NLF forces extra space and time to recover.[56]

The aim of the invasion of Laos, according to Nixon, the defence
secretary, Melvin Laird, and the US State Department, was 'to protect
the Vietnamization program'. But the South Vietnamese population
strongly opposed it even before it started. Words of the invasion had
leaked out days before it took place. According to most Saigon daily
newspapers, on 5 February 1971, three major organizations in South
Vietnam (the Women's Committee to Demand the Right to Life, the
People's Movement for Self-Determination and the People's Front in
the Struggle for Peace) strongly denounced the expansion of the war
into Laos in a joint declaration. In its 9 and 11 February 1971 issues,
Tin Sang reported that on 8 February tens of thousands of people
marched in Saigon to protest. Representatives from many groups
(women, students, workers and religious) demanded that their hus-
bands, sons and brothers be returned to their families. Many of the
marchers were arrested and beaten. Saigon combat police and US
military police also attacked the Saigon students' dormitories. On 14
February, demonstrators burnt 15 US army vehicles in Saigon and
distributed 250 000 leaflets denouncing Nixon for expanding the war

into Laos.[57] The invasion of Laos also met with strong opposition among South Vietnamese governmental circles. An example can be seen in an article by Deputy Ho Ngoc Nhuan, a Catholic, in the 11 February 1971 issue of *Tin Sang*. It reads in part:

> It is exceedingly difficult to understand why, when the Saigon government is not yet able to pacify and control the territory of South Vietnam, and has had to ask the Koreans, the Thais, the New Zealanders and the Australians to stay here as long as possible, its own troops are sent outside of the country to stop infiltration. Such an expedition has turned the question of the presence of foreign troops in South Vietnam upside down: Has this presence become unnecessary? Are the foreign troops fighting to protect us, or are we fighting to protect them?

The invasion of Laos invited not only strong anti-Thieu and anti-American activities throughout South Vietnam but also resulted in a military defeat of the first magnitude. Only a few weeks after US helicopters ferried South Vietnamese troops into the Laotian panhandle for a daring test of Vietnamization, about 15 000 ARVN soldiers were put out of action, 496 planes and helicopters, 586 tanks, armoured cars and trucks, 144 artillery pieces and over 5000 other weapons had been destroyed or captured. The Americans admitted a total of 167 US pilot and crewmen casualties.[58]

The débâcle in Laos led to a series of devastating defeats in the northern sectors, the strategic Central Highlands and certain parts of the Mekong Delta, and helped the NLF to regain its strength. According to General Tran Van Tra and many other sources, the Southern revolutionary infrastructure was entirely rebuilt to pre-Tet levels by the end of 1971.[59] Some North Vietnamese books and articles published since 1990 have come around to the view that the escalating urban opposition to the Saigon regime in the south also contributed to the recovery of the NLF and brought about subsequent military and political successes. An example of this is the lead article in the April 1991 issue of the *Journal of Military History* in which the author, Mr Tran Vu, discusses the magnitude of, and the reasons for, the communist military success in 1971. He analyses several communist victories in South Vietnam and points out that the ARVN suffered 232 000 casualties. Vu insists that this proves that through increased NLF activities in the south

our main force units were again able to return one by one to the
battlefronts and to reinforce the base areas along the western corridor of the central provinces, in the Highlands, in the eastern provinces of the south, and in the Mekong Delta. The enemy's resolute
effort to push our main forces units beyond the borders [of the
south] therefore had failed miserably by this time.

He goes on to say that these guerrilla activities against the pacification and Phoenix programmes helped double the population in the
liberated areas to nearly three million and expand the contested areas
to 7240 villages that comprised over 11 million inhabitants. This not
only provided the revolutionary forces with contiguous areas throughout the South from which to operate, but also helped solve their
logistics and supply. Vu credits the large opposition movements of
women, students, workers and intellectuals in the United States for
isolating the Saigon regime and for causing doubts about the Vietnamization programme among officials in Saigon and the United States.
All these factors led to further defeats for the allies in 1972 which,
along with timely diplomatic initiatives by Hanoi and the NLF, finally
forced the Nixon administration to agree to sign the Paris peace
accords.[60]

The Fifth and Final Period, 1973–75

Although both the United States and the Thieu government were
forced to sign the Paris agreement, neither believed that carrying it
out to the letter would not lead to an eventual political takeover by the
Vietnamese revolutionaries. Therefore, in spite of the fact that the Paris
agreement established two parallel and equal parties in South Vietnam
– the Saigon regime and the Provisional Revolutionary Government –
and that the two parties were supposed to reach a political settlement
under conditions of full democratic rights without US interference
(articles 1, 4, 9 and 11), the United States and Thieu consistently denied
the PRG any political role in South Vietnam. Article 12 of the Paris
agreement also stipulates that a 'National Council of National Reconciliation and Concord' would be created with 'three equal segments'.
    The third segment was supposed to be composed of non-aligned
'neutralists', or a 'third force' as it was then known. But as soon as

the Paris Agreement was signed Thieu reiterated, with American acquiescence – if not to say outright support – his 'Four Nos' policy: no recognition of the enemy, no coalition government, no neutralization of the Southern region of Vietnam and no concession of territory. Later on, in an interview published in the 15 July 1973 issue of *Vietnam Report*, an English-language publication of the Saigon Council on Foreign Relations, Thieu stated: 'The Vietcong are presently trying to turn areas under their control into a state endowed with a government, which they could claim to be the second such institution in the south ... In the first place, we have to do our best so that the NLF cannot build itself into a state, a second state within the south.' In the same interview Thieu also ruled out any role for the third segment, branding all third-force people as pro-PRG. In a 13 November 1974 speech, Thieu said that all government means had to be used to prevent the creation of a Third Force.[61]

To match Thieu's 'Four Nos', the Politburo in Hanoi imposed the 'Five Forbids' on all the military forces from the North as well as PRG forces in the south. They were forbidden to attack the enemy; to attack enemy troops carrying out land grab operations; to surround outposts; to shell outposts; and to build combat villages. Except for rare instances of local defiance, Hanoi's approach prevailed for almost a year after the agreements were signed.[62] Le Duc Tho later admitted in an article published in the March 1988 issue of the *Journal of Military History* that a number of problems after the signing of the Paris agreement had influenced the cautious attitude of the Vietnamese policy-makers, resulting in their defensive posture during the post-agreement period. One was that both the Soviet Union and China cut off all military aid to Vietnam and that China, for ulterior motives, also cut off all economic aid. Another was the fact that

some high [Northern] cadres who went to the south to explain the situation had placed too much emphasis on maintaining a peaceful stance for the sake of reconstruction ... Therefore, at that time there were many cases in which our [Southern] brothers simply withdrew from, or at best tried to maintain, the areas attacked by the enemies but did not fight back.[63]

The Saigon government, however, was not subjected to any of the constraints faced by Hanoi and the PRG. After the signing of the Paris agreement the United States supplied the Thieu government with so many arms that, as Major General Peter Olenchuck testified before the Senate Armed Services Committee on 8 May 1973, 'We shortchanged ourselves within our overall inventories. We also shortchanged the reserve units in terms of prime assets. In certain instances, we also diverted equipment that would have gone to Europe.'[64] In fiscal year 1974, Congress gave Saigon $1 billion more in military aid. Saigon expended as much ammunition as it could – $700 million worth. This left a stockpile of at least $300 million, a violation of the Paris agreement, which stipulated that equipment could only be replaced on a one-to-one basis. For fiscal year 1975, Congress again authorized $1 billion in military aid, but appropriated $700 million – about what was actually spent in 1974.

Thieu was certainly encouraged by the American military aid, and immediately carried out the so-called 'military operations to saturate the national territory' (*hanh quan tran ngap lanh tho*) through indiscriminate bombings and shelling as well as ground assaults on PRG-controlled areas. The 16 February 1974 issue of the *Washington Post* quoted Pentagon officials as saying that the Thieu armed forces were 'firing blindly into free zones [i.e. PRG-controlled areas] because they knew full well they would get all the replacement supplies they needed from the United States'. A study by the US Defense Attaché Office in conjunction with the Saigon Joint General Staff and the US Pacific Command revealed that

> the countryside ratio of the number of rounds fired by South Vietnamese forces [since the signing of the Paris Agreement] to that fired by communist forces was about 16 to 1. In Military Regions II and III, where South Vietnamese commanders have consistently been the most aggressive and where some U.S. officials said that random 'harassment and interdiction' fire against communist controlled areas was still common, the ratio was in the order of 50 to 1.[65]

In addition to the shelling, on average about 15 000 bombs were dropped and 10000 different military operations were conducted into the countryside every month. A classified study by the province of Long An has documented that in the post-Paris-agreement period every village under the control of the NLF was bombed from four to five times and struck by an average of about one thousand artillery shells a day. Repeated assaults by large forces, which sometimes reached up to several divisions, were conducted and, as a result, from

May to August 1973 the revolutionary forces in the province had to battle the Saigon troopers 3300 times.[66]

The military aggressiveness of the Saigon government, however, also inflicted untold death and suffering on the civilian population, as well as exposing Saigon's own armed forces to danger and death. As early as 30 August 1973 the French newspaper *Le Monde* reported that the Saigon high command had stated that about 41 000 of its troops had been killed and 4000 were missing since the signing of the Paris agreement. Saigon was never known for inflating its own casualty statistics; and the casualty rate climbed continuously as Thieu increased his attacks on the rural areas.

Worse still, because of the increase in economic aid to the Thieu regime in 1973 and 1974 it felt confident enough to carry out an 'economic blockade' designed to inflict hunger and starvation on the PRG areas.[67] Thieu was frequently quoted as exhorting his armed forces to do their utmost to implement the 'economic blockade' in order to defeat the 'communists' by starving them out.[68] This blockade, which was also known as the 'rice war' in the American press at the time, included prohibitions on the transport of rice from one village to another, rice milling by anyone except the government, storage of rice in homes and the sale of rice outside the village to any except government-authorized buyers.

Widespread hunger and starvation were the results. According to reports by Saigon deputies and Catholic priests, up to 60 per cent of the population of the central provinces were reduced to eating bark, cacti, banana roots and the bulbs of wild grass. Children and the aged were the first victims. In some central Vietnam villages deaths from starvation reached 1 to 2 per cent of the total population each month.[69] On 30 September 1974 *Dai Dan Toc* quoted official reports to the National Assembly by a number of deputies as saying that in the four districts of Huong Dien, Vinh Loc, Phu Thu and Phu Vang in Thua Thien province alone 21 596 persons had died of hunger by mid-1974 out of a total population of half a million. In the same issue of the newspaper there are also heart-rending excerpts from official reports of deputies from the provinces of Quang Tin, Quang Ngai, Phu Yen and Binh Dinh on the acute problem of hunger and starvation there. Even in the wealthiest section of Saigon itself, Tan Dinh district, a poll conducted by Catholic students in late summer 1974 disclosed that only 22 per cent of the families had enough to eat. Half of the families could only afford a meal of steamed rice and a meal of gruel a day; the remaining went hungry.[70] And in the rice-rich Mekong Delta, acute rice shortages became commonplace in many provinces.[71]

As for the economy, Thieu's policies precipitated a major depression. On 25 February 1974, *Hoa Binh* ('Peace', a conservative Catholic daily newspaper in Saigon) quoted Deputy Premier Phan Quang Dan as complaining that there were from three to four million unemployed persons in the Saigon-controlled areas alone. Through Thieu's Vietnam, firms were firing workers in droves. The employers frequently mistreated and insulted their workers to force them to quit. Even foreign companies, which enjoyed many special privileges such as exemption from all income taxes, had to cut back their workforce by 30 per cent.[72]

Hunger and unemployment increased crimes, suicide and demonstrations throughout the areas under Saigon's control. On 11 September 1974 *Dien Tin* commented on the problem of suicide as a result of hunger and unemployment with the following words:

Faced with these kinds of suicides, people expect the government, especially the Department of Social Affairs, to express some kind of positive attitude. On the contrary: beyond ignoring the whole thing, they bad-mouth these dead people . . . What are we waiting for? Why not organise a movement for aiding the miserable – a movement to save people from hunger?

A Committee for Hunger Relief was created partly as a result of this call, but the Minister of the Interior immediately outlawed this organization for fear that it might become a rallying point for the hungry and the frustrated.[73] The Saigon regime saw this Committee for Hunger Relief as such a threat that it repeatedly carried out repression against it and consistently prevented it from giving food to the hungry in all parts of the country.[74] The corruption and callousness of the Saigon regime caused *Dong Phuong*, a conservative Saigon daily, to write the following in an editorial on 27 September 1974:

We are told that the South Vietnamese population is hungry and that many families have died while several million people in the central provinces are hanging on with a meal of rice and a meal of roots. Many people have even died from the grass and cacti they had to eat . . . The hunger and suffering of several million inhabitants of South Vietnam have occurred beside rice bins which are filled to the top and within sight of the abundance, wealth, callousness and festivities of the majority of officials who are corrupt, who speculate and hoard rice, and of a minority who enrich themselves on the war and on the blood of the soldiers...Therefore, the most pressing responsibility facing us is not just to promote a movement of hunger relief. The entire people must also struggle hard for the eradication of corruption, the elimination of injustices, the implementation of democratic freedoms, the establishment of peace, and the decapitation of those who have created so many tragic situations for our people.

Demonstrations demanding jobs and food occurred almost daily. Here are a few random examples taken from a single Saigon daily to illustrate the intensity of the urban struggles by August and September of 1974. The 30 August 1974 issue of *Dien Tin* reported that 1000 disabled veterans and other inhabitants of Do Hoa village in Thua Thien province blockaded the streets with barbed wire, demanding that the government provide them with food and jobs. Later on 19 September, 116 trade unions in Saigon and Cholon met to demand food and clothes and an end to mistreatment and unwarranted layoffs (*Dien Tin*, 20 September 1974). Two days later, on 21 September, the whole workforce of Saigon, Cholon and Gia-dinh demonstrated for food, clothes and temporary relief (*Dien Tin*, 22 September 1974). While this was going on, huge numbers of workers in Danang, the second largest city in South Vietnam, marched in the streets and then went on a mass hunger strike (*Dien Tin*, 22 and 24 September 1974).

The demonstrations were met with selective but extremely harsh repression. On 1 November 1974, for example, Father Nguyen Ngoc Lan, a progressive Catholic priest, and a number of deputies were severely beaten in a demonstration in the streets of Saigon.[75] The next day, disabled veterans were also beaten in a demonstration.[76] In a demonstration in Chanh Tam district of Saigon on the following day, Thieu's police forces fired into the crowd, killing one person and wounding many others. These forces also burnt houses and destroyed religious shrines. When the people of the area and religious leaders protested, the Thieu regime simply said it was conducting a regular military operation against the communists in the area.[77]

The death and suffering caused by Thieu's military attacks and 'economic blockade' not only intensified the general population's hatred of Thieu's regime; they also forced the PRG to fight back. In the summer of 1974, the PRG's counterattacks forced Thieu's armed forces to make one 'tactical withdrawal' after another. Even in the heavily defended delta provinces, Saigon was forced to abandon 800 fire-bases and forts in order to 'increase mobility and defense'.[78] The northern half of Long An province, which was considered the gateway to the Mekong Delta, was largely liberated and Saigon forces could travel on the main roads only from 6 o'clock in the morning until 4 o'clock in the afternoon. The province of Kien Tuong, which was immediately west of Long An and south-west of Saigon, was largely liberated.[79]

But instead of drawing some lessons from the whole experience and responding to the demands of the PRG as well as the general population of Vietnam to return to the Paris Agreement, both the Thieu regime and the Ford administration tried their own tricks to obtain more aid from Congress to shore up the already hopeless situation. For its part, the Ford administration tried to set in motion a plan they had long held in reserve. This was the replacement of Thieu by a right-wing coalition capable of winning more aid from the Congress and keeping some control of the country. High CIA agents were sent in droves to South Vietnam in September and October 1974.[80] The US embassy in Saigon publicly encouraged a coalition of conservative forces within the Catholic, Buddhist, Cao Dai and Hoa Hao churches to give the appearance of widespread popular backing for Thieu's successor regime.[81] The whole rightist Catholic opposition to Thieu was based on the narrow accusation against Thieu on six specific charges of corruption and called itself the Anti-Corruption Campaign; Father Tran Huu Thanh, the Campaign's chairman, was quoted by the *Washington Post* as saying that the reasons for the Catholic actions were that 'South Vietnam also needs a clean government so our allies will trust us and will send foreign aid and investment.'[82]

Perhaps impressed by the show in Saigon and by the Ford administration's promise that there would soon be a regime worth supporting, on 17 and 18 December, the Congress authorised $450 million in economic aid to Saigon for the financial year 1975, which represented a $100 million increase over the amount authorised for 1974. The PRG evidently interpreted this action by Congress as a renewed commitment to the Saigon regime. In answer, they increased their counter-attacks against Thieu's aggressive military stance, and by early January 1975, eight districts and a province fell into PRG's hands. But the United States and Saigon used this opportunity to accuse Congress of having weakened South Vietnam militarily by its reduction of aid requests and clamoured for supplemental appropriations.

It was already clear to most Saigon observers, however, that more aid would at best only prolong the agony, if not to cause the Saigon government to collapse that much quicker. Following are a few excerpts from statements made by the more conservative public opinion makers in South Vietnam.

Huynh Trung Chanh, a deputy in the Lower House, wrote the following in an editorial in the 17 January 1975 issue of *Dien Tin*:

> The leaders of the Republic of Vietnam are now spreading the view that the present deteriorating situation is due to the lack of aid. But the reality of the situation is that the difficulty is not because of a lack of aid but *because of lack of support of the people* [original emphasis]. In previous years, aid was overly abundant and yet what was ever solved? Now, if there were supplemental aid in order to meet this military situation, then the difficult period will only be prolonged and in the end nothing will be solved.

Even Father Nguyen Quang Lam, an ultraconservative Catholic priest known by his famous pen name of Thien Ho (Heaven's Tiger), wrote the following in the 10 February issue of *Dai Dan Toc*:

> Yesterday I wrote that whether there is an additional $300 million or $3,000 million in aid, South Vietnam will still not be able to avoid collapse... In the afternoon a reader called me up and said that I should have put it more strongly. I must say that the more the aid, the quicker the collapse of South Vietnam. All I had to do was to take a look at our society... Come to think of it, the reader has a point there. The American dollars have really changed our way of thinking. People compete with each other to become prostitutes, that is to say, to get rich in the quickest and most exploitative manner... No wonder whenever our soldiers see the enemy they run for their lives, even though they might have a basement full of ammunition which they could presumably fire till kingdom comes.

It is clear from the above Saigon statements by even the more conservative and anti-communist elements that the Saigon regime was on the verge of collapse and that there was no longer any mood for any kind of military confrontation. When the communist forces finally carried out their offensive beginning in March 1975, one province after another fell hardly with a fight. As it turned out, North Vietnamese troops were sent rushing into the South to snatch political power, not from the South Vietnamese government but from the Southern revolutionaries.[83]

4

THE UNITED STATES AND VIETNAM

David L. Anderson

From the Geneva conference of 1954 to the withdrawal of US forces from Vietnam in 1973, the United States sought to provide an American solution for a Vietnamese problem. Vietnam's problem was to define its post-colonial identity as an independent state in the context of a world divided by cold war hostility. If Vietnam became united under the socialist leadership of North Vietnam, the presumption in Washington was that this success by the Democratic Republic of Vietnam (DRV) would strengthen the world's communist ranks, which were headed by the Soviet Union and the People's Republic of China (PRC). If, however, the pro-Western regime in Saigon could maintain its separate existence then South Vietnam would remain a cold war bastion like those in other divided countries – West Germany, South Korea and Taiwan. Presidents Eisenhower, Kennedy, Johnson and Nixon shared this belief in South Vietnam's vital strategic importance to the United States, and each in his own way sought to guarantee the survival of the Saigon regime.

The Truman Doctrine of March 1947 proclaimed that 'the free people of the world' look to the United States for 'support in maintaining their freedom'.[1] Clashing US and Soviet interests in Europe prompted Harry Truman's remarks, but his rhetoric was global. By its close in 1953, the Truman administration had extended from Europe to Asia the concept of American containment of communist tyranny. In 1949, the creation of NATO and the communist victory in China's civil war profoundly affected Washington's thinking about South-East Asia. The need for French military co-operation in Europe overshadowed US dislike for French efforts to restore colonial control in Indochina. Opposing France was the communist-led Viet Minh. With Chinese aid available, the Viet Minh posed a real danger of a French defeat and a communist success in Vietnam. These considerations led the Truman administration in February 1950 to recognize the French-backed government of Bao Dai in Vietnam and to increase aid to France's military effort. When communist North Korea invaded South Korea a month later and Truman sent US troops into the conflict, the application of containment to Asia seemed prudent and necessary to Washington.[2]

Dwight D. Eisenhower continued Truman's policy of assisting France against the Viet Minh. The new administration sought a limited US commitment, but it portrayed the stakes as extremely high. In Indo-China, Eisenhower declared, France was holding 'the line of freedom' against the global communist assault. In April 1954 he made his famous 'falling dominoes' analogy that declared the maintenance of a pro-Western Vietnam as vital to the security of all of South-East Asia. When the French military effort collapsed at Dien Bien Phu, however, Eisenhower chose not to authorize a last-minute US armed intervention. He and his advisers viewed the outcome of the French–Viet Minh war as more of a French failure than a Viet Minh success.[3]

After a cease-fire and temporary north–south partition of Vietnam was arranged at the Geneva conference, the Eisenhower administration moved to Americanize foreign assistance to South Vietnam. Secretary of State John Foster Dulles created the South-East Asia Treaty Organization (SEATO) in September 1954. Ostensibly a collective security arrangement, SEATO more accurately represented an international sanction for US intervention in Indo-China, something that had not existed during the siege of Dien Bien Phu. In 1955 the Eisenhower administration decided to give 'wholehearted support' to the efforts of Ngo Dinh Diem to build a separate, non-communist government in South Vietnam. A devout Roman Catholic, Diem had lived briefly in the United States and had met some influential Americans. His potential ability to attract American support played a major part in Diem's selection by Bao Dai as prime minister for the government in the South. Because Diem was intensely anti-French and lacked any significant political following among the Buddhist majority in South Vietnam, Paris gave him little chance for success and withdrew its remaining forces from the South. In a rigged election in October 1955, Diem deposed Bao Dai and became president of the Republic of Vietnam (RVN).[4]

For the remainder of the decade, the Eisenhower administration laboured to build a viable nation in South Vietnam. Diem remained in power, and an outward semblance of order and prosperity emerged. Washington boasted of Diem's miracle in South Vietnam. In reality, the Saigon government rested on an extremely narrow political base of Ngo family loyalists and Catholic refugees who had fled from North Vietnam in 1954. Arrests, imprisonments and executions were used to silence political opponents. The Southern economy would have collapsed without the $200 million in aid provided annually by the United States. The modestly affluent consumer culture of refrigerators and motor-bikes in the cities contrasted sharply with rural poverty that left some families with $25 annual income after payment of rent and taxes.[5]

Economic deprivation and Saigon's police repression aided communist cadres in organizing an armed insurgency in the South to challenge Diem's regime. In league with Hanoi, the Southern resistance formed the National Liberation Front (NLF) in 1960. Dubbed the Viet Cong by Diem's government, the NLF recruited followers, received supplies and reinforcements from the North, and mounted armed attacks and terrorist assaults intended to undermine the Saigon government.[6]

When John F. Kennedy became president of the United States in January 1961, the policy of building a South Vietnamese state to contain the spread of communism in South-East Asia was failing. Neither Truman's containment policy nor Eisenhower's nurturing of Diem gave sufficient weight to Vietnamese nationalism. Global calculations of American, Soviet and Chinese power did not adequately account for domestic realities in Vietnam. Diem was an anti-foreign nationalist who clearly hated the French, resented his dependence on the Americans and took great pride in the tradition of Vietnamese resistance to Chinese domination. He frequently lectured visiting Americans for hours about the history of his country. His anti-foreignism did not translate into political popularity, however, because his arrogant manner, clannishness and Catholicism weakened his ability to compete with the charismatic Ho Chi Minh and the disciplined cadres of the Viet Cong and DRV.

Kennedy entered the White House convinced of the importance of the so-called Third World in the cold war conflict. He and his advisers recognized that the United States needed to pay closer attention to the internal political struggles in Vietnam and other developing nations. Crises elsewhere in the world, however, prevented reassessments of Vietnam in terms of its own history and circumstances. Disasters in

Cuba and Berlin and compromise in Laos put global and domestic pressure on Kennedy to stand firm somewhere, and Vietnam seemed to be the place. Hence, despite doubts about Diem's regime, Kennedy plunged ahead with a belief that determination would prove sufficient. As the historian Gary Hess has written, 'four words – commitment, credibility, consequences and counterinsurgency – are central' to Kennedy's decision to link the security interests of South Vietnam and the United States.[7] From Truman and Eisenhower, Kennedy inherited a commitment to assist those Vietnamese threatened by the ideology and control of the DRV. To renege on that commitment would have been, in Kennedy's view, a sign of weakness that would damage the global credibility of the United States to counter Soviet and Chinese-backed aggression. The embarrassing débâcle at the Bay of Pigs in Cuba and the construction of the Berlin Wall during the early months of Kennedy's presidency made the Kennedy team fear the consequences of inaction in South-East Asia. They felt pressure to convince global adversaries and domestic critics that the United States had an answer to the challenge in South Vietnam. The Kennedy response was counterinsurgency warfare.

Although the Kennedy Counterinsurgency Plan for South Vietnam contained military, economic, psychological, covert and financial sections, the moves to implement the plan marked a clear militarization of US assistance to Diem. Eisenhower's aid policy had capped South Vietnamese armed forces at 150 000 and kept uniformed US military personnel in South Vietnam under 900. In May 1961 Kennedy authorised a 200 000-man ceiling for the South's regular military forces and an expansion of local self-defence forces. Four hundred US Army Special Forces (Green Beret) troops went to the South's Central Highlands to train Montagnard tribesmen in anti-guerrilla warfare. To reassure Diem of continued US support, Kennedy sent Vice-President Lyndon Johnson to visit Saigon. The president also directed the Pentagon to examine 'the size and composition of forces which would be desirable in the case of a possible commitment of US forces to Vietnam'.[8]

These demonstrations of American resolve failed to impress the DRV and NLF. During the summer, infiltration from the North doubled and Viet Cong attacks increased and reached into the vicinity of Saigon itself. In October the president sent two of his closest White House advisers, Walt Rostow and Maxwell Taylor, to assess the situation. They found the Diem regime suffering from a lack of confidence and recommended a 'limited partnership' between Washington and Saigon to enable the Army of the Republic of Vietnam (ARVN) to take the military initiative against the guerrillas. They urged specifically that an 8000-man U.S. military taskforce be deployed to Vietnam. Concerned that such a move would greatly increase US risks, other Kennedy aides – Chester Bowles, W. Averell Harriman and George Ball – favoured negotiation with Hanoi. Kennedy accepted neither the taskforce nor negotiation. He agreed with the idea of 'limited partnership', but in his view negotiations would undermine American's already tarnished credibility.[9]

The limited partnership or 'joint effort', as termed in the president's official authorization, meant that US aid would not only continue but would increase. During 1962 the number of US military advisers reached 9000.[10] Modern US military technology and equipment, including helicopters and armoured personnel carriers, added to the ARVN's mobility and fire-power. To provide an effective command structure for this mounting military effort, Washington created the Military Assistance Command, Vietnam (MACV). Annual US economic and military aid to South Vietnam tripled. To combat the insurgency in rural areas, MACV and the RVN constructed a number of 'strategic hamlets'. These fortified villages were designed to provide security from NLF terror, insulation from communist propaganda and tangible evidence of Saigon's concern for peasant welfare. This flurry of US largesse and innovation created a façade of progress in the counter-insurgency effort. Washington expressed cautious optimism that the American solution for Vietnam was making headway.

The battle of Ap Bac, south-west of Saigon, dramatically dispelled this image in January 1963. An NLF battalion routed an ARVN force approximately ten times its size. Furthermore, the ARVN were equipped with the best American equipment and had tactical air cover. What Saigon's forces lacked was a will to fight, because there was very little popular support for Diem among the people in the South. On the contrary, there was strong resentment of Diem among the nation's Buddhists. The usually apolitical Buddhist clergy were challenging the regime's oppression and its favouritism for Catholics, and some monks even burned themselves to death in powerful anti-government protests. This 'Buddhist crisis' ended hope among US leaders that Diem could ever create an effective government. American officials, including the president, began to consider a change of leadership in Saigon.[11]

The ire of the Buddhists, and of many US officials, focused principally on Diem's brother, Ngo Dinh Nhu. Diem's closest personal adviser,

Nhu directed the regime's secret police activities, including attacks on Buddhist pagodas, which he declared to be dangerous subversive centres. On 24 August 1963, a State Department cable to Ambassador Henry Cabot Lodge in Saigon authorized the ambassador to demand that Diem remove Nhu from the government. This instruction also permitted the embassy to inform disgruntled South Vietnamese generals that the United States would not interfere with a coup if Diem failed to oust his brother. It was clear that the Kennedy administration was giving up on Diem but not giving up on finding an American solution for South Vietnam under new leadership.[12]

Despite the 'green light' from Washington, no coup occurred in August or September, and Diem and Nhu defied pressure from Lodge to make changes in the regime. In October, Taylor and Secretary of Defense Robert McNamara met in Saigon with Diem and Nhu and separately with some of the generals. They reported to the president that a coup was unlikely, that some progress was being made in counterinsurgency and that Diem was not going to get rid of Nhu. They recommended increasing pressure on the Saigon government by withholding various types of US assistance, including reducing the number of US advisers. Perhaps Diem could be induced to relax his repressive policies that were fuelling dissent. In discussing the report, Kennedy's aides argued over how best to handle Diem. Undecided himself, the president agreed to allow the increased pressure.

The US squeeze on Diem and Nhu and the 'green light' from August prompted the generals to resume scheming. Aware of talk of a coup, the US embassy did not interfere. The plotters seized power in Saigon on 1 November 1963, and after an attempt to escape, Diem and Nhu were murdered by soldiers sent to put them under arrest. There is no evidence that US leaders desired or anticipated the killing of the brothers, but Washington was not surprised by the coup itself.[13]

Kennedy's own brutal death on 22 November made it impossible to know how he would have dealt with the South Vietnamese leaders who succeeded Diem. Some Kennedy aides later argued that his persistent doubts about the American course in Vietnam would have led him, if re-elected in 1964, to have withdrawn the United States from the conflict and avoided the massive escalation that occurred in 1965. Kennedy's actual record from January 1961 to November 1963 shows, however, that he bears significant responsibility for further Americanizing and militarizing the South Vietnamese government's battle with the North Vietnamese and NLF. As long as he lived, Kennedy maintained that the security of South Vietnam was vitally important to the security of the United States. He never expressed doubt that America could somehow defend its own self-proclaimed interest in Vietnam. When Kennedy died, over 16 000 American military advisers were in South Vietnam, and over 100 Americans had been killed in action there while he was president. Diem's failure to gain a popular following had frustrated the American goal to build a nation around him, but when Diem and Kennedy were murdered in 1963, there had been no US reassessment of the strategic value of South Vietnam.[14]

Johnson had much the same perception of Vietnam as did Kennedy. Like his predecessor's policies, Johnson's views were summarized by four words – commitment, credibility, consequences and combat. For the new president, the commitment undertaken by Truman and renewed by Eisenhower and Kennedy continued in full force. Four days after Kennedy's murder, Johnson approved National Security Action Memorandum No. 273 that restated, in language very similar to Truman's, the US pledge to assist the South Vietnamese 'to win their contest against the externally directed and supported communist conspiracy'.[15] Drafted by the NSC before Kennedy's death, this document placed Johnson's policies firmly in the containment tradition. Determined not to lose Vietnam as Truman had been accused of losing China, Johnson instructed Ambassador Lodge to give the leaders in Saigon his personal promise that the United States 'intends to stand by our word'.[16]

The credibility of US purpose and global power was at stake, but so too was the credibility of the Johnson administration with the American public. Disdainfully referring to North Vietnam as a 'ragged ass little fourth rate country', Johnson could not conceive that Hanoi could thwart Washington's ability to impose an American solution in Vietnam.[17] Eventually US determination would, in his view, overwhelm the communists' bogus promises of national liberation. As the magnitude and cost of this task grew under Johnson's leadership, however, Americans began to doubt their president's word. Citizens increasingly questioned whether the administration was honestly portraying the progress and prospects of the war. By the time Johnson left office, his domestic credibility was as tattered as was America's international image.

In large measure it was Johnson's fear of negative consequences that propelled his sense of commitment and his concern with credibility. Despite his blustering and overbearing personality, Johnson was personally and politically insecure. Johnson knew his own strength was in domestic politics and not international and military affairs. He was overawed by the expertise of the military brass and of what he called the 'Harvards' in the foreign policy establishment. Beyond his personal fear of failure was his overarching passion for domestic reform. He worried that his dream of a Great Society within America would founder if the nation turned its attention to a major war in Asia. Ironically, it was this preoccupation with the consequences of a large war – whether successful or unsuccessful – that led him into the combat he preferred to avoid.[18]

Because Johnson wanted only a limited war, he constantly asked his advisers how much US military aid was enough. Invariably they recommended increases, because conditions within South Vietnam continued to deteriorate. By the spring of 1964, vast areas of South Vietnam were under NLF control, the strategic hamlet programme was essentially moribund and the infiltration of men and *matériel* from the North had grown. Simply assisting the South against the North was not enough. In June, Johnson sent one of America's most accomplished combat officers to head MACV – General William C. Westmoreland. The new commander immediately requested more men. Washington allowed the number of US military personnel to surpass 23 000.

While MACV's size increased in the South, Johnson's top aides turned their attention to the North. Not only was counterinsurgency warfare not working well in the South, but McNamara, Rostow, Secretary of State Dean Rusk and other senior aides remained convinced that Hanoi, not the NLF, was the true enemy. Pressure on the North, they reasoned, would strengthen the South, but such coercion had to be covert because the United States could not assault the DRV without provocation. Through the spring and summer of 1964, the United States secretly gathered intelligence, spread propaganda and supported South Vietnamese commando raids on the coast of North Vietnam as part of a covert operation codenamed OPLAN 34A. Seemingly unimpressed by this harassment, Hanoi stepped up its aid to the NLF, and the Pentagon began to prepare contingency plans for air strikes against North Vietnam as a possible next step.[19]

The pretext that Johnson needed to launch selective bombing of the North came in early August. On 2 August, North Vietnamese torpedo boats closed on the *USS Maddox*, a destroyer in the area of the Gulf of Tonkin where the OPLAN 34A raids had been occurring. The *Maddox* and US carrier-based aircraft fired on the torpedo boats. On the night of 4 August, the *Maddox* and another destroyer, the *USS Turner Joy*, reported another North Vietnamese attack. More reports immediately cautioned that poor weather conditions and other factors raised doubts that an attack had occurred. After reviewing many messages, Admiral US Grant Sharp, commander in chief of US Pacific forces, concluded that 'no doubt now existed that an attack on the destroyers had been carried out'.[20] With that assurance, the White House did not hesitate to order retaliatory air strikes against North Vietnamese naval facilities.

At the same time, Johnson sought and obtained a congressional resolution authorising 'all necessary measures to repel any armed attacks against the forces of the United States and to prevent further armed aggression'.[21] This Tonkin Gulf Resolution passed the House and Senate with only two dissenting votes and became the principal legal authority for the massive American war effort that subsequently emerged in Vietnam. In August 1964 Johnson was not envisaging a huge buildup. The resolution and the bombing were intended to convey strong messages to Hanoi and to American voters. Johnson's firm but limited handling of the Gulf of Tonkin incident helped him to decisively defeat the Republican candidate, Barry Goldwater, in the November 1964 election. The near unanimity in Congress and Johnson's landslide victory revealed solid political support for the president's moves in Vietnam.

In South Vietnam, however, these demonstrations of American determination did not improve the Saigon government's prospects. In fact, the DRV and NLF interpreted the US action as preliminary to expanded fighting and accelerated their military preparations in the South. Political instability mounted as Buddhists and Catholics continued to clash and various civilian and military leaders in Saigon jockeyed for power. After the bombing threshold was crossed in August, a majority of Johnson's inner circle recommended the use of more American air power. The under-secretary of state George Ball pointed out that bombing the North did not directly pressure the insurgents in the South, and he also warned that a major air campaign could force China, the USSR, or both to intervene directly to rescue their socialist allies in Hanoi. Most of the president's aides believed, however that bombing should be tried to bolster Southern morale and to intimidate the North. As for the Soviets and Chinese, there was also a presumed risk in doing nothing. The USSR had new leaders and the PRC had new nuclear weapons. A collapse in Saigon at this juncture could have encouraged Moscow and Beijing to challenge the United States elsewhere in the world.[22]

In 1965 Johnson made the fateful decision to Americanize completely the combat against Hanoi and its Southern adherents in the NLF. This Americanization took two forms: (1) a sustained and gradually increasing US air bombardment of targets in South and North Vietnam; and (2) the deployment to South Vietnam of entire US combat divisions with supporting elements. These moves began a three-year escalation, which reached prodigious proportions. US bombing tonnage eventually exceeded Second World War levels, and US troops in South Vietnam surpassed the half-million mark in 1968.

The air war began in February 1965. A Viet Cong attack on the American base at Pleiku provided a reason for a retaliatory air strike. Within forty-eight hours Washington ordered 'sustained reprisal' bombing. Codenamed 'Rolling Thunder', this bombing campaign became a regular and expanding feature of the American war in Vietnam. US fighter-bombers from bases in Thailand and from aircraft carries in the Gulf of Tonkin and the South China Sea attacked military bases, supply depots and infiltration routes in North and South Vietnam. During the first year of Rolling Thunder, there were 25 000 sorties flown against North Vietnam. In 1966 the number was 79 000 and in 1967 it reached 108 000 sorties, delivering almost 250 000 tons of explosives. The target lists expanded from strictly military targets to include farms, factories and transportation lines in North Vietnam and the Ho Chi Minh Trail supply route in Laos.[23]

From the beginning of the bombing, American strategists debated the effectiveness of air power in defeating a political insurgency in a predominantly agricultural country. Despite the American bombs, dollars and military advisers, the Viet Cong continued to inflict heavy casualties on the ARVN, and the political situation in Saigon grew worse. In March 1965, two battalions of US Marines landed at Danang to protect the US air base there. By June 1965, there had been five governments in the South since Diem's death, and the newest regime headed by General Nguyen Van Thieu and Air Marshal Nguyen Cao Ky inspired little confidence. Assistant Secretary of State William Bundy lamented that the Thieu–Ky government was 'absolutely the bottom of the barrel'.[24] To stave off defeat, the JCS endorsed Westmoreland's request for 150 000 US troops to take the ground offensive in the South. The Pentagon clearly wanted control of the ground war.

Johnson well understood the gravity of such action, and from 21 to 28 July wrestled with his decision. He sought advice from several sources but not from the Saigon government itself. In the words of

South Vietnamese diplomat Bui Diem, the 'unselfconscious arrogance of the American approach' was 'appalling'.[25] All of Johnson's senior advisers except Ball favoured meeting Westmoreland's request. McNamara, for example, assured the president that, if the United States were to 'expand substantially the US military pressure' and 'launch a vigorous effort' at negotiations, this programme would likely 'bring about a favorable solution to the Vietnam problem'.[26] Johnson decided to commit the forces and, on 28 July, announced that 50 000 troops would go to South Vietnam immediately. By the end of the year, there were 184 300 US personnel in the South.

The United States had crossed the line from aiding and advising the South Vietnamese military to actually fighting the war against the DRV and NLF, but Johnson sought no declaration of war. He rejected recommendations by the Joint Chiefs that he mobilize the reserves and National Guard and resisted McNamara's proposal for levying war taxes. The president believed that his conservative opponents in Congress would use such military mobilization as a reason to postpone his beloved Great Society programme for America. Consequently, the administration resorted to the military draft to meet manpower needs and doubled monthly draft calls up to 35 000. The $20 billion annual expenditure on the war came from deficit financing with its inevitable inflationary effect.[27]

Even as it stepped up military escalation, Washington professed readiness to negotiate a settlement with Hanoi. Johnson announced in a speech at Johns Hopkins University on 7 April 1965 that the United States would enter into 'unconditional discussions' and offered an incentive of a billion-dollar economic development project for the Mekong River Valley similar to America's famous Tennessee Valley Authority.[28] In May and again during the Christmas holiday season, the United States conducted brief bombing pauses as gestures to begin talks. As long as Johnson remained president, however, combat not compromise was the reality. Neither the United States nor the DRV would take a meaningful first step toward real negotiations. Having been frustrated by compromise at the Geneva conference of 1954, the Politburo absolutely rejected the legitimacy of the RVN and of the US presence in the South. Northern negotiators insisted that no talks were possible as long as US forces were in Vietnam. Conversely, Washington declared that the DRV and its NLF agents were conducting a war of aggression against the South. The United States would not remove its troops until Hanoi ceased infiltration of the South and recognized the existence of the Saigon government. Both sides chose to accept armed conflict rather than to retreat from their basic positions.[29]

While US planes bombed targets in North Vietnam, Westmoreland went on the offensive against the Southern insurgents. The general formed his battle plan within the doctrine of limited warfare, which meant gradual escalation of bombing and incremental troop deployments. Politically, the president did not want the war to intrude into American domestic life. Internationally, the risks of a wider war with China and the Soviet Union meant that the United States would not go all out to annihilate North Vietnam. Thus, Westmoreland chose a strategy of attrition in the South, that is, of inflicting heavier losses on the enemy than Hanoi could replace. Using air mobility and massive fire power, the MACV commander intended to exhaust the enemy while limiting US casualties.[30]

Responding to the American escalation, Hanoi deployed into the South units of the People's Army of Vietnam (PAVN), which was the regular North Vietnamese Army (NVA). In October, General Vo Nguyen Giap, the PAVN commander, launched a major offensive in the Central Highlands, south-west of Pleiku. Westmoreland responded with the 1st Air Cavalry Division. Through much of November, in the battle of the Ia Drang Valley, US and North Vietnamese forces engaged each other in heavy combat for the first time. Westmoreland used helicopters extensively for troop movements, resupply, medical evacuation and tactical air support. US Air Force tactical bombers and even huge B-52 strategic bombers attacked enemy positions. The Americans ultimately forced the NVA out of the valley and killed ten times as many enemy soldiers as they lost. The battle convinced Westmoreland that search-and-destroy tactics using air mobility would work in accomplishing the attrition strategy. Yet, soon after the PAVN departed, so too did the air cavalry. Clearly, control of territory was not the US military objective.[31]

During 1966 the Americanization of the war continued in earnest. Keeping with Johnson's 'enough but not too much' formula, the US force level that year reached 385 000, organized into seven combat divisions and other specialized units. With US aid, the ARVN also expanded to eleven divisions. While MACV prepared for future large-unit search-and-destroy operations, army and marine units conducted smaller operations. Although the 'body count' – the estimated number of enemy killed – mounted, attrition was not changing the political equation in South Vietnam. The NLF continued to exercise more effective control in many areas than did the government.[32]

In 1967, Westmoreland was ready to implement his big-unit, attrition strategy for what he believed would be military victory. He assigned Saigon's troops primarily to occupation, pacification and security duties in populated areas. This arrangement freed large US combat formations numbering in the tens of thousands to sweep rural areas. US forces inflicted heavy casualties on the enemy and destroyed large amounts of supplies. MACV declared vast areas to be 'free-fire zones', which meant that US and ARVN artillery and tactical aircraft, as well as B-52 'carpet bombing', could target anyone or anything in the area. Chemical defoliants sprayed from aircraft laid bare thousands of acres of natural vegetation and food crops in suspected NLF-controlled areas. By the end of 1967 there were 485 000 US troops in Vietnam.[33]

Under mounting public pressure to show results, Johnson ordered Westmoreland to Washington in November 1967 to give a progress report. The general dutifully announced that, although much fighting remained, a cross-over point had arrived in the war of attrition, that is, the losses to the NVA and Viet Cong were greater than they could replace. He told a group at the Pentagon that 'the ranks of Viet Cong are thinning steadily', and he publicly asserted that 'we have reached an important point when the end begins to come into view'.[34] This assessment was debatable. Although NVA and Viet Cong losses were three times those of the US and ARVN forces from 1965 to 1967, enemy force levels in the South had actually increased. There was considerable evidence also that the so-called other war for political support in South Vietnam was not going well. Corruption, factionalism and continued Buddhist protests plagued the Thieu–Ky government. Despite incredible losses, the NLF still controlled many areas. Diplomatic compromises proposed by third countries such as Poland and Great Britain met firm resistance from both Washington and Hanoi. The war was at a stalemate. The escalation had increased the costs of the war in lives and money, but failed to diminish the North's threat to the South.[35]

The continuing vulnerability of the South to sudden collapse became alarmingly apparent when the NLF launched the Tet Offensive in the early morning hours of 30 January 1968. In one of the greatest military surprises since Pearl Harbor, NLF units struck throughout South Vietnam in simultaneous attacks on urban areas and military installations. Guerrillas even breached the US embassy compound in Saigon. Heavy fighting raged throughout the South for three weeks. Westmoreland claimed military success because the NLF failed in its goal to incite a popular uprising, many in the urban population actually rallied behind the Thieu government, no vital territory was permanently lost and extremely heavy casualties were inflicted on the attackers.

Based on news reports from Vietnam, many Americans concluded conversely that Tet was a defeat or at least a reality check. Having heard the administration's assurances of progress in November, citizens interpreted the stunning magnitude of the offensive as evidence that the end was not near. Journalists and others expressed doubts that government claims about success could be trusted. At the least, Tet demonstrated that much more American blood and treasure would be lost even if Washington were able ultimately to convince Hanoi to accept a separate Southern regime. Such additional costs, for many, were unacceptable. After Tet, more and more Americans simply wanted the United States out of Vietnam.[36]

Many writers have advanced a 'stab in the back' argument, which alleges that the pessimistic reporting and analysis of the Tet fighting turned a military success into psychological defeat. Actually, Tet was a military as well as psychological defeat from which the US effort to impose its power on Vietnam never recovered. Despite Westmoreland's public confidence, military leaders privately acknowledged that the enemy offensive exposed serious weaknesses in the American war effort. The massive American air and ground war had not deterred infiltration into the South. The Tet combat had weakened the ranks of the Viet Cong, but the PAVN could and would continue to pour a virtually limitless supply of men into the RVN. US and ARVN losses had been high, and the fighting generated thousands of refugees, further destabilizing the South. In an 'eyes only' message to Westmoreland on 1 March, Army Chief of Staff General Harold K. Johnson concluded: 'We suffered a loss, there can be no doubt about it.'[37]

Seeing the deep erosion of public support for the war, Johnson decided in March 1968 to end the escalation of American forces in Vietnam. After Tet, Westmoreland and JCS Chairman General Earle Wheeler requested 206 000 additional troops beyond the over 500 000 already in Vietnam. The president turned to his new secretary of defence, Clark Clifford, for a thorough policy re-evaluation. McNamara had just left the administration, privately despairing of any good outcome in Vietnam. Clifford consulted the Wise Men, a group of former government officials. When the majority of them favoured de-escalation and disengagement, the president recognized that a limit had been reached. He approved only 13 500 more soldiers for Westmoreland. In a television address on 31 March 1968, Johnson announced limits on the bombing, and named Ambassador W. Averell Harriman to head a new effort to start peace talks. Johnson also revealed that he would not seek re-election. The war he did not want had driven him from office.[38]

Despite the conciliatory tone of Johnson's speech, his administration was far from ready to compromise with Hanoi. Although the DRV surprised Washington by agreeing quickly to begin talks in Paris, both sides continued to wage heavy combat. In April and May US and ARVN troops carried out the largest ground operation of the war, in a massive sweep near Saigon. The United States suffered its highest annual total of killed in action in 1968, with over 14 000 deaths. US bombing exceeded one million tons during the year. In June General Creighton Abrams replaced Westmoreland as MACV commander, and late in the year he began to shift US strategy from attrition to greater use of small-unit operations, an accelerated pacification programme, and Vietnamization, that is, improving the ARVN's ability to do more of the fighting.[39]

While the United States went through the tumultuous 1968 election to choose Johnson's successor, negotiations in Paris went nowhere. Johnson reluctantly agreed to a bombing halt in October to try to get talks moving, but Thieu created innumerable procedural delays. Even without South Vietnamese obstruction, meaningful progress was unlikely. Johnson consistently refused to retreat from the long-standing US opposition to recognition of the NLF and creation of a coalition government in the South. The DRV and NLF had successfully withstood the large-scale Americanization of the war, but the withdrawal of the United States from Vietnam remained to be accomplished.[40]

Richard M. Nixon campaigned for the presidency pledging to bring 'peace with honor' in Vietnam. He felt honour-bound by the same concepts – commitment, credibility and consequences – that had influenced Kennedy and Johnson before him. He would be forced eventually to add 'compromise' to that list. As a congressional critic of Truman's alleged 'loss' of China, Nixon had been militant in his commitment to America's pledge to oppose communist tyranny. As vice-president in 1954, he had urged a hesitant Eisenhower to use US troops or air power in Indochina to aid the French. After losing the presidential contest to Kennedy in 1960, Nixon publicly supported Kennedy's subsequent decision to increase US aid to Vietnam. When controversy swirled around Johnson in 1967, Nixon wrote that 'without the American commitment in Vietnam, Asia would be a far different place today'.[41]

Upon taking office, Nixon and his chief national security aide, Henry Kissinger, understood that the voters expected them to end American involvement in Vietnam. They interpreted that mandate, however, as requiring them to find a way to maintain US credibility. To simply pull out would have far-ranging consequences. America's friends and enemies would be closely watching how the United States extricated itself from the war. Like the administrations that preceded them, Nixon and Kissinger began with a certainty that there was an American solution – its vast arsenal including nuclear weapons – that could still coerce the DRV into a compromise settlement. Ultimately it was Washington, not Hanoi, that made the key concession – the acknowledgement that the Vietnamese would determine their own fate. Kennedy attempted counterinsurgency, Johnson waged combat, and Nixon finally resorted to compromise.

In 1969, the US war effort remained massive, but the basic decision to de-escalate had already been reached. With the ground war stalemated, the new administration turned increasingly to air bombardment and secretly expanded the air war to neutral Cambodia. Publicly the White House announced in June the withdrawal of 25 000 US troops and heralded Vietnamization as working. In fact, South Vietnam's armed forces remained problem- plagued. To bolster the South, the administration leaked to the press dire threats of a 'go for broke' air and naval assault on the North – possibly including nuclear weapons. Kissinger also began secret meetings with North Vietnamese representatives in Paris, hoping to arrange a diplomatic breakthrough. Hanoi's leaders refused to be intimidated by Nixon's rhetoric and continued to demand US withdrawal from the South and abandonment of Thieu. The DRV's stubbornness enraged the president, but his staff convinced him that a 'savage' attack on the North would not produce diplomatic results.[42]

Like the diplomatic efforts, the ground war in the South was also stymied. In May 1969 the 101st Airborne Division fought and won a major ten-day battle at Hamburger Hill in the A Shau Valley. The Americans suffered over fifty killed but dislodged two NVA battalions, only to be compelled to abandon the ridge a few days later. Such experiences devastated morale among US troops and created open dissension in the ranks. Hamburger Hill marked the end of the erstwhile attrition strategy. The related pacification programme was no better. US troops would move into an area, and NLF political activity would vanish only to reappear immediately upon the relocation of the American unit. As one American official observed: 'It is only occupation, not pacification.'[43]

Seeking a 'big play' to counter the diplomatic, military and public relations frustrations that he faced, Nixon ordered US troops into Cambodia in April 1970. Enemy use of neutral Cambodian territory along the South Vietnamese border for infiltration and base areas was not new. The US thrust across the border lasted until June, and was more a demonstration of daring and determination than of tactical progress. The incursion momentarily disrupted NVA operations but had serious negative consequences. It sparked major protests in the United States and it prompted increased North Vietnamese assistance to Cambodia's brutal Khmer Rouge in their war against the US-backed government of Lon Nol. Meanwhile, US troop reductions continued, with only 334 600 in South Vietnam as 1970 ended.[44]

Throughout 1971 Nixon continued to emphasize Vietnamization but, after the long Americanization of the war, progress was slow. Washington reduced its troop level to 156 000 by December and poured aid and *matériel* into the South. The ARVN became one of the best-equipped forces in the world. American planes continued heavy bombardment of supply lines in Laos and Cambodia and air strikes against targets in North Vietnam, including raids near Hanoi and Haiphong. Still the will and ability of South Vietnamese forces to take charge of the warfare did not improve. In March 1971 the ARVN launched a major thrust into Laos backed by US tactical air support. This operation, LAM SON 719, ended in confusion and retreat. A façade to provide an honourable cover for US withdrawal, Vietnamization offered little hope for future South Vietnamese success in battle.[45]

Similarly, Kissinger laboured secretly to gain a face-saving diplomatic formula for the United States. In May 1971, for the first time, the Nixon administration offered to separate the arrangement of a ceasefire from the political talks about the Saigon government. The DRV's Le Duc Tho countered with language accepting an end of US support for Thieu rather than demanding his removal. Neither side rejected or accepted the other's proposals. The impasse continued.[46]

During the first half of 1972, both the United States and DRV made their own big plays to end the American war in Vietnam. With the US troop level down to about 100 000, and these mostly in non-combat units, General Giap began a major spring offensive against provincial capitals and ARVN bases throughout northern and central South Vietnam. The US command responded with ferocious air strikes against the attackers including use of B-52 heavy bombers. Nixon also authorized large-scale bombing of North Vietnam and the mining of Haiphong Harbour. The offensive failed to topple the Saigon government, and Hanoi discovered that, although diminished, US fire power was still dangerous.

For his part, Nixon went on a global diplomatic offensive. In February he made a turning-point visit to the People's Republic of China, which reversed over twenty years of American refusal to communicate with Beijing. In May Nixon travelled to Moscow and signed a nuclear arms limitation agreement with the Soviet Union. Although much tension remained in US–China and US–Soviet relations, these diplomatic breakthroughs took some of the danger out of the cold war concerns that were at the foundation of the US presence in Vietnam. On the other hand, Nixon's hopes that Moscow and Beijing would urge Hanoi to compromise were not realized.[47]

Neither the United States nor North Vietnam had gained the negotiating advantage that it sought, and thus both returned to the bargaining table. In October they discussed a cease-fire, the return of the US prisoners of war, the temporary continuation of Thieu's government, and permission for NVA units to remain in the South. Although the language appeared to contain significant concessions by both sides, it was the United States that had moved furthest. Upon implementation of the terms, US ground and air forces would be completely withdrawn and the PAVN would remain in the South to face the RVN's notoriously ineffective forces. Thieu strongly protested at US disregard for its Saigon ally. He managed to delay Nixon's acceptance of the agreement, and Hanoi appeared ready to reintroduce tougher demands. Nixon gave Thieu a personal, secret promise that the United States would respond with 'full force' to any DRV violations of a signed agreement. In December the United States unleashed another deluge of bombs on the North including B-52 attacks on Hanoi itself. On 27 January 1973, the United States, the DRV, the RVN and the Provisional Revolutionary Government representing the NLF signed in Paris the Agreement Ending the War and Restoring the Peace in Vietnam. The terms were essentially those drafted in October.[48]

Nixon's compromise peace finally ended the futile quest of over twenty-five years to find an American solution for Vietnam's post-colonial political and social structure. The departure of the last American troops left the outcome to be decided by the Vietnamese themselves. Nixon maintained that the 1973 accord was 'peace with honor', because US forces parted with the RVN government still in place and well stocked with US arms. Although Kissinger claimed to support Nixon's assessment, he made other comments suggesting more cynically that the diplomatic settlement provided a 'decent interval' between the end of US operations and the final political resolution. During that interval Nixon resigned the presidency under the cloud of the Watergate accusations. For US policy in Vietnam, the end came on 30 April 1975 when US helicopters lifted the last remaining US personnel from the roof of the American embassy as the North Vietnamese army occupied the RVN government buildings in Saigon.[49]

The United States renewed its commitment in Vietnam year after year because of assessments of credibility and consequences for US policy outside Vietnam. Successive American leaders worried about how American strength and reliability was being perceived in friendly and hostile capitals around the world and among Americans themselves. With the international order framed by hostile US and Soviet rhetoric and the US and Chinese clash in Korea still echoing throughout Asia, some cautious intervention by the United States in Vietnam was understandable after the Geneva conference. Despite US economic and military power, however, Washington's ability to shape the domestic structure of Vietnam was always limited. US policy moved from counterinsurgency to combat and finally to compromise; but it never was able to translate American power and good intentions into political viability in Saigon. In fact, as the US war in Vietnam grew to heroic proportions, any credibility of the RVN as an independent state vanished and the danger of direct American conflict with China and the USSR increased.

Despite the apocalyptic rhetoric of the Truman Doctrine and the domino theory, the Vietnam War was always a limited war for the United States. For the Vietnamese, on the contrary, the war was total. Their lives and futures were at complete risk. In the political and economic interconnections of the twentieth-century world, a powerful nation like the United States could not leave events in any region entirely beyond its notice and influence. Washington, however, lost its sense of proportion. What should have been a modest American interest in South-East Asia became major. American leaders tended to think of the conflict in absolute terms of all or nothing. After the war,

Americans continued to debate the idea of 'No More Vietnams'. For some that negative adage meant no US intervention anywhere, and for others it meant no more limited, losing intervention anywhere. Experience showed, however, that both notions were faulty. The United States was a nation among nations, and it could neither avoid nor dominate the world around it.

5

THE ANTI-VIETNAM WAR MOVEMENT IN THE UNITED STATES

Tom Wells

A large-scale movement against the Vietnam War developed in the United States. The movement was less a unified army than a rich mix of political notions and visions. The tactics used by anti-war activists were diverse. Though youth predominated, the peace movement came to include a wide cross-section of American society.

The US government took the anti-war movement quite seriously. Officials followed the movement closely and persistently, and took multitudinous steps to counteract it. The movement disrupted officials' lives by restricting their public activity, and it infiltrated their immediate families. The movement had a major impact on US policies in Vietnam. As the cutting edge of domestic anti-war sentiment as a whole, it played a significant role in constraining, de-escalating and ending the war. It also promoted the Watergate scandal, which itself played an important role in ending the war.

Yet the movement could have been even more effective. The failure of many protesters to recognize their actual political power hurt their cause, as did infighting among them.

History and Character of the Movement

Though the first American protests against the war took place in 1963, the anti-war movement did not begin in earnest until nearly two years

115

later, when the United States began a sustained bombing campaign against North Vietnam.[1] In the spring of 1965, 'teach-ins' on the war were held on numerous college campuses. Many of the teach-ins were debates involving the participation of government spokesmen and other war supporters. The teach-ins awakened large segments of the academic community to the war, and many students took their first public act against it after attending one. Unhappy with the results of the debates, the Johnson administration soon stopped participating in them, opting to send speakers only to 'responsible' forums.[2] The spring of 1965 also witnessed the first national demonstration against the war. 20 000 people, mainly students, attended the demonstration, organized by Students for a Democratic Society (SDS), a politically diverse, left-leaning organization. Many peace activists were then protesting the war in their own communities. That fall some hundred thousand people participated in International Days of Protest in several dozen cities, and 30 000 attended a rally sponsored by SANE in Washington. The first national anti-war coalition was formed, only to die shortly from infighting. A Quaker named Norman Morrison immolated himself in front of the Pentagon, near the office window of the defence secretary, Robert McNamara, who later called the suicide 'a personal tragedy for me'.[3]

As the war expanded, so did the anti-war movement. The tactics ranged from legal demonstrations, grassroots organizing and congressional lobbying to civil disobedience, draft resistance and political violence. Some protesters met overseas with the Vietnamese enemy. Quakers and others provided medical aid to Vietnamese civilian victims of the war in both Vietnam and the United States. Some US servicemen protested, at considerable personal risk; in 1966 three army privates who became know as the 'Fort Hood Three' refused their orders to serve in Vietnam and consequently spent two years behind bars. Clergy and Laymen Concerned About Vietnam, a national organisation of religious dissenters, was formed the same year. So was the Student Mobilization Committee, a national student anti-war coalition. The following year a national organization of draft resisters was born; 'the Resistance' would subsequently hold several national draft-card turn-ins. Some students joined 'We Won't Go' groups on campuses; other young men even rejected their induction orders. The civil rights leader Martin Luther King Jr came out against the war in 1967, adding a powerful new voice. Many prominent liberals also spoke out, encouraging others to do the same.[4] Nearly 600 business executives, many of whom were concerned about the war's impact on the economy, signed an open letter to Johnson asking him to stop the conflict. Members of the US Congress, 'in search of a stance that took account of the growing distaste' for the war, increasingly challenged US policies in Vietnam.[5] Organized by a series of national 'Mobilization' committees, mass anti-war demonstrations were growing in size: in April 1967 more than 300 000 Americans protested against the war in New York. It was the largest demonstration in US history to that point. 50 000 protesters surrounded the Pentagon the following October, provoking nearly 700 arrests. Militant protest, including sit-ins, blockades, the destruction of draft files and the use of 'mobile tactics' in city streets, was spreading, as was revolutionary sentiment among youth. Some peace activists were organizing within the US military.

Senator Eugene McCarthy announced in late 1967 that he was challenging President Johnson in the 1968 Democratic presidential primaries. The growth of the anti-war movement played no small part in McCarthy's decision to enter the race. In particular, a protest by Clergy and Laymen Concerned About Vietnam in early 1967 had seemed to McCarthy 'a significant expression of a widening new judgment' on the war and gave him 'some assurance' that 'there was some solid base upon which to oppose the war'. 'The number were not great, but what they represented was something the administration could not very easily ignore', McCarthy recalled later.[6] McCarthy's strong showing in the March 1968 New Hampshire Democratic primary was widely seen as a major defeat for Johnson and a repudiation of his war policies.

The American public was meanwhile losing heart for the war in rapidly growing numbers. Many citizens were shaken by the war's cost in American lives and resources and sceptical that it could ever be won. Some were undoubtedly influenced by the peace movement's non-stop criticism of the conflict. More than a few were tired of the domestic strife Vietnam was breeding. By the fall of 1967, opinion polls indicated that, for the first time, more people thought US intervention in Vietnam had been a mistake than did not.[7] As the former national security adviser McGeorge Bundy told President Johnson that November, public discontent with the war was now both 'wide and deep'.[8] Blacks and women were especially disapproving of the conflict.[9] Later research found that anti-war sentiment was inversely correlated with people's socio-economic level.[10] Many Americans also disliked the protesters. A December poll found that 40 per cent opposed even the right to hold peaceful demonstrations.[11] Small groups of counterdemonstrators often gathered at protests, and the movement was frequently denounced by media commentators and public figures.

The anti-war movement peaked during the Nixon administration. After a slump following raucous protests at the 1968 Democratic convention and Nixon's election, a hundred thousand people marched in the spring of 1969 in New York, and Quakers and others held sit-ins at draft boards and publicly read the names of American war dead. Militant protest, including building occupations, the trashing of property and bombings of buildings, continued to spread. In October the Weatherman, an ultra-left splinter group of SDS (which had become a 'revolutionary' organization), held its infamous 'Days of Rage' demonstrations in Chicago, in which the mostly young protesters attempted to fight police in the streets. The same month witnessed an outpouring of dissent unprecedented in US history: more than 2 million people joined in Vietnam Moratorium activities around the country. Many were protesting against the war for the first time. Also for the first time, the press sympathized with a protest.[12] The following month, over 500 000 people demonstrated in Washington, and 150 000 protested in San Francisco (the largest number in that city's history) despite rain. GI dissent was growing. In Vietnam, some US soldiers were mutinying and even murdering ('fragging') their own officers, and drug use was widespread.[13]

In the spring of 1970, the US invasion of Cambodia and the killing of student demonstrators by National Guardsmen at Kent State University in Ohio provoked an enormous display of campus protest. A national student strike shut down over 500 colleges and universities. The protests were overwhelmingly peaceful, though violent demonstrations, including the burning of Reserve Officers' Training Corps (ROTC) buildings, erupted on many campuses. Other Americans protested against the invasion and killings in cities across the country. Many lobbied White House officials and members of Congress. Over 100 000 demonstrated in Washington, despite only a week's prior notice. Senators John Sherman Cooper and Frank Church sponsored legislation (later passed) prohibiting funding of US ground forces and advisers in Cambodia. Many union leaders spoke out against the war for the first time, and workers joined protests in unprecedented numbers. However, construction workers in New York assaulted a group of peaceful student demonstrators, and (with White House assistance) union leaders organized pro-administration rallies.[14]

In April 1971, despite an increasingly divided and flagging move-ment, half a million people demonstrated against the war in Washing-ton, 200 000 in San Francisco. Significantly, many members of Congress endorsed the protests. Vietnam Veterans Against the War, who had earlier held public hearings on US war crimes in Vietnam, staged dramatic demonstrations in Washington, including the return of their war medals. Others engaged in a mass civil disobedience protest known as 'May Day', resulting in a police dragnet and 12 000 arrests (a subsequent class action suit by the American Civil Liberties Union won $12 million in damages for wrongfully arrested persons). Daniel Ellsberg, a former Pentagon official, released a secret history of US decision-making in Vietnam called the *Pentagon Papers* to the *New York Times*. The morale and discipline of US soldiers in Vietnam were then deteriorating seriously: drug abuse was rampant, and combat refusals, racial strife and fraggings were mounting. 'By every conceivable indi-cator, our army that now remains in Vietnam is in a state approaching collapse,' a retired marine colonel observed in the *Armed Forces Jour-nal*.[15] According to a Harris poll, most Americans now felt that the war was 'morally wrong'.[16]

With US troops returning from Vietnam, the anti-war movement gradually declined between 1971 and 1975. The many remaining activists protested continued US bombing, the plight of South Viet-namese political prisoners and US funding of the war. Much of their activity involved lobbying Congress. They also pressured President Nixon to honour the Paris peace treaty.

The US Government and the Movement

US government officials paid close attention to the anti-war movement from its inception. They considered it a particularly visible and nagging sign of domestic dissatisfaction with the war, a threat to their base of domestic support and a source of encouragement to the Vietnamese enemy. They also came to consider it a threat to American social stability. Officials recognized that the protesters were, in fact, the cut-ting edge of domestic anti-war sentiment as a whole.[17] 'It was the noisy public opinion . . . that would have created concern', remembered H. R. Haldeman, the Nixon's administration's powerful White House chief of staff, 'the heavy attempt, as the president put it, to make policy in the streets.'[18] Or, as another official said of the protesters, 'They were noisy and they squeaked a lot, and when the wheel squeaks that's the one you pay attention to.'[19] According to Richard Helms, the Director of Central Intelligence during the war, the large 'mobs' in Washington were 'particularly' noteworthy, 'because this is a threatening action when you put mobs in the streets'.[20]

Even Presidents Johnson and Nixon took a keen interest in the movement's doings. The reports they requested and received on upcoming protests, particularly large national ones in Washington, exhibited considerable detail.[21] Nixon and Haldeman, who desired intelligence on all of their political enemies, received multiple reports on some demonstrations the day they occurred.[22] So closely was Nixon following the movement's activities that a week before leaders of the 1969 Vietnam Moratorium protest publicly announced their plans to hold it, he asked his close aide, John Ehrlichman, to come up with a 'game plan' to counter it.[23] Lyndon Johnson, for his part, demanded daily reports from the Justice Department on the planning of the October 1967 demonstrations at the Pentagon nearly three weeks in advance of it. Johnson's reading consisted of detailed descriptions of the anti-war activities planned, the protest leaders and their organizational affiliations, and the administration's preparations for the demonstration. He also received multiple reports on the protest the day it took place.[24]

The US government took many steps to blunt the movement.[25] The Johnson administration sent officials to campuses and other locations to debate anti-war speakers. To enhance its prospects at these events, it often demanded favourable formats (e.g. undesirable debating foes, including the political scientist Hans Morgenthau and Senator Wayne Morse, were rejected). Officials secretly helped organize and aid pro-war groups – ostensibly 'citizens' committees' – which undertook a host of supportive propaganda activities, including passing out literature on campuses, running speakers' bureaux, mobilizing pro-war Americans and circulating pro-war bumper stickers. The government helped organize pro-war demonstrations and other supportive activity, including written statements by notables, speeches by other backers and newspaper advertisements. To foster the impression of public support, the Nixon administration even sent pro-war letters and telegrams to itself. It also aided conservative student groups, including the College Republicans and Young Americans for Freedom. Government operatives of various institutional stripes infiltrated, wire-tapped and burglarized the movement, as well as opening some of its mail. They also aggravated the movement's internal divisions through assorted undercover operations, including anonymous 'poison pen' letters playing one group off against another. The Selective Service System revoked the student draft deferments of many protesters, until appeals courts repudiated this practice. Officials sometimes met with protesters to try to placate them and learn more about them. (In a famously clumsy attempt to communicate with anti-war youth, Nixon himself once took an early morning trip to the Lincoln Memorial, where protesters were gathered for an impending demonstration. The sleepless president talked to the protesters mainly about sports and travel, very little about 'the war thing', as he put it afterwards.)[26] The Nixon administration initiated a draft lottery to defuse youthful protest. It even orchestrated physical attacks on some demonstrators. And the government attempted publicly to link protesters to foreign communists in order to discredit them.

The government's red-baiting of protesters was not just talk for public consumption, however. Numerous officials really believed foreign communists were aiding and abetting the anti-war movement.[27] Many reasoned that the Soviet Union could not be expected to pass up such a propitious opportunity to harm its superpower rival. Some believed that the efficient manner in which the peace activists seemed to organize their protests required the involvement of an outside force. 'I don't care what anybody says, some of the demonstrations were *not* spontaneous!', the Johnson aide George Christian later commented. 'They had an efficient network of some kind.'[28] More than a few officials felt the movement's funding was suspect. 'You know damn well that if you charter fifty or sixty buses, and you're spending all your time rioting, you're not going to be able to [fund] it yourself,' one observed.[29] Both Presidents Johnson and Nixon strongly believed foreign communists were fomenting the movement. Richard Helms recalled:

> There's no doubt that President Johnson, if he wasn't convinced at least he was very much concerned, that the antiwar opposition *was* promoted by the communists, by foreign elements. And he wanted this thoroughly investigated. And he put a lot of pressure on the CIA and the FBI to try and find out about it. And when he would come back with reports that we couldn't find any evidence of this, that hardly changed his mind. He still felt that there was a strong foreign

influence in all of this. Otherwise, Americans wouldn't be behaving the way they were.

Nixon, Helms said, 'had the same feeling'.[30]

A lengthy CIA analysis on the movement's 'international connections' stated directly that 'We see no significant evidence that would prove communist control or direction of the US peace movement or its leaders.' The only 'extensive' government contacts that anti-war activists maintained were with Hanoi, the CIA reported. The movement was simply 'too big and too amorphous to be controlled by any one political faction', communist or otherwise: 'the most striking single characteristic of the peace front is its diversity'. The CIA's researchers perceptively noted that American communists 'seem more concerned about countering each other than about countering the non-communists'.[31]

Officials had other theories of anti-war protest which, while not completely without merit, also reflected misunderstanding of it. Some felt the militant demonstrators were trying to prove their manhood. Others felt draft resisters were cowards or nuts (at one meeting Johnson pointed to FBI reports alleging that many draft-card burners were 'crazy people who had previous history in mental institutions'). Some officials, including Nixon and his national security adviser, Henry Kissinger, believed permissive child-rearing practices were partly responsible for the dissent. 'This is like dealing with thumb-sucking,' Kissinger told his aides. According to other officials, many protesters were simply seeking thrills or conforming to the latest fad. They were 'people who want to get excited about something, and they don't really give much of a darn what it is they're excited about,' Haldeman perceived. 'And they move from one cause to the next. They get fired up on civil rights, then on antiwar, then on ecology, and it moves from one thing to another.' The Nixon aide Ray Price believed they were 'strangers to linear logic' and engaging in 'an orgy of right- brain indulgence'. Some officials felt the dissent was partially a response to youth's difficulty navigating a complex society. According to the Johnson administration's Walt Rostow, 'the high number of dissident leaders and followers who come out of sociology and the soft subjects' was a 'very significant' factor in student protest. 'They are accustomed to dealing in generalities and abstractions,' Rostow stated at a cabinet meeting in 1968. 'The hard subject people, economists and engineers, do not seem to have the same trouble fitting in. They can find their place.'[32]

The peace movement also had painful personal consequences for many US officials. Protesters disrupted their lives by restricting their public activity in the United States. Most officials attracted demonstrators when speaking in public, and many also encountered them outside their homes and on vacations. For example, protesters rocked Robert McNamara's ski lift in Colorado, and one woman came up to him in a lodge and yelled that she hoped that the ketchup on his hamburger reminded him of blood. Others later set fire to a house he owned in Colorado. (After McNamara left office, a young man even tried to throw him off a ferry at night, repeatedly hitting him and pinning him against a railing.)[33] It became 'almost a game' to limit prior notice of President Johnson's public appearances so that 'the Students for a Democratic Society and other campus militants did not have time to organize a protest', George Christian later revealed. These confrontations 'were to be avoided at all costs'.[34] While many officials were undoubtedly unaffected by such harassment, it sapped other officials' strength for the war. Christian recalled:

> The security problems became so intense. You couldn't very well reconcile yourself to demonstrations and potential demonstrations and things when the intelligence reports and the police reports that we were getting indicated there was a violent streak in all this stuff, and that there was actually a danger of bodily harm, for the president in particular and for his surrogates in some cases. So it was pretty serious business...And I'm sure the effect was worse on some others than it was on the president. Not that they were afraid of getting hurt or anything like that, but I mean just the signs of what was going on, the evidence that the country was torn up...The cabinet officers and others who travelled around a lot...probably saw a heck of a lot more of it than those of us in the White House did...The wear and tear on the will of the government to carry on with the policy was not just wear and tear on the president.

Christian said that Johnson's view was that 'they may wear everybody else down, but I'm going to be the last one up here to go under'. Yet Christian believed that Johnson's 'inability to move about the country freely without having demonstrations' contributed to his pivotal 1968 bombing halt over North Vietnam and decision not to run for re-election.[35]

The movement also infiltrated officials' social circles. Many had friends who turned against the war. Most painful of all to officials was the strife the war bred inside their families. Many had sons, daughters or wives who opposed the conflict.[36] McNamara, for one, suffered an agonizing split with his only son, Craig, over the war and consequently was estranged from him for years. To express his disagreement with his father's policies in Vietnam, Craig even put a small 'enemy' flag of the National Liberation Front on the wall of his bedroom; on the opposite wall he hung an upside down American flag. His dad was furious. 'It must have just really hurt my folks,' Craig later reflected. 'It must have been devastating.'[37] Many children of officials participated in the October 1967 protest at the Pentagon. Three of the four children of senior Pentagon official Paul Nitze – who was the government's self-proclaimed 'mastermind of the planning of the defense of the Pentagon' for the demonstration – joined the protest.[38] During a Vietnam Moratorium march outside the White House in 1969, National Security Council staffer William Watts was inside the building writing a presidential speech announcing a major escalation in Vietnam, only to walk out to the White House gate during a break and see his wife and children march by. 'I felt like throwing up,' he remembered. 'There they are demonstrating against me, and here I am inside writing a speech.' 'You talk about a sense of siege mentality inside,' Watts said, 'it was pretty strong...It was very painful to be on the other side of the fence'.[39] Among the many other government officials who had children opposed to the war were Dean Rusk, Nicholas Katzenbach, John Ehrlichman, H.R. Haldeman and Melvin Laird. The dissent that officials experienced inside their families probably contributed to the sense of besiegement many came to feel and may even have altered some officials' perceptions of the war's merits. 'I'm quite sure that the strong opposition of [McNamara's] own children to the war had a very definite impact on him,' senior Pentagon official Paul Warnke said. 'I think Craig in particular. He was very opposed to the war and very disapproving of his father. If you ever have sons that are of the age of reason, you will find that their opinion is very important to you.' Warnke added, 'If you have a close relative, particularly a child, who feels that the policy is incorrect, any responsive parent has to give some thought to it. If you're a good parent, you don't just automatically figure that you know best.'[40] At the least, opposition to the war inside officials' families heightened their awareness of public opposition as a whole.

The anti-war movement exerted a major influence on US policies in Vietnam.[41] During the Johnson administration, it played a significant role in restraining the US bombing of North Vietnam and the level of US troop deployments, and in discouraging US invasions of North Vietnam, Cambodia and Laos. The movement was certainly not the only factor restraining the administration. In particular, besides the resistance of the Vietnamese, officials' perceptions that substantial escalation would not bring significant military gains were also compelling, as was fear of provoking direct Chinese or Soviet intervention in the conflict. Nevertheless, officials knew that unleashing the war would further incite the protesters, which would also nourish the discontent of the public as a whole. In addition, the movement fed the mounting unease with the war of key administration officials, including the new secretary of defence, Clark Clifford, and also Paul Nitze and the White House aide Harry McPherson, in late 1967 and early 1968. Clifford, who was the most influential player in the administration's reversal of its policy in 1968, when it halted the bombing of North Vietnam and effectively put a lid on US troop deployments, recalled later: 'It was a period of the deepest concern because of the very sharp divisions among our people. It was very distressing.' Clifford wrote, 'I was more conscious each day of domestic unrest in our own country. Draft-card burnings, marches in the streets, problems on school campuses, bitterness and divisiveness were rampant.'[42] As we have seen, the movement also fuelled Eugene McCarthy's presidential bid, which shaped official perceptions that the public had turned against the war. Further, it had a significant effect on the group of influential private Johnson advisers known as the Wise Men, who also exerted an important influence on the administration's policy reversal. They told Johnson in March 1968 that Americans would not stand for more of the same. 'The divisiveness in the country was growing with such acuteness that it was threatening to tear the United States apart,' one of the Wise Men commented afterward.[43] And while it was domestic anti-war sentiment as a whole that forced the administration to change course in Vietnam, the movement was the most important manifestation of that sentiment. It was visible, influential, disruptive and persistent. As Thomas Powers has aptly written, 'If the opposition had remained only a state of mind, a condition of the public not unlike atmospheric pressure . . . detectable only by the barometers of opinion pollsters, then Johnson's policy of escalation would not have ended as and when it did.'[44] This policy reversal was the major turning point in the war.

During the Nixon administration, the movement fuelled US troop withdrawals from Vietnam. Through his 'Vietnamization' programme, which entailed withdrawing U.S. troops and strengthening the South Vietnamese army, Nixon hoped to calm domestic opposition to the conflict and thereby buy time for his effort to force a favourable outcome to the war. As Morton Halperin has argued, Nixon and Kissinger recognized 'that they were sitting on a very volatile political situation, that people thought that Johnson was moving toward withdrawing us, and that if they had any sense that Nixon was not, the whole thing would blow up.'[45] The movement also continued to inhibit both the US air and ground wars in Indo-China. Nixon, too, was painfully aware that major escalation would provoke angry protests. In particular, the movement exerted a substantial influence on Nixon's decision not to carry out a threat he made to the North Vietnamese of a massive military blow in 1969. As Nixon subsequently divulged, he felt that the Vietnam Moratorium protest that fall had undermined the credibility of his threat (which he called his 'November 1 ultimatum'). Moreover, the anti- war protests that erupted following the 1970 US invasion of Cambodia and Kent State shootings, shaped Nixon's decision to withdraw US forces from Cambodia earlier than he had wanted to. 'The enormous uproar at home was profoundly unnerving,' Kissinger recalled. 'The panicky decision to set a June 30 deadline for the removal of our forces from Cambodia was one concrete result of public pressures.'[46] By organizing inside the military, the movement also nourished the deterioration in US troop discipline and morale in Vietnam, which provided additional impetus to US troop withdrawals. Further, it put pressure on the administration to negotiate a settlement of the war. And it gave impetus to congressional legislation that cut off US funds for the war.

The anti-war movement accomplished none of these feats alone. Its power was always tied to broader political forces. It sounded the dominant note in a powerful cacophony of anti-war voices in the United States. In fact, the movement's *precise* impact on US policies is impossible to pin down. Nevertheless, that impact was clearly considerable. In addition, the movement nurtured broad anti-war sentiment in the country. Although the citizenry's defection probably sprang mainly from the war's length and cost, the movement provoked doubts about the merits and wisdom of US policies among the public and élites, including in Congress and the media, who, in turn, influenced other Americans.[47] As John Oakes, the editor of the *New York Times*'s influential editorial page during the war, commented later, 'It would be crazy to argue that that kind of thing didn't have any impact on my mind and on the minds of my associates... I would have had to have been deaf, dumb and blind not to have felt... an impact... *Of course* an impact – just like the air you breathe has an impact.'[48] Tom Wicker, a *Times* columnist during the war, remembered the effect that four middle-class housewives who obstructed the shipment of napalm bombs in 1966 had on him:

> They had a very profound impact on me. Because these were very ordinary women. I mean, they may be remarkable for all I know, but they weren't government officials or anything like that, or big entrepreneurs. They were housewives. And that they were willing to go to jail, with all that that entailed for housewives – and they had children and families and everything – because they'd stopped those trucks from moving... struck me very forcefully. I said, 'There's something going on in this country when people will do that.' And I had tended up to that point to take peace activists to be more like [later *Los Angeles Times* columnist] Bob Scheer was then. You know, kind of academic lefties who were not very practical and so forth. But when I really began to get a look at people like that I saw that [the anti-war movement] was quite a different thing from what I had imagined ... I began to get a look at the actual composition of the peace movement, and saw that it was a very, very broad spectrum of the public, even by 1966.[49]

When asked in an interview whether campus protesters influenced him, Notre Dame University's president, Father Theodore Hesburgh, responded:

> There's no question about it. I have said very often that this is the only case I know of in the history of the country where the younger people pulled their elders around to a position they didn't really go with in the beginning. I think that's true. I think the young people really turned the tide on this one... Most of us underwent a complete transformation from A to Z.[50]

The threat the anti-war movement seemed to pose to American social stability also fostered public and elite discontent with the war. Many people got sick of the domestic turmoil the war was generating. Vietnam 'really *was* tearing apart American society', recalled John Oakes, and anti-war violence and illegalities 'certainly' fuelled the *New*

York Times' pleas for an end to the war, he said.[51] The cost in domestic
social peace that protesters were exacting for the conflict also had a
'considerable' effect on Arthur Schlesinger, a former Kennedy administration official and a prominent liberal critic of US policy. The war
'was leading to all kinds of disruptions and concerns which were very
alarming', Schlesinger remembered.[52] The turbulence also disquieted
the Wise Men, who were 'shaken by the opposition in this country',
Richard Helms recalled.[53]

Of course, the distaste that many Americans felt for protesters may
have led some to support the war longer and more strongly than they
would have otherwise. The Nixon administration would, in fact, play
on this distaste to try to rally support for its policies and tarnish
Democratic critics of the war. 'Smear the liberals with the left – and
keep at it,' Haldeman's notes of a meeting with Nixon during the 1971
May Day protest record.[54] That strategy probably met with some
success, given, among other events, Nixon's trouncing of the anti-war
Senator George McGovern in the 1972 presidential race. Yet unfavour-
able attitudes toward protesters and being influenced by their arguments are not mutually exclusive (most of the élites I interviewed for a
book on the anti-war movement were displeased with many protesters
yet indicated that the movement had influenced them).[55] Perhaps
more important, many people grew so tired of the demonstrators
and the disorder they were causing that they wanted the war to end
so that society would return to 'normal'.

Officials paid only minimal attention to the particular forms of protest. True, they preferred small protests to large ones, and felt media
coverage added political import to the demonstrations. And unruliness
apparently hurt the peace movement's public image; as Haldeman,
who considered all forms of protest unwelcome, later put it, 'If they
were going to do something *anyway*, the less attractive they were in the
process of doing it, the more harm they did themselves, was the feeling.' But tactical differences were generally of little significance to
officials. Most viewed the protesters as cut from the same cloth. In
Haldeman's words, they tended to put all protesters 'in the same
bag'.[56] Richard Helms told me:

> I realized as a socialist that you are interested in being more precise
> about who had influence in the dissident movement and who didn't,
> but from the vantage point of Washington I think it was the *totality* of
> the turn-off that was the pressure on [officials]. I mean, certainly the

sight of the demonstrations, the letters, the telephone calls – all of the things putting pressure on the administration. There's no doubt about that. But I don't think that President Johnson or Nixon tried to sort out which groups this was coming from. Just the fact that there was a lot of it.[57]

The movement also promoted the Watergate scandal, a series of abuses of governmental power which themselves played a significant role in ending the war.[58] The movement influenced Nixon's decisions to bomb Cambodia secretly, starting in 1969, and then to lie to Congress about it, a consideration in the subsequent proceedings to impeach him. Public exposure of the bombing prompted the Nixon White House to wiretaps illegally a number of officials and reporters in an effort to stop leaks to the press. These wiretaps were among the 'White House horrors' (as Nixon's Attorney General, John Mitchell, later characterized the adminstration's abuses of power) subsequently revealed to the public.[59] The movement, particularly its militant wing, and Nixon's conviction that foreign communists were behind the dissent, engendered the infamous 'Huston Plan'. A Scheme, approved by Nixon, for a more aggressive – and illegal – domestic intelligence programme, this was another White House horror and a consideration in the Watergate inquiries.[60]

Peace activists inspired Daniel Ellsberg, whose public release of the *Pentagon Papers* prompted Nixon to set up a secret unit of White House operatives known as the Plumbers. Ostensibly established to plug leaks, the Plumbers acted to try to discredit Ellsberg and his perceived co-conspirators through various illegal acts, including breaking into Ellsberg's psychiatrist's office to secure damaging material on him. The Plumbers' activity was also a major factor in the impeachment proceedings.[61] Ellsberg's leak further inspired a bizarre White House plot to firebomb the Brookings Institution and, amid the resulting 'confusion', pilfer classified documents that Ellsberg's co-conspirators were apparently keeping there. This plot – also approved by Nixon – was yet another 'White House horror'.[62] And the evidence that the Pentagon Papers provided of high-level duplicity on Vietnam probably fed domestic scepticism of Nixon during the Watergate hearings. Many Americans were less likely to believe their political leaders than before. The movement also fed the Nixon White House's paranoia about its political enemies, which played no small part in hatching the Watergate break-in itself. As White House counsel John Dean later testified,

Watergate was 'an inevitable outgrowth' of 'excessive concern over the political impact of demonstrators' and leaks, and 'an insatiable appetite for political intelligence'. Finally, the Watergate revelations undermined Nixon's authority in Congress and thus his ability to wage war. Renewing the US bombing of Vietnam then (as Nixon had planned) would have added fuel to the investigations into his conduct, and members of Congress, unhappy with that conduct and emboldened by his weakness, would no longer provide him the money he requested to fund the war.[63]

Internal Problems of the Movement

Despite its considerable accomplishments, however, the anti-war movement could have been even more effective. For the protesters weakened themselves through both infighting and failure to appreciate their power.[64]

The movement's diversity was a double-edged sword. Although it compounded the movement's numbers, it engendered fierce and lasting disputes among protesters that tore peace organizations apart. Often, participants at anti-war meetings could agree on little more than their opposition to US intervention in Vietnam. To the chagrin of others, some protesters seemed more intent on fighting each other than on fighting the war. 'It was supposed to be a peace movement and we were tearing each other apart.'[65] The national 'Mobilization' anti-war coalition consequently was slow to develop and always difficult to maintain; it went through a series of metamorphoses and eventually split bitterly into opposing factions. Gripped by harsh factional warfare, the national student anti-war coalition also eventually split in two. So did Students for a Democratic Society, then the dominant radical youth group. Many local anti- war groups were also riddled with internal conflict. US government operatives fanned the movement's schisms, but they were largely internally generated.

The strife inside the movement wreaked considerable damage. It sapped energy from the movement that could otherwise have gone into building it. It turned off recruits, demoralized activists, created personal enemies and led protesters to drop out; more than a few people left the movement to avoid combat. The strife also lengthened already long anti-war meetings, and many people simply tired of attending them. It hurt the movement's public image, too. Moreover, the infighting stalled anti-war planning and hampered nationally co-ordinated peace activity. And splits in anti-war groups not only weakened the movement but stoked perceptions of powerlessness among activists. The Trotskyist Socialist Workers' Party (SWP) was the most divisive force. Its zealous effort to control the movement's politics and rigid insistence that anti-war groups take the 'correct line' poisoned the atmosphere of countless anti-war meetings. The SWP's bitter rivalry with the American Communist Party, a long-time political enemy, was mainly responsible for the spiteful tone of many disagreements in anti-war committees. The SWP was largely to blame for the splits in both the adult and the student national anti-war coalitions, as its political rigidity and gladiatorial approach to coalition work left little room for compro-mise. For many activists, it simply became impossible to work with members of the group. 'Every time that there would be a convention or steering committee meeting, they would have two or three hundred people thrown in as ringers, with all these phoney organizations,' one coalition leader recalled.[66]

The SWP was not the only source of divisions in the movement, however. Indeed, there were strategic and tactical differences of every conceivable nature. There were disputes between liberals and radicals, new leftists and old leftists, advocates of electoral politics and its critics, anti-communists and communist supporters, and between assorted radical youth groups. There was also conflict between advocates of an exclusive focus on the war and those with multi-issue orientations, and there were many fights of a petty nature.

Perceptions of political powerlessness also hurt the movement. For many protesters, the fight against the war brought mounting and profound political frustration. Despite the movement's steady expan-sion, the bloodshed in Vietnam only increased. The White House seemed heedless of anti-war protest. The threat of even greater escala-tion fed activists' distress. So did domestic support for the war; though public opinion had largely turned against the war by 1968, Nixon, mainly through withdrawing US troops, was able to rally majority support for his policies for significant stretches. The building frustra-tion in the movement bred feelings of desperation in many circles. For some opponents of the war, the desperation even begot self- sacrifice. 'What more can we possibly do?' was a common cry. The frustration was greatest among younger protesters, many of whom lacked under-standing of how much hard work was required to bring about political change. And the frustration was particularly pronounced in periods following large national demonstrations, when, despite the dissent, little if anything seemed to change. Few activists fully appreciated the potential political power they possessed.

The failure of many protesters to appreciate their power spawned defections from the movement. Many quit protesting because they decided it was futile. Their misperception bred lethargy, stagnation and despair in the movement's ranks, impeding the organization of protests and the maintenance of anti-war sentiment. It also promoted perceptions that it would take a revolution to stop the war and thus growing revolutionary rhetoric, which hurt the movement's public image. Moreover, this misperception hampered efforts to sustain outpourings of dissent, particularly in the early 1970s, when, amid Nixon's various escalations of the war (e.g. the US invasion of Cambodia and the later mining of Haiphong Harbour), cynicism about the efficacy of anti-war protest was especially widespread. Not least important, it aggravated dissension over strategies and tactics, further depleting energies, hardening internal divisions and reducing the movement's capacity for coordinated action. Moreover, some Americans never protested because they felt it was futile.

In short, infighting and failure to appreciate the movement's power served to limit the size, frequency and scope of anti-war protest. A still larger, stronger movement would have imprinted the war's unpopularity and cost in domestic peace even more forcefully on the minds of US officials. It would have also exerted greater influence on the American public. Consequently, the domestic political restraints on the war would have been even greater.

6

DEVELOPING AN ALLIANCE: THE SOVIET UNION AND VIETNAM, 1954–75
Ilya V. Gaiduk

On 21 July 1954 at the former headquarters of the League of Nations, the Palais des Nations in Geneva, delegates of the nine states participating in the conference on Indo-China gathered for the final plenary session. This session crowned an almost three-month-long marathon of hard negotiations, back-stage activities, secret meetings and public declarations with an agreement on settlement of the conflict in Indo-China. As in the days of the League of Nations, the great powers, now Great Britain, France, the USSR, the Unites States and the People's Republic of China (PRC), played a decisive role in defining prospects of the future peace in the faraway region; as before, the United States refused to associate itself with the conference's final documents.

There were several such documents in Geneva. Three cease-fire agreements put an end to the eight-year military dispute over the future of the French colonial empire in South-East Asia between France and the communist-led Viet Minh, along with the national movements in Laos and Cambodia. The final declaration embodied the principles of maintaining peace in the region and the respective obligations of the participants of the conference. Six unilateral declarations, two each from France, Laos and Cambodia, completed the list of documents that soon became a subject of controversy and source of antagonisms.

This controversy stemmed from the fact that the final declaration that should have been regarded as the main document of the conference was not signed by its participants. They only expressed opinions upon it. The problem lay also in the refusal of the delegations of the United States and the Republic of Vietnam to associate their governments with its terms. The vague and evasive language of the document only added to the future difficulties relating to its realization in practice.[1]

However, in July 1954 the results of the Geneva conference seemed satisfactory to the great powers who imposed their will on the countries of Indo-China. Even the US leaders, despite all their recalcitrance during the conference and the refusal to be bound by its decisions, could have derived encouragement from the provisions of the final declaration that left the United States 'room to manoeuvre against communist expansionism in South-East Asia'.[2] Likewise, the communist powers – the Soviet Union and communist China – may have regarded the outcome of the diplomatic struggle in Geneva positively, though their optimism was based on somewhat different views on the situation that was created in Indochina as a result of the agreements reached at the Palais des Nations. Especially for Moscow, the cessation of hostilities in Indochina opened a new perspective for its policy, not only towards this region but also in the sphere of its relations with the West.

From the beginning of the Geneva conference the Soviet delegation demonstrated a relatively high degree of flexibility in the negotiations on the settlement of the conflict between the French and the Viet Minh. In his talks with the Western delegates, as well as in speeches at official sessions the head of the Soviet delegation, the USSR foreign minister, Vyacheslav Molotov, did not cease to repeat the strong Soviet desire to reach an agreement which put an end to the long war in the Indochinese countryside. These declarations were accompanied by practical steps in mediating between the French and the Vietminh representatives, with the help of the Chinese, in order to find a compromise. Molotov's activities during the conference were noted by its participants and observers as well as by scholars who analysed developments in Geneva in May–July 1954.[3]

Undoubtedly, such efforts were dictated by the general trend of Soviet foreign policy, which after Stalin's death was undergoing gradual transformation in the direction of achieving more understanding with the West and of abandoning an exclusively confrontational model of relations with the outside world. In this situation the new Soviet leadership regarded the conflict in Indo-China as capable, if not of undermining, at least of hindering the process of détente with the West, of aggravating plans to ease tensions in Europe and other regions, which, unlike faraway South-East Asia, were of more importance for Moscow, and of blurring prospects of economic cooperation with the capitalists.

Moreover, the Soviet leaders had every reason to fear that the continuation of the war in Indochina would lead to an even greater US involvement in the conflict in the region as a result of the French inability to resolve the problem by themselves. Such a development could transform the Indo-China war into an issue of cold war global confrontation and a focal point in Soviet–American rivalry, an outcome hardly desirable for Moscow in the situation soon after the Korean War had demonstrated the danger of an escalation in local conflicts.

Therefore, when Molotov confided to Anthony Eden, the British foreign secretary, during one of their last meetings in Geneva, that, unlike with Korea, 'he never lost hope for success' in the Indo-China question,[4] he did not express just his personal conviction but also revealed his Moscow colleagues' determination to do everything possible to reach an agreement on Indo-China that would bring peace in the region. Partition of Vietnam and neutralization of Laos and Cambodia served as the best possible compromise to this end.

The Soviet leaders could not fail to understand the weaknesses of the Geneva accords. They hardly regarded the peace in Indo-China as permanent or long-term. As had happened before, the diplomats in Geneva were concentrating mostly on symptoms of the disease, not on its cause. And the remedy they prescribed could only postpone eventual crisis. Recognition of this fact, however, did not prevent the Soviet leaders from feeling a cautious optimism, because they envisaged a number of factors that might delay a climax, at least until after there was a more favourable situation for Moscow to deal with.

First, the Geneva agreements secured France's predominant role in Indo-China, which could serve as a guarantee against growing American involvement in the region. As long as France, the Soviet leadership may have been speculating, with all its ambitions and jealousies toward foreign penetration, preserved its position in Indo-China, then the issue remained outside the immediate concern of the two superpowers and, consequently, would not serve as a stumbling-block on the road of Soviet–American rapprochement.

An additional guarantee in Moscow's plans against possible intervention of the Indo-China problem in the East–West dialogue was the Soviet intention to delegate the primary responsibility for relations with the newly born socialist state – the Democratic Republic of Vietnam (DVR) – to the faithful and powerful Soviet ally in Asia, the PRC.

The Chinese delegation in Geneva headed by Zhou Enlai proved its effectiveness in dealing with the Vietnamese communists, bringing pressure on them and obtaining necessary concessions from sometimes obstinate Vietminh representatives. Moscow was going to continue this practice of a division of labour in the period to come and share the burden of supporting a new ally with Beijing, thus killing two birds with one stone.

And, finally, the experience the Soviet leaders had with other divided states, such as Germany and Korea, seemed to support their hope that it was possible to preserve the *status quo* for a relatively long period to the mutual satisfaction of the cold war rivals, who retained parts of each country in their respective spheres of influence. Moscow expected that Vietnam would follow the same pattern, and the formal establishment of the DRV, with the territory north of the 17th parallel, should be working to this end. Although, in his statement at the final plenary session of the Geneva conference, Molotov drew attention to the peaceful reunification 'as soon as possible', which according to the national interest of the Vietnamese people was the 'new most important task',[5] it became obvious from Soviet policy toward the DRV after the conference that this task was not on Moscow's agenda, at least at that time. In fact, in its relations with North Vietnam after the Geneva conference the Soviet Union seemed to be preoccupied more with the necessity to strengthen the DRV as a sovereign and independent state, a new member of the socialist community, than with the concern about preparation of conditions for reunification. During negotiations with their Vietnamese counterparts, either in Moscow or in Hanoi, Soviet officials, after having paid tribute to the 'struggle for unification of the country' concentrated instead on the problems of economic development and the political prestige of the DRV. For example, in a draft of the Communist Party of the Soviet Union (CPSU) Cental Committee directives prepared by the Foreign Ministry in connection with Ho Chi Minh's forthcoming visit to Moscow in July 1955, the principal goal of the Soviet–North Vietnamese summit was defined in a somewhat contradictory way. It put the issue of the support of the 'Vietnamese friends' in the reunification of Vietnam in between the assurances of the Soviet assistance to Hanoi 'in strengthening in every possible way the DRV and its international positions,' and the 'reconstruction of the people's economy of the Republic.' Furthermore, the Foreign Ministry did not elaborate on the question of reunification, except for several expressions of solidarity with the views of Hanoi on this problem.[6]

Such an ambivalent attitude of the Soviet leadership toward the issue is most revealing if one takes into account that exactly at the time when Ho Chi Minh was on his way back to Hanoi after his official visit to Moscow was over, Molotov left the Soviet capital for an East–West summit conference in Geneva scheduled for 18 July. During the summit the leaders devoted most of their time to Germany and arms control. The Soviet foreign minister raised the issue of Vietnam only once, in his conversation with Eden on 23 July. Having received from his British opposite number an assurance that Britain, France and the United States would recommend to Diem that he send the DRV a direct communication of his position on elections, Molotov seemed satisfied.[7] This satisfaction remained undisturbed despite the fact that, contrary to the provision of the Geneva final declaration, that consultations would be held on the subject of the nationwide election 'between the competent representative authorities of the two zones from the 20 July 1955 onwards',[8] this important deadline passed without any developments in the sphere of negotiations between the two governments of Vietnam. Only later, in response to South Vietnamese leader Ngo Dinh Diem's statement of 9 August, in which Diem openly refused to engage the Hanoi regime in direct correspondence, did Moscow formally protest against the violation of the Geneva accords. But again this protest was not followed by any practical steps. Obviously, the Soviet leaders had already reconciled themselves to the existence of the two Vietnams.

In the meantime Soviet–North Vietnamese cooperation in various spheres was taking shape. Already, on his way home from the Geneva conference, the head of the Viet Minh delegation and the DRV vice-premier, Pham Van Dong, had made a stopover in Moscow and conducted negotiations with the Soviet authorities. He raised the question of Moscow's assistance to Hanoi in economic recovery and military aid. He also asked that a Soviet military group be sent to Vietnam to help fulfil the agreement on the cessation of hostilities.[9] The Soviet leaders reacted immediately and positively to this request. The South-East Asia department of the Foreign Ministry recommended that Pham Van Dong be assured that the Soviet Union (1) would provide all possible assistance in delivering the necessary goods to the DRV at low prices and (2) would send a military group, under the guise of aides to the Soviet military attaché.[10]

The problems of economic and military assistance to the DRV were discussed in detail during Ho Chi Minh's visit to Moscow in the summer of 1955. In the final communiqué of the visit, the Soviet government assumed an obligation to grant North Vietnam 400 million roubles to restore the DRV economy, including twenty-five industrial and municipal factories. In addition, Moscow agreed to provide North Vietnam with consumer goods, and to render assistance in geological explorations and in medical service. The two sides expressed readiness to develop trade relations with each other.[11] The forms of economic cooperation, however, were not confined only to grants and commodities sent from the Soviet Union to the DRV. Moscow dispatched specialists to North Vietnam and invited the Vietnamese to be educated in the USSR. Already, by the end of 1955, 273 Soviet specialists had been sent to the DRV. They worked in prospecting expeditions, medical groups and construction brigades. At the same time Vietnamese students entered Soviet universities and colleges.[12]

Soviet–North Vietnamese military cooperation also gained momentum in the first months after the termination of the war on the Indo-Chinese peninsula. In early August 1954, the DRV ambassador in Moscow, Nguyen Long Bang, asked in his conversation at the Soviet Foreign Ministry that the Soviet military attaché be sent to North Vietnam at the same time as the Soviet ambassador, 'or even earlier than him'. Bang justified his request by the DRV military command's need for the advice of Soviet military representatives in fulfilment of the agreement on the cessation of hostilities in Vietnam.[13] From this conversation, onwards the North Vietnamese embassy literally bombarded Soviet officials with similar requests. Only when Moscow officially assigned General Pavel Buniashin to this post on the 14 October 1954 was Hanoi satisfied.[14]

The Soviets were prepared not only to send military advisers to Vietnam but also to allocate sums of money for the North Vietnamese armed forces. At the time of the Soviet–DRV summit in July 1955 Moscow decided to provide Hanoi with 30 million roubles of long-term credit that would be used in payments for equipment and materials for the army during the period 1955–6.[15]

However, Moscow showed some restraint in involving itself in full-scale military cooperation with North Vietnam. Following its scheme for the division of labour, the Soviet leaders were ready to delegate the prime responsibility in this sphere to Beijing, rather than to assume burdens and risks relating to deeper involvement. As a result, in response to incessant requests from Hanoi for closer military relations, Moscow consistently referred to the necessity for the DRV to develop such relations with the PRC. The Soviet authorities accounted for their reluctance with arguments that the Chinese were more experienced in dealing with the specific conditions of the region and therefore they could be more helpful. Such arguments, for example, were put forward by the Soviet general staff on the eve of Ho Chi Minh's visit to Moscow in 1955. According to the Soviet military authorities, the establishment in Hanoi of the joint Soviet–Chinese military mission for the coordination of the process of building the DRV armed forces was not expedient. The argued that

> At the present time, there are Chinese military advisers in the People's Army of the Democratic Republic of Vietnam who know well the specifics of that country and its army and who have a long-time experience in rendering assistance to the Vietnamese comrades in the issues of military building, education and training of the troops.

The Soviets, in their turn, would be ready to provide the 'Vietnamese friends' with their advice, but only through the command of the People's Liberation Army of China.[16] The Soviet political leaders took into account the recommendations of their military colleagues, and included in the directives for the negotiations with Ho Chi Minh a paragraph formulated in the same vein.

Moreover, Moscow did not wish to yield to its Chinese allies the leading position in dealing with the DRV in other spheres as well. For example, when in 1956 the Vietnamese requested Soviet participation in drawing up a project for the economic development plan, the Soviet ambassador in Hanoi assured his counterparts that the Soviets would be ready to help Hanoi in this matter, but 'it is necessary to take into account that our abilities are limited, since the [Soviet] specialists here do not yet know conditions and prospects of Vietnam. It is necessary to enlist the PRC specialists to help.'[17] It is therefore not surprising that in the 1950s the PRC became number one on the list of allies and supporters of the DRV among the socialist countries. By the end of the decade Beijing provided about 60 per cent of the socialist help provided to North Vietnam. Moscow was far behind with its almost 30 per cent.[18]

Such conduct obviously showed the deliberate policy of the Soviet leadership, who did not regard Vietnam or the rest of the region of South-East Asia as its priority, concentrating instead on the problems of East–West relations and the situation in Europe. Moscow could afford to let its policy towards Indo-China drift without active intervention as long as the *status quo*, maintained by the Geneva conference, remained unshakable. However, almost from the outset the basis of such an inert policy began to shatter. The first blow was struck by the French withdrawal.

Nobody had expected French power to disintegrate so rapidly in its former Indo-Chinese colonies, particularly Vietnam. In the latter case their departure was accelerated by the anti-French attitude of the South Vietnamese leader, Ngo Dinh Diem, who openly aligned his regime with the United States in the hope that American support and assistance would help him maintain his power in the South.[19] As a result of the French withdrawal during 1955, Washington stepped up its presence in Vietnam. American advisers had to replace the French military as training officers in the South Vietnamese army. They increased the flow of aid to Diem and intensified political contacts with his regime. Already in June 1956 the United States exceeded the limit of 342 US trainers imposed by the Geneva agreements by sending to Vietnam 350 extra American servicemen. During the years 1955–60, South Vietnam received from Washington more than $2 billion in aid, thus becoming the third-ranking non-NATO recipient and the seventh worldwide. The economic aid mission in Vietnam was the largest anywhere.[20]

Moscow perceived these developments in Vietnam with apprehension. In May 1955 Molotov sent the CPSU Central Committee a memorandum, in which he drew attention to the changes in the situation in South Vietnam. He noted the US activities in the country, aimed at 'eliminating the French from Vietnam'. According to the memorandum, the Americans were trying to undermine the economic position of France, intensifying their efforts to oust the French from the army and strengthening their political influence. The Soviet foreign minister proposed that the situation should be discussed with the Vietnamese, Chinese and French 'friends', as well as with the Polish representatives in the International Control Commission (ICC), in order to work out countermeasures against such US actions. In a draft of the telegram to Paris, the foreign minister instructed the Soviet ambassador to ascertain the opinion of the French 'friends' on the expediency of steps aimed at masking the 'aggressive American actions in Vietnam' through the mass media 'or by any other way which you would consider appropriate'.[21] Of course, Moscow was hardly able to stop the irreversible process, especially in view of the absence of efficient leverage against it.

Soon, however, the Soviet leaders had to deal with another tendency that threatened not only their policy toward Indochina but the very basis of their Asian strategy and their position in the world communist movement. This was the estrangement between the two communist giants, the USSR and communist China, which developed into open rivalry during the next decade. Although the destructive effect of the disagreement between Moscow and Beijing for the Soviet positions in Indo-China was not obvious in the 1950s, the Soviet leaders had to revise their country's actions with respect to the region, while taking into consideration the fact that they now faced in Asia not an ally to whom it was possible to delegate concerns of secondary importance, but a rival who was waiting for any blunder they might make to reap a profit for itself.

With the two premises of the Soviet policy toward Indo-China disappearing, Moscow's whole strategy in the region seemed to lose its coherence, especially because the Soviet leaders could not rely on such an unknown factor as the North Vietnamese willingness to live with a peace that rested 'on a bed of nails,' as Lloyd Gardner characterizes the Geneva provisions on the partition of Vietnam.[22] From the outset, the Vietnamese communists were far from pleased with this particular outcome of the 1954 conference on Indo-China and were utterly determined to eliminate this unfortunate result as soon as circumstances would allow. Nor did they not conceal this intention even from their Soviet allies. Only one year after the Geneva conference, a top-ranking North Vietnamese official, Truong Chinh, told a Soviet diplomat in conversation that he could see no way to reunify the country by peaceful means. Because each zone of Vietnam had its own government and army, which were antagonistic to each other, he reasoned, any attempt of one zone to impose its will on the other or make it acquiesce would lead to war.[23]

Hanoi followed this logic and prepared the country for an eventual military solution of the Vietnamese problem. In June 1956 the politburo of the Vietnamese Workers Party (VWP) adopted a resolution which, along with peaceful struggle in the south, admitted the necessity to develop armed resistance against the Saigon regime. Next year a military unit was created in one of the zones of South Vietnam that became later a core of the regular army of the communist forces.[24] At the same time Hanoi supported local resistance through the party bureau on South Vietnam, which was established in October 1954 for coordination of the struggle in the south.[25]

By the end of the decade all hopes for a peaceful reunification of the country had evaporated, particularly after Diem maintained his power and proclaimed himself president of a newly created Republic of Vietnam (RVN). In the situation of the mounting repression by the Saigon regime of the South Vietnamese communists and their allies, Hanoi finally abandoned its peaceful course and turned toward military struggle.

The Fifteenth Plenum of the VWP declared that the main method of the revolution in the South Vietnam was that of violence. The Third Congress of the party, which took place in September 1960, ratified this plenum's decision.[26]

Moscow was informed about the transformation of its Vietnamese allies' views on their future. In their report on the Third Congress of the Lao Dong party (VWP), Soviet diplomats in Hanoi drew the attention of their superiors to the emphasis that Le Duan, the rising leader of the North Vietnamese politburo, made on the revolutionary movement in the South. The report concluded that 'although the Vietnamese friends regard unification of the country by peaceful means as very important, they nonetheless reserve a not unimportant place for the reunion of the country by way of revolution in South Vietnam'.[27]

It appeared that the moment had come for a substantial reconsideration of Soviet strategy in Indo-China in general, and of Soviet policy toward the North Vietnamese allies in particular. However, the Soviet leaders were in no hurry to reverse their political course in the region. Notwithstanding the inflammatory speeches in support of the national liberation movement delivered by Premier Nikita Khrushchev in Moscow, and promises of economic and even military aid to the DRV, the Soviet leaders seemed to be more preoccupied with problems other than the Vietnam reunification. Although they noted with some apprehension the growing militancy in Hanoi, they had to deal with other pressing issues even in South-East Asia, such as the situation in Laos, which diverted their attention from the needs of the Vietnamese leadership; moreover, its nationalism, which had become obvious by the early 1960s, only added to the reluctance of Moscow to make a choice in favour of unconditional support of the struggle of the Vietnamese communists. As became clear after the Soviet–Vietnamese high-level negotiations in Moscow in January – February 1964, the Soviet leaders did not exclude the possibility of close cooperation between the two countries, but saw that its development would be a difficult and time-consuming process.[28]

However, events in South-East Asia threatened Moscow's passive attitude toward the conflict. The tension in the region was growing during the spring and summer of 1964, and led to the first serious crisis in early August when North Vietnamese patrol boats in the Gulf of Tonkin allegedly attacked US vessels that were on electronic reconnaissance in the international waters close to the shores of the DRV. Washington immediately reacted by authorizing retaliatory strikes against the North Vietnamese patrol boat bases and a supporting oil complex. The US Congress adopted a resolution that provided the president with power 'to take all necessary steps, including the use of armed forces', to assist non-communist states in South-East Asia (primarily, South Vietnam) against Hanoi's aggression.[29]

The Tonkin Gulf incidents sharpened a dilemma faced by the Soviet leadership: either to abandon the DRV and to occupy a position of non-involvement in Indo-China or to plunge into direct confrontation with the United States in alliance with independent and nationalistic North Vietnam, while having almost negligible opportunity to influence developments there and risking total collapse of its policy of rapprochement with the West. Both alternatives seemed unacceptable to the Kremlin. The former threatened to undermine the Soviet position in the world communist movement and *vis-à-vis* Moscow's allies, while the latter might increase radically the hostilities of the cold war and the danger of nuclear war. Moscow had therefore chosen a middle way: to provide its North Vietnamese allies with the necessary aid, including military assistance, but at the same time to undertake efforts in order to find a diplomatic solution of the conflict in Vietnam, using its relations with both warring parties.

Such a policy, which was taking shape in the last months of 1964 and emerged in its final forms during the first period of the US escalation of its involvement in the conflict in 1965, remained unchanged throughout the war in Vietnam. As a result of a number of agreements between the USSR and the DRV, Moscow sent to North Vietnam substantial and ever growing aid, gradually becoming a principal DRV supplier. The Soviets provided their Vietnamese allies with industrial and telecommunication equipment, trucks, medical supplies, machine tools, iron ore and non-ferrous metals. In its supplies to the DRV the USSR was initially in second place among the socialist countries, yielding only to China. For instance, by the beginning of 1967 Moscow provided 36.8 per cent of the aid, while China's contribution exceeded 50 per cent. However, in 1968 Soviet assistance grew to 50 per cent of socialist aid, worth a total of more than half a billion dollars, as compared with $370 million in 1964.[30]

Soviet–North Vietnamese military cooperation played a decisive role in Hanoi's plans for the war against the United States and its Saigon allies. In 1965, according to a memorandum prepared by the US Department of State Bureau of Intelligence and Research, the Soviet Union radically increased its military support to the DRV.[31] In 1966–7 Moscow assumed an obligation to deliver 500 million roubles' worth of equipment for the North Vietnamese armed forces (approximately $550.5 million), and to reach a limit of 1 billion roubles for the military shipments since the beginning of 1953. But in reality the Soviets exceeded this limit, providing in 1968 aid that totalled 1.1 billion roubles for the whole period from 1953. In 1968 military aid to North Vietnam comprised two-thirds of the overall Soviet assistance to the DRV, and amounted to 357 million roubles ($396.7 million).[32]

The Soviet Union was responsive to the requests from Hanoi for various kinds of armament and ammunition. Its main concern was to defend a fraternal socialist country in South-East Asia from US air attacks. For this purpose, Moscow sent to the DRV surface-to-air missiles, jet planes, air rockets, anti-aircraft guns and other hardware for DRV air defence. Furthermore, Moscow tried to satisfy Hanoi's requirements in military advisers and in well-trained cadres who were able to man modern weapons delivered from the USSR. Every year of the Vietnam War, more than a thousand Soviet military experts arrived in the DRV to help the 'Vietnamese friends' organize the defence of their country against American attacks. These were mostly technicians and missile complex operators. However, there were also pilots and air instructors from the Soviet Union, who took part in combat missions against the Americans.[33]

At the same time, Hanoi sent to the Soviet Union thousands of soldiers and officers who were to be trained in Soviet military colleges. In 1966, for example, 2600 Vietnamese had been dispatched to the USSR to be prepared for service in the air and in anti-aircraft defence. The total effect of the cooperation in this sphere was that only in 1966 were cadres for four anti- aircraft regiments and technicians for an aircraft regiment trained in the Soviet Union, as well as some pilots among those North Vietnamese who joined the People's Army of Vietnam.[34]

Notwithstanding this impressive aid to North Vietnam, its growth did not correspond directly to the level of the Soviet influence in that country. Although Moscow was now somewhat able to strengthen its position in the DRV as compared with the early 1960s, it remained flimsy. One of the factors that precluded a rapid change of the situation in the Soviet favour was a strong Chinese influence in North Vietnam. The PRC was a faithful ally of Ho Chi Minh's regime. Beijing had assisted the Viet Minh during the first Indo-China war against the French. After the war against the French colonizers China had provided, with Soviet blessing, the fledgling communist state in the Northern zone of Vietnam with the assistance necessary for the Vietnamese Communist Party to consolidate its power and to accumulate resources for the war against the Saigon regime and its American supporters. According to Soviet estimates, from 1955 to 1965 the PRC provided the DRV with 511.8 million roubles' worth of economic aid, roughly $569 million. More than half of this sum was sent to Hanoi in the form of grants.[35] Although during the years after the US escalation of the war in Vietnam, China lost its leading position in the sphere of aid to the DRV, having given up its place to the Soviet Union, it nevertheless provided substantial assistance to the Vietnamese allies.

But what was no less important, the North Vietnamese leadership shared with its Chinese counterpart many ideological views, including the assessment of the conflict in South-East Asia and the international situation, of the role of the world communist movement and the national liberation struggle, the assessment of *détente* and the prospects of peaceful coexistence between socialism and capitalism. There was strong pro-Chinese feeling among the top leaders of the DRV. While politicians sympathetic to the Soviet Union had been removed from their posts in the period of estrangement between Moscow and Hanoi in the early 1960s, pro-Chinese leaders retained their power even after 1965. This trend manifested itself in the freedom of Chinese propaganda in the DRV, whereas Soviet propaganda was confined to exhibitions and film screening on occasion of national holidays. There were no obstacles in the way of Chinese anti-Soviet campaigns, despite vigorous protests by the Soviet embassy in Hanoi. The Chinese diplomats and other officials enjoyed more freedom in North Vietnam than their Soviet colleagues. The DRV leaders visited Beijing frequently to ask advice from Mao Zedong and Zhou Enlai on important foreign policy problems.

The Vietnamese communists' own specific beliefs and prejudices only added to the difficulties the Soviets faced in their policy toward the DRV. As Douglas Pike put it, throughout the Vietnam War, Hanoi maintained an 'ultra-hardline, fundamentalist view' of its enemy in the south, of its contribution to the world revolutionary process, and, as a result, of the socialist countries' responsibilities to them:

> Each Communist nation, large or small, said the Hanoi theoretician, has both national interest and international duty. In dealing with these, the small nation (read DRV) must be free to decide its interest or obligations, which should never be forced on it by a larger nation (read USSR or China). However, the small nation also has the right to expect support from the big nations. Thus staked out was the claim that the USSR (and China) must support the DRV in the name of international proletarianism but – in the same spirit – may not levy requirements on the DRV, as that would violate the principle of self-determination.[36]

The Soviet embassy in Hanoi characterized such an attitude as a 'narrow national' approach to the role of the USSR in the world arena, in general, and in the Vietnamese question, in particular.[37]

This attitude showed itself in almost all spheres of Soviet–DRV relations. In the political arena, the North Vietnamese leaders were reluctant to share with their Soviet colleagues information on the situation in Vietnam and Indo-China. They concealed the facts of the internal life of the Lao Dong party (the VWP) and developments in their relations with Beijing. Hanoi tried to avoid revealing to Moscow its plans for the war with the United States, or its views on possible ways of securing a settlement of the conflict. The latter policy was especially annoying for the Soviets who, from the beginning of the war in South-East Asia, were looking for a peaceful settlement of the conflict.

Soviet propaganda on behalf of the DRV and economic and military aid to North Vietnam were combined in Moscow's policy toward the Vietnamese conflict with persistent efforts to find a diplomatic solution of the war that would guarantee against transformation of the conflict into global confrontation and, at the same time, that would preserve North Vietnam as a friendly socialist country allied with Moscow. This inclination of the Soviet policy-makers went as far back as November 1964, when the USSR ambassador in Hanoi stressed in his report to Moscow that 'in the present situation, as always, the main attention should be directed to searching for ways towards a political settlement in Vietnam and in the whole of Indochina.'[38] To reach this goal, the Soviet leaders exerted pressure on the warring parties, the United

States and North Vietnam, which was aimed at persuading them to abandon their military ambitions and to agree to negotiations. They mobilized their allies and appealed to the Western countries for assistance in drawing the rivals to the conference table. They played the role of mediator between Washington and Hanoi, forwarding their messages to each other, facilitating the exchange of useful information and prompting other countries to do the same. All this activity took place mostly behind the scenes, because the Soviet Union tried by every means to avoid being seen as an official intermediary.

Such efforts by the Soviet diplomats proved to be successful, because negotiations between the United States and North Vietnam started in Paris in May 1968. Moscow could regard the Paris peace talks as its own success. What was more important, these talks were, for the Soviet leadership, a guarantee that while the conflict might not remain within the bounds of Vietnam at least it would not develop beyond Indo-China. It was therefore, essential for Moscow to prevent a collapse of the negotiations, to keep participants at the conference table. With this purpose, the Soviet diplomats actively involved themselves in resolving numerous deadlocks in the negotiations in Paris and in helping to reach an agreement on the cessation of the US bombing of DRV territory and on full-scale talks between all the participants in the war, including the Saigon regime and the National Liberation Front of South Vietnam (the Viet Cong).

The US diplomats involved in the negotiations with the DRV representatives in Paris valued this role of the Soviet Union highly. The head of the American delegation at the first stage of the peace talks, Averell Harriman, in his conversation with Valerian Zorin, the Soviet ambassador to France, expressed his conviction that 'we could not have a real settlement without Soviet help, and he was glad the Soviets had shown this willingness to help.'[39]

While trying to push the North Vietnamese and American negotiators in Paris to agreement, Moscow continued its policy of strengthening the Soviet position in the DRV. Soviet aid to Vietnam appeared to be an important factor to this end. Although the amount of military aid decreased after the start of the peaceful negotiations, as a result of the decline of the activity on the battlefield, it still amounted to $200 million in 1969. The North Vietnamese armed forces, according to a Soviet embassy report, were rearmed and equipped mostly by the Soviet Union and became one of the most powerful in the region. From 1969 to 1971, Moscow signed seven agreements with the DRV on economic cooperation and assistance, three of them supplemental aid to the North Vietnamese economy and defence.[40]

Although, as in previous years, the Soviet assistance to Hanoi was not converted proportionally into political influence, by the early 1970s Moscow scored a significant success in its relations with the DRV. A number of North Vietnamese contacts with the Soviet Union was growing. Exchange of delegations of various levels between the DRV and other socialist countries allowed the Soviet policy-makers to consider the issue of coordination of Moscow's policy with that of its allies in order to tie North Vietnam to the Soviet bloc. In June 1970 the Soviet embassy in Hanoi sent to Moscow a memorandum that discussed the prospects of such coordination. The main idea of the lengthy memorandum was to assess the possibility of inclusion of North Vietnam in the Soviet orbit, of gradual reorientation of the DRV policy from Beijing to Moscow, and of increasing the influence of the DRV in South-East Asia.[41]

Thus, while in 1964–5 the main task for Moscow was to bridge the gap in Soviet-North Vietnamese relations created by previous overcautiousness with respect to Hanoi, and to strengthen its position in Vietnam as a counterbalance to the Chinese influence, by the end of the decade the Soviet leadership had moved to the next stage of its policy in the region. The ultimate goal was to make Vietnam a partner and the outpost of Moscow in South-East Asia, especially when China, which played such a role in the 1950s, had resolutely broken with the Soviet system. This idea was put forward even more clearly in another Soviet embassy memorandum a year later. Soviet diplomats in Hanoi believed that

> now, when the WPV [Workers Party of Vietnam] has been strengthened on the way to independence, when the Party course is developing, in general (though still slowly) in a favourable direction for us, when the DRV has become the leading force in the struggle of the peoples of Indochina, we will possess comparatively more possibilities for establishing our policy in this region. It is not excluded that Indochina may become for us the key to the whole of South-East Asia. In addition, in that region there is nobody, so far, we could lean on, except the DRV.[42]

These Soviet plans help to explain why Moscow was so sensitive to any accidents that could jeopardize its relations with the North

Vietnamese. The Soviet leaders consistently refused to yield to American pressure and to convince Hanoi to agree to US conditions for peace, even if those conditions were not totally unacceptable to them. They continued providing the DRV and its allies in South Vietnam with military aid, despite Washington's vigorous protests. Notwithstanding complaints about Vietnamese duplicity, intransigence, and egoism, they never considered the issue of disengagement from the war, for Vietnam gradually became for Moscow not only a question of ideology but also an issue of geopolitics.

It is therefore not surprising that, even before the war in Indochina was over, the Kremlin actively considered the prospects of Soviet political penetration in other regions in South-East Asia. For instance, in November 1972 the CPSU Central Committee discussed the situation in the communist movement in Thailand. They examined a proposal for establishing in that country a patriotic front following the example of similar organizations in Vietnam and Laos, and expressed readiness to assist the Vietnamese and Laotian communists in their efforts in this direction.[43]

A broader perspective opened before Moscow when the Paris agreement on ending the war and restoring peace in Vietnam was signed in January 1973. This agreement put an end to direct US involvement in the conflict in Indo-China. But it did not bring peace in the region. The war continued in Vietnam between the North and the South for two more years, and its outcome depended on which regime proved to be more viable, more capable of converting aid sent from the outside into decisive victories on the battlefield, and on the political scene.

The North Vietnamese leadership was obviously sure of the support of its Soviet comrades in the struggle against the Saigon regime. On his way back from the International Conference on Indo-China that took place in March 1973, the DRV foreign minister, Nguyen Duy Trinh, during his meeting in Moscow with one of the top Soviet leaders, spoke of a 'comprehensive development of cooperation between the two countries'. A month later, in a conversation devoted to the problems of Soviet assistance in realization of the DRV economic recovery programme between the Soviet ambassador to Hanoi, Ilia Shcherbakov, and Le Thanh Nghi, the DRV deputy prime minister, the Vietnamese drew the attention of his counterpart that the

successful building of Socialism in the DRV will exert great influence on all countries of South-East Asia. In connection with this, the authority and influence of the Soviet Union in this region of the world will be strengthened as well.[44]

Moscow could hardly overlook such a hint.

In fact, circumstances were favourable for the Soviet Union to undermine significantly Chinese influence in South-East Asia and to consolidate its position in the region. In its top-secret estimate of the prospects of USSR–DRV relations, the Soviet foreign ministry noted the growth of 'pragmatic elements in the Vietnamese comrades' assessment of the USSR role' in the realization of Hanoi's plans. The officials in Moscow predicted that these elements would persist, 'since the WPV–DRV leadership regards development of rather close relations with the USSR as a kind of counterweight to Beijing's hegemonic aspirations in Indochina'. It was by Hanoi's fear of the Chinese influence that the foreign ministry explained the North Vietnamese leadership's gradual abandonment of its war policy of balancing between the Soviet Union and the People's Republic of China and its intention to rely exclusively on Soviet aid in the military and economic spheres.[45]

Doubtless, the Soviets tried to bolster this tendency by new promises of support and assistance to the DRV. When the DRV leaders, Le Duan and Pham Van Dong, visited Moscow in July 1973, they not only received assurances from the Soviet side that it would help Hanoi in economic recovery and in the development of energy, coal mining, trade and other branches of the North Vietnamese economy, but also obtained the USSR's obligation to continue providing military aid to Hanoi. In November 1973, the two countries signed a new military agreement.[46] By signing this agreement Moscow virtually approved Hanoi's plans to overthrow the government of South Vietnam and establish a North Vietnamese political regime throughout the country.

In the meantime the Soviet leadership continued to work out its strategy in South-East Asia. In June 1973 the Soviet Foreign Ministry suggested publicly emphasizing the leading role of the Vietnamese communists in Indo-China and South-East Asia, 'without affecting, of course, the independence of other Marxist parties in the region'.[47] On 17 January 1974 the CPSU politburo adopted a resolution 'On the Main Directions of the Activity Aimed At the Strengthening of the USSR Position in Indochina'. In February of the same year the CPSU Central Committee considered its secretary Boris Ponomarev's proposal to use the influence of the Workers Party of Vietnam in promoting

Soviet influence in the communist movements in such countries as Thailand, Malaysia, Indonesia and the Philippines.[48]

Thus, the collapse of the Saigon regime in April 1975 and the subsequent reunification of Vietnam under Hanoi rule became the final solution of the Vietnam problem, which neither diplomacy at the Geneva conference nor the military intervention of the United States was able to resolve. The victory of April 1975 was the last brick crowning the edifice that represented one of the cold war alliances, the legacy of which will probably remain for several generations.

7

CHINA AND THE VIETNAM WARS

Chen Jian

It is by now well known that the People's Republic of China (PRC) was deeply involved in the Vietnam wars (both the French and the American). From 1950 to 1975, Beijing provided the Vietnamese communists with substantial military, financial and other material support. In addition to delivery of a large quantity of ammunition and military equipment, high-ranking Chinese military and political advisers participated in the Viet Minh's decision-making during the French war, and, from 1965 to 1970, Beijing despatched as many as 320 000 Chinese engineering and air defence troops to North Vietnam, significantly enhancing Hanoi's capacities in fighting against the Americans.

Why and how did the PRC provide substantial support to the Vietnamese communists? What were the basic considerations underlying this support? How did these considerations, as well as the specific forms of Chinese support, change along with China's changing domestic and international situations? Finally, why did China and Vietnam, despite the magnitude of Beijing's support, turn into enemies after the end of the Vietnam War? This chapter, with the insights gained from newly available Chinese source materials, is able to offer a brief yet comprehensive account of China's involvement in the Vietnam wars.

Contacts Between Chinese and Vietnamese Communists Before 1950

China and Vietnam are neighbours. The Chinese Communist Party (CCP) and the Vietnamese communists had close connections in history. From the 1920s to the 1940s many Vietnamese communists, including Ho Chi Minh, frequently carried out revolutionary activities in China, and some of them joined the CCP.[1]

When the Democratic Republic of Vietnam (DRV) was established in September 1945, following the successful August Revolution, the CCP decided to send the majority of its Vietnamese members back to their own country to promote the Vietnamese revolution. The Chinese communist guerrilla forces in Chinese–Vietnamese border areas occasionally assisted the Viet Minh's military operations. However, having to take its own revolution as the top priority, the CCP was unable to offer direct support to their Vietnamese comrades before 1949. Because of technical difficulties, there existed no effective telegraphic communication between the Chinese and Vietnamese communist leaderships during this period.[2] The Vietnamese communists had to fight a war against the French basically by themselves.

Planning China's Support to the Viet Minh, Late 1949 to Early 1950

The victory of the Chinese revolution in late 1949 changed the international environment of the Vietnamese revolution. For the purposes of promoting the PRC's international reputation and enhancing its southern border security, the CCP leadership was willing to play an outstanding role in supporting the Viet Minh. From late June to early August, Liu Shaoqi, the CCP's second most important leader, secretly visited Moscow and had a series of meetings with Stalin and other Soviet leaders. A main part of their discussions covered how to promote an Asian revolution in general and the Vietnamese revolution in particular. The Chinese and Soviet leaders reached a general consensus that it was primarily the CCP's responsibility to provide support to the Vietnamese revolutionaries. On 24 December 1949, during a meeting between Mao Zedong and Stalin in Moscow, the two leaders confirmed the above arrangement.[3]

The Vietnamese communists were also eager to gain support from their Chinese comrades. In August 1949, Ho Chi Minh wrote a letter to Mao Zedong, introducing the situation in Vietnam and asking for Chinese aid in all forms. The letter was delivered to the CCP leaders in Beijing in October. On 24 December 1949, Liu Shaoqi chaired a CCP Politburo meeting to discuss China's support to Vietnam, which made the decision to invite a high-ranking Vietnamese delegation to Beijing to 'discuss all important issues'. It also decided to send Lao Guibo, a People's Liberation Army (PLA) commander with extensive experience in dealing with complicated situations, to Vietnam as the CCP's general representative.[4] After Hoang Van Hoan, a Central Committee member of the Indo-China Communist Party (ICP; after February 1951, the Vietnamese Workers' Party or VWP) arrived in Beijing early in January 1950 to establish direct contacts with the CCP, the PRC formally acknowledged the DRV and established diplomatic relations with it on 18 January.[5]

Ho could not wait until the arrival of the CCP representative. After walking for seventeen days, he secretly arrived at Jingxi, a small Chinese border town, on 16 January 1950. It took him another twelve days to travel to Beijing, where he met with Liu Shaoqi. As both Mao Zedong and Zhou Enlai were then visiting the Soviet Union, Ho left Beijing for Moscow on 3 February to meet the Chinese and Soviet leaders.[6] This secret trip to Moscow brought Ho mixed achievements. Stalin agreed to recognize Ho's government, but was reluctant to provide more substantial support to the Viet Minh. He turned Ho to the Chinese. To Ho's great satisfaction, Mao and Zhou, first in Moscow and then in Beijing (Ho returned to Beijing together with Mao and Zhou), promised him that the CCP would do its best 'to offer every assistance needed by Vietnam in its struggle against France'.[7] Ho returned to Vietnam in March, knowing that he could now count on the firm backing of the PRC.

In April 1950, the ICP Central Committee formally asked for military advisers and other support from the CCP. On 17 April, the CCP leadership ordered the establishment of the 'Chinese Military Advisory Group' (CMAG). By late July, the CMAG, composed of 79 experienced PLA officers, was formally established, with General Wei Guoqing as the head.[8]

Before the Chinese advisers went to Vietnam, Mao Zedong, Liu Shaoqi and other CCP leaders had several conversations with them, revealing the basic considerations underlying Beijing's decision to support Ho's cause. The CCP leaders emphasized that after the victory of the Chinese revolution, it was the CCP's internationalist obligation to support their Vietnamese comrades. They believed that the victory of the Vietnamese revolution would greatly promote the cause of an 'Eastern Revolution' following the Chinese model. They also believed that a confrontation between China and the United States would occur sooner or later, and that the victory of the Vietnamese revolution would greatly strengthen the PRC's capacities in a confrontation with the United States.[9] These specific ideological commitments and security concerns formed the foundation of Beijing's Vietnam policy in the early 1950s.

China's Involvement in the First Indo-China War, 1950–54

China's actual involvement in Vietnam began with the Border Campaign in the fall of 1950. The idea of the campaign first emerged during Ho's early 1950 visit to Beijing, and the Chinese and Vietnamese communist leaders quickly caught its merits: a victory in such a campaign would enable the Viet Minh's base areas to be directly backed by the PRC. In July 1950, the CCP decided to despatch General Chen Geng, one of the PLA's most talented high commanders, to Vietnam to help the yet inexperienced Vietnamese to organize the campaign.[10] Chen arrived at the Viet Minh's Viet Bac base area in mid-July. After a series of meetings with Ho Chi Minh, General Vo Nguyen Giap and other ICP leaders, Chen proposed that the campaign should follow the line of 'concentrating our forces and destroying the enemy troops by separating them', a strategy that had been proven effective during China's civil war. The Vietnamese accepted Chen's plan.[11] In order to prepare for the campaign, from April to September 1950, Beijing delivered to the Viet Minh more than 14 000 guns, 1700 machine guns, about 150 pieces of different types of cannon, 2800 tons of grain and large quantity of ammunition, medicine, uniforms and communication equipment.[12]

The Border Campaign began on 16 September and ended with a huge Viet Minh victory. By 13 October, the Vietnamese communist forces had eliminated seven battalions (about 3000) of French troops, forcing the French to give up the blockade lines along the Vietnamese–Chinese border. As a result, the PRC's vast territory now became the Viet Minh's strategic rear, placing the Vietnamese communists in an unbeatable position. General Chen and other Chinese advisers played a major role in directing the Viet Minh's operations during the campaign. After fulfilling his tasks, Chen left Vietnam in early November 1950 to take a new assignment in Korea.[13]

Encouraged by their victory in the Border Campaign, the Viet Minh's military commanders (General Giap in particular), as well as the Chinese advisers, believed that they were in a position to lead the war to the Tonkin delta area. They hoped that by conducting a series of victorious offensive campaigns against the French defensive system there, they would create conditions for a total Viet Minh victory on the Indo-China battlefield.[14]

However, the Viet Minh's three offensive campaigns ('Tran Huong Dao', 'Hong Hoa Tham' and 'Quang Trung') in the delta area, which lasted from late December 1950 to June 1951, failed to reach their original goals. In face of firm French defence, supported by superior artillery fire, the Viet Minh's troops suffered heavily and had to give up head-on attacks against fortified French positions by mid-1951. The Viet Minh high command, as well as the Chinese advisers, realized that it was still premature to wage a 'general counteroffensive' aimed at seizing the delta area.[15]

Consequently, the Viet Minh's strategy experienced an important change in 1952, with its emphasis shifting from the delta area to upper Laos and north-western Vietnam. While it is still unclear who, the Vietnamese or the Chinese advisers, first proposed this important strategic change, Chinese sources available now reveal that by early 1952 the CMAG had taken the competition over north-western Vietnam as a top priority. On 16 February 1952, the CMAG proposed to the Viet Minh high command that it should treat 'the preparation for conditions for future combat tasks in the North West' as its main task for 1952. The same day, Luo Guibo summarized in a report to the Chinese Central Military Commission that it was necessary for the Viet Minh to focus on liberating Son La, Lai Chau, and Nghia Lo, all in north- western Vietnam, in 1952, and preparing for seizing north-western Vietnam and upper Laos in 1953.[16]

From October to December 1952, the Viet Minh's troops successfully conducted the north-west campaign, which resulted in their occupation of Nghia Lo, Son Lo, southern Lai Chau and western Yen Bay. From late March to May 1953, the Viet Minh's troops further conducted the Xam Neua Campaign in Upper Laos, leading to their control of Xam Neua and part of Xiang Khoary and Phong Sali. The Chinese advisers were actively involved in the planning and organization of these campaigns. In the meantime, Beijing continued to provide a large quantity of military and other material support to the Viet Minh.[17]

In the fall of 1953, the VWP leadership realized that the war had reached a potential turning point. In a cable to the CCP Central Committee on 13 August 1953, it asked the Chinese 'to provide advice' concerning 'the understanding of the current situation, as well as our strategies for future operations'.[18] On 27 and 29 August, the CCP Central Committee sent two telegrams to Luo Guibo and the VWP Central Committee, proposing that the Vietnamese should continue to carry out the 'north-western strategy' and should not shift to the delta area, to which the VWP Politburo agreed.[19] In late October and early November 1953, Chinese military advisers (especially Wei Guoqing), together with Viet Minh commanders, worked out the operation plans for 1954 along these lines, which were approved by the VWP Politburo on 3 November.[20]

All of the above formed an important background element for the Dien Bien Phu campaign. On 20 November 1953, the French dropped six parachute battalions to Dien Bien Phu, a previously little-known village in the mountains of north-western Vietnam, to prevent further communist advance in that region. The Chinese advisers immediately realized that this presented a challenge, as well as a good opportunity, for the Vietnamese communist forces. They proposed that the Viet Minh's troops should seize this opportunity to surround French troops at Dien Bien Phu and, if possible, destroy them there. On 6 December, with the Chinese advisers' active participation, the VWP leadership made the decision to initiate the Dien Bien Phu campaign.[21]

Although Chinese and Vietnamese sources have differed on the actual role the Chinese advisers had played during the Dien Bien Phu campaign (while the Vietnamese sources pointed out that the Chinese had provided some bad advice, the Chinese sources emphasized that most of the guidance from Chinese advisers had been positive in nature), one thing is certain, namely that Beijing tried its best to guarantee a Viet Minh victory in the campaign. Top Chinese leaders, such as Mao Zedong, Zhou Enlai and Liu Shaoqi, carefully followed every development at Dien Bien Phu. During the latter stage of the campaign, Mao even made specific instructions on how to deal with possible sudden attack by French parachute troops on the Viet Minh's supply lines.[22] Beijing also accelerated its military delivery to the Viet Minh during the winter and spring of 1953–4, rushing more than 200 trucks, over 10 000 barrels of oil, over 100 cannons, 3000 pieces of various types of guns, 2 400 000 gun bullets, over 60 000 artillery shells and about 1700 tons of grain into the hands of the Viet Minh.[23] In order to cut off Dien Bien Phu from French airborne support, Beijing sent four Vietnamese anti-aircraft battalions, which had been trained in China, back to Vietnam. All of this significantly strengthened the Viet

Minh's military capacity, contributing to its resounding victory at Dien Bien Phu.

To summarize, China's involvement in the First Indo-China War was deep. Beijing provided large quantities of ammunition and military equipment to the Viet Minh, helped the Viet Minh train military commanders and troops, and the Chinese advisers participated in the Vietnamese communist leadership's decision-making processes. Thus it is fair to say that China's support had played a decisive role in the shaping of a series of Viet Minh victories during the war, such as those in the border campaign, the north-west campaign and, especially, the Dien Bien Phu campaign.

Yet the high degree of solidarity between the Chinese and Vietnamese communists during this period did not mean that no problem existed between them. In actuality, even at the height of their cooperation, there were signs of contradictions and, in some cases, conflicts between the two sides. Members of the CMAG, for example, complained that the Viet Minh's troops were too inexperienced to realize some of their strategic designs. General Chen Geng mentioned in his diary that General Giap and a few of his Vietnamese colleagues lacked the 'Bolshevik-style self- criticism' and were unhappy with the Chinese criticism of their 'shortcomings'. On one occasion, Chen even described Giap as 'slippery and not very upright and honest' to his Chinese comrades.[24] The Vietnamese, on the other hand, were not satisfied with some of the Chinese adviserss' suggestions, especially those concerning carrying out land reform and political indoctrination in Vietnam following China's experiences, which, in their view, did not fit Vietnam's special situation. As we may now see, the potential divergence between the Chinese and the Vietnamese would surface further at the Geneva Conference of 1954.

The Geneva Conference, 1954

Beginning on 26 April 1954, an international conference was held in Geneva to discuss the Korea and Indo-China problems. On 8 May the discussions on Indo-China began. Different opinions existed between the PRC and DRV delegations at the conference: while the Vietnamese hoped to pursue a solution that would leave a clear communist domination not only in Vietnam but in Laos and Cambodia as well, the

Chinese, supported by the Soviets, were more willing to reach a compromise.

Beijing's strategy towards the Geneva conference reflected several of its leadership's basic considerations at the moment. First of all, with the end of the Korean War, Beijing's leaders sensed the need to devote more of the nation's resources to domestic issues, such as the introduction of the first five-year plan and the liberation of the nationalist-controlled Taiwan. They thus did not want to see the continued escalation of conflict in Indo-China. Second, with their Korean War experience, Beijing's leaders saw in the wake of the Dien Bien Phu siege the possibility of a direct American military intervention in Indo-China and hoped to prevent it from happening.[25] Third, Beijing's leaders also believed that a reconciliatory Chinese approach at the Geneva conference would help to strengthen Beijing's new claim on peaceful coexistence as the foundation of the PRC's international policy, while at the same time creating opportunities for 'breaking up the American blockade and embargo' against the PRC.[26]

Beijing's considerations were consistent with a central concern of the leaders in Moscow, who, after Stalin's death, also needed to focus on domestic issues and avoid a confrontation with the West in Asia. In the first three weeks of April, Zhou Enlai visited the Soviet Union three times to discuss the Chinese–Soviet strategy at the Geneva conference. These discussions resulted in a consensus: although the imperialist countries, the United States in particular, would try to sabotage the conference, if the communist side adopted a realistic strategy then it was still possible that a peaceful solution of the Indo-China problem could be worked out.[27]

The Vietnamese communist leaders, according to Chinese sources, originally posed no opposition to Beijing's views. From late March to April 1954, Ho Chi Minh and Pham Van Dong led a Vietnamese delegation to visit Beijing and Moscow (together with Zhou Enlai). In discussions with them, Mao Zedong, Liu Shaoqi and Zhou Enlai particularly introduced China's experience gained from the negotiations to end the Korean War, emphasizing that it was necessary to maintain 'realistic expectations' for the Geneva conference, to which, according to Chinese sources, the Vietnamese leaders agreed.[28] However, the victory at Dien Bien Phu made the Vietnamese believe that they were in a position to squeeze more concessions from their adversaries at Geneva. Pham Van Dong, head of the DRV delegation, announced at the conference that in order to settle the Indo-China problem, the Viet

Minh would ask for establishing its virtual control of most parts of Vietnam (through an on-the-spot truce, followed by a nationwide plebiscite which they knew that they would win), and pursuing positions for communist forces in Laos and Cambodia (by treating the settlement of the Laos and Cambodia problems as part of a general settlement of the Indo-China problem).[29]

Behind the scenes of the Geneva conference, Dong's unyielding approach caused potential tensions in the relations between the Chinese and the Soviets, on the one side, and the Vietnamese communists, on the other. In several discussions between the Chinese, Soviet and Vietnamese delegations, Zhou Enlai pointed out that Dong's attitude reflected how the inexperienced Vietnamese had been out of touch with reality. In justifying his willingness to accept the solution of dividing Vietnam into two areas, with the North belonging to the communists and the south to the French and pro-French Vietnamese, waiting for a national plebiscite, Zhou emphasized that this would allow the Viet Minh to have the entire north and gain back the south after the plebiscite. On the Laos and Cambodia problems, Zhou, after some investigation into the situation, favoured a separate solution, which, he believed, would simplify the whole issue and make the total settlement of the Indo-China problem possible. But Dong was not ready to accept Zhou's arguments.[30]

At this moment a major change occurred in France: the French parliament, reflecting the public's impatience with the immobility at Geneva, ousted Prime Minister Laniel and replaced him with Pierre Mendès-France, who, as a long-time leading critic of the war in Indo-China, promised that he would lead the negotiations to a successful conclusion by 20 July or resign. Zhou seized this opportunity to push the negotiations at Geneva forward. On 15 June, the Chinese, Soviet and Vietnamese delegations held a crucial meeting. Zhou pointed out that the key to the deadlock of the conference lay in the Vietnamese refusal to admit the existence of their forces in Laos and Cambodia. He warned that this would render the negotiations on the Indo-China problem fruitless, and that the Vietnamese communists would also lose an opportunity of achieving a peaceful solution of the Vietnam problem. Zhou proposed that the communist camp should now favour the withdrawal of all foreign forces, including the Viet Minh's, from Laos and Cambodia. The Soviets strongly supported Zhou's proposal, and the Vietnamese, under the heavy pressure of the Chinese and Soviets, finally yielded.[31] On 16 and 17 June, Zhou communicated the change of the Communist attitude towards Laos and Cambodia to the French and the British. To prepare for further discussions, the foreign ministers' meeting on the Indo-China problem at Geneva adjourned for three weeks from late June.

In order to coordinate with the Chinese, Ho Chi Minh, accompanied by Truong Chinh and Vo Nguyen Giap, visited China and met Zhou Enlai on 3–5 July in Liuzhou, a city in the south. Zhou particularly emphasized the danger involved in a possible direct American intervention in Indo-China, arguing that this would greatly complicate the situation there and reduce the Viet Minh's achievements. He thus convinced Ho that it was in the interests of the Vietnamese communists to reach an agreement with the French at the Geneva conference. The two sides reached a consensus on strategies towards the next phase of the conference: on the Vietnam problem they would favour dividing the country temporarily along the 16th parallel, but as Route Colonial Nine, the only line of transport linking Laos to the sea port, was located north of the 16th parallel, they would be willing to accept some slight adjustment of this solution; on the Lao problem, they would try to establish Xam Neua and Phong Sali, two provinces adjacent to China, as the concentration zone for pro-communist Laos forces; on the Cambodia problem, they would allow a political settlement that would probably lead to the establishment of a non-communist government.[32]

When Ho returned to Vietnam, the VWP Central Committee issued an instruction on 5 July (known as the '5 July Document'), which reflected the agreements Ho reached with the CCP.[33] In mid-July, the VWP Central Committee held its sixth meeting. Ho endorsed the new strategy of solving the Indo-China problem through a cease-fire based on 'temporarily' dividing Vietnam into two areas, which would supposedly lead to the unification of the whole country after the withdrawal of French forces and a nationwide plebiscite. It is notable that Ho criticized the 'leftist tendency' among Party members which ignored the danger of American intervention.[34]

The foreign ministers' meeting at Geneva resumed on 12 July. Zhou found that Dong was still reluctant to accept the new negotiating line and had an overnight meeting with him to try to persuade him of the necessity of reaching a compromise. He used America's intervention in the Korean War as an example to emphasize the tremendous danger involved in a direct American military intervention in Indo-China. Zhou promised, 'with the final withdrawal of the French, all of Vietnam will be yours'. Dong finally yielded to Zhou's arguments.[35]

Consequently, a settlement of the Indo-China problem was reached at Geneva on the early morning of 21 July (but the dividing line was established along the 17th parallel, not the 16th).

Beijing's Attitude Toward the 'Southern Revolution', 1956–62

The 1954 Geneva agreement on Indo-China concluded the First Indo-China War, but failed to end military conflicts in South-East Asia. When it became clear that a peaceful reunification through the plebiscite scheduled for 1956 would be indefinitely blocked by Washington and the government in Saigon, the Vietnamese communist leadership decided in 1959–60 to resume 'armed resistance' in the South. Policy-makers in Washington, perceiving that the battles in South Vietnam and other parts of South-East Asia (especially in Laos) represented a crucial contest against further communist expansion, continuously increased America's military involvement there. Consequently, the Second Indo-China War came into being.

Beijing neither hindered nor (until 1962) encouraged Hanoi's efforts to 'liberate' the South by military means. After the signing of the Geneva agreement, the leaders in Beijing seemed more willing than their comrades in Hanoi to accept the fact that Vietnam would be indefinitely divided. In several exchanges of opinion between top Beijing and Hanoi leaders in 1955–6, the basic tone of the Chinese advice was that the urgent task facing the Vietnamese communists was how to consolidate the revolutionary achievements in the North.[36] In December 1955, Beijing decided to recall the CMAG, and all members of the group returned to China by mid- March 1956.[37] In the summer of 1958 the VWP Politburo formally asked the CCP's advice on strategies for the 'Southern revolution'. In a written response, the CCP leadership emphasized that 'the most fundamental, most important and most urgent task' facing the Vietnamese revolution was 'how to promote socialist revolution and reconstruction in the North'. 'The realization of revolutionary transformation in the South,' according to Beijing, 'was impossible at the current stage'. Beijing therefore suggested that Hanoi should adopt in the South a strategy of 'not exposing our own forces for a long period, accumulating our own strength, establishing connections with the masses, and waiting for the coming of proper opportunities'.[38]

In 1959–61, the nationwide famine following the failure of the 'Great Leap Forward' in China forced the Beijing leadership to focus on dealing with domestic issues. During Zhou Enlai's meetings with Ho Chi Minh and Pham Van Dong in Hanoi in 1960, he advised the Vietnamese that they should adopt a flexible approach in the South by combining political struggles with military struggles. He emphasized that even when military struggle seemed inevitable, it was still necessary for political struggle to take an important position.[39] All of this indicated that 'to resume the resistance' in the South was basically an initiative by the Vietnamese themselves.

However, Beijing took no active steps to oppose a revolution in South Vietnam. The relationship between the PRC and the DRV was very close in the late 1950s and early 1960s. The close connection with Hanoi, as well as Beijing's revolutionary ideology, would not allow the Chinese to go so far as to become an obstacle to the Vietnamese cause of revolution and reunification. The late 1950s and early 1960s also witnessed in China the continuous propaganda that Beijing was a natural ally of the oppressed peoples of the world in their struggles for national liberation. It would be inconceivable, in such a circumstance, for Beijing to play a negative role toward the Vietnamese revolution. Further, from a strategic point of view, as Sino-American relations experienced several crises during this period, especially in the Taiwan straits in 1958, the Chinese leaders would not ignore that intensifying revolutionary insurgence in South Vietnam could extend America's commitment, thus improving China's position in its confrontation with the United States in East Asia.

Under these circumstances and in response to Hanoi's requests, China offered substantial military aid to Vietnam during the period 1956–63. China's arms shipments to Vietnam included 270 000 guns, over 10 000 artillery pieces, 200 million bullets of different types, 2.02 million artillery shells, 15 000 wire transmitters, 5000 radio transmitters, over 1000 trucks, 15 planes, 28 naval vessels and 1.8 million sets of military uniforms.[40] Without a direct military presence in Vietnam, Beijing's leaders used these supports to show to their comrades in Hanoi their solidarity.

Beijing's Decision to Increase Aid to Hanoi, 1963–4

China's policy toward Vietnam began to turn more radical in late 1962 and early 1963. In the summer of 1962 a Vietnamese delegation led by

Ho Chi Minh and Nguyen Chi Thanh, visited Beijing. The Vietnamese summarized the situation in South Vietnam, emphasizing the possibility that with the escalation of military conflicts in the South, the United States might use air and/or land forces to attack the North. Alarmed, Beijing's leaders offered to equip an additional 230 battalions for the Vietnamese.[41]

Beijing made general security commitments to Hanoi throughout 1963. In March, a Chinese military delegation headed by Luo Ruiqing, the PLA's chief of staff, visited Hanoi. Luo said that if the Americans were to attack the DRV, the PRC would come to its defence.[42] In May, Liu Shaoqi visited Vietnam. In his meetings with Ho Chi Minh and other Vietnamese leaders, Liu promised them that if the war expanded as the result of their efforts to liberate the South, they 'can definitely count on China as the strategic rear'.[43] In September 1963, the leaders of four communist parties (Zhou Enlai from China, Ho Chi Minh, Le Duan and Nguyen Chi Thanh from Vietnam, Kayone Phomvihane from Laos, and D.N. Aidit from Indonesia) held an important meeting in Conghua, in China's Guangdong province. In addressing the meeting, Zhou Enlai pointed out that South-East Asia had been the focus of a confrontation between international revolutionary and reactionary forces. He encouraged communist parties in this region to promote an anti-imperialist, anti-feudalist and anti-compradore capitalist revolution by mobilizing the masses and conducting armed struggles in the countryside. He also promised that China, as the great rear of this 'Revolution in South-East Asia', would try its best to support the anti-imperialist struggle by the people in South-East Asian countries.[44] At the end of 1963, after the Johnson administration demonstrated its intention to expand American military involvement in Vietnam, military planners in Beijing suggested that the Vietnamese strengthen their defensive system in the Tonkin delta area. Hanoi asked the Chinese to help in completing the construction of a new defence works there, and Beijing agreed.[45]

Beijing extended its security commitments to Hanoi in 1964. In June, Van Tien Dung, the DRV's chief of staff and the person in charge of the military struggle in the South, led a delegation to Beijing. Mao told the delegation that Vietnam's cause was also China's, and that China would offer 'unconditional support' to the Vietnamese Communists.[46] On 3–5 July, Chinese, Vietnamese and Laotian Communist leaders held another important meeting in Hanoi to discuss how to strengthen coordination between them if the war in Indo-China expanded.[47] In assessing the possible development of the situation, the three delegations agreed that the United States might continue to expand the war in Vietnam by sending more land forces to the South and, most possibly, using the air force to attack important targets in the North. Zhou Enlai, head of the Chinese delegation, promised that China would increase its military and economic aid to the Vietnamese, help to train Vietnamese pilots, and, if the Americans were to escalate the war, China would offer support to the DRV 'by all possible and necessary means'. He particularly stated that 'if the United States takes one step, China will take one step; if the United States sends troops [to attack the DRV], China will send troops too.'[48] These promises indicate that Beijing's leaders were more willing than ever before to commit China to the cause of the Vietnam revolution.

Profound domestic and international causes shaped Beijing's adoption of a more aggressive strategy toward the escalating conflicts in South-East Asia. Beijing's decision was closely related to the increasing confrontation between China and the Soviet Union (support to Hanoi became a test case of 'true communism' for Beijing and Moscow in the 1960s). It also reflected Beijing's new understanding of the central role China was to play in promoting revolutionary movements in Asia, Africa and Latin America – by supporting Hanoi in the making of a 'Revolution in South-East Asia', Beijing hoped to demonstrate that China deserved the reputation as the emerging centre of the world revolution.

In a deeper sense, Beijing's enthusiastic attitude toward Hanoi in the mid-1960s had to be understood in the context of the radicalization of China's political and social life, as well as in that of Mao's desire to create strong dynamics for such radicalization. In late 1962, Mao urged the whole party 'never to forget class struggle' at a crucial party meeting. In early 1963, a 'Socialist Education' movement began to sweep across China's cities and countryside. Mao constantly emphasized that 'class struggle did not extinguish in China', rather according to the CCP chairman, 'the danger of capitalist restoration in China' was always there. In 1963 to 1964 Mao insisted, on a series of occasions, that China was facing an international environment full of crises, and that the imperialists and the international reactionary forces were preparing wars against China. By stressing the necessity for China to prepare politically and militarily for the coming international crisis, Mao justified his attempt to begin a mass mobilization on an unprecedented scale at home.[49]

In the meantime, Mao also used the party's international strategy in general and its Vietnam policy in particular to win an upper hand in a potential confrontation with other party leaders who had failed to follow his own 'continual revolution' programmes. He took Wang Jiaxiang, head of the CCP's External Liaison Department, as the first target of his criticism. In June 1962, Wang submitted to the party's top leadership a report on international affairs, in which he argued that China should not allow itself to be involved in another Korean-style confrontation with the United States in Vietnam.[50] Mao quickly characterized Wang's ideas as an attempt to conciliate imperialists, revisionists and international reactionaries, while at the same time reducing support to those countries and peoples fighting against imperialists. He emphasized that his policy, by contrast, was to fight against the imperialists, revisionists and reactionaries in all countries, and, at the same time, to increase support to anti-imperialist forces in other countries.[51] Mao would later use these accusations to challenge and overwhelm his other more prominent 'revisionist' colleagues in the party's central leadership, especially Liu Shaoqi and Deng Xiaoping, during the Cultural Revolution. Under these circumstances, it is not surprising that Beijing began to adopt a more radical policy toward Vietnam.

Beijing's Response to the Tonkin Gulf Incident, August 1964

The above analysis will help in understanding Beijing's response to the Gulf of Tonkin incident in August 1964. On 5 August, the day after the second incident, Zhou Enlai and Luo Ruiqing cabled Ho Chi Minh, Pham Van Dong and Van Tien Dung, advising them to 'investigate and clarify the situation, discuss and formulate proper strategies and policies, and be ready to take actions'. Without going into details, they proposed closer military collaboration between Beijing and Hanoi to meet the American threat.[52]

Beijing's military mobilization began immediately after the Gulf of Tonkin incident. On 5 August, the Central Military Commission and the General Staff ordered the Military Regions in Kunming and Guangzhou (the two military regions adjacent to Vietnam), and the PLA air force and naval units stationed in southern and south-western China, to enter a state of combat readiness, ordering them to 'pay close attention to the movement of American forces, and be ready to cope with any possible sudden attack'.[53] Starting in mid-August, the PLA air force headquarters moved a large number of air and anti-aircraft units into the Chinese–Vietnamese border area. On 12 August, the head-quarters of the air force's Seventh Army was moved from Guangdong to Nanning, so that it would be able to take charge of possible opera-tions in Guangxi and in areas adjacent to the Tonkin Gulf.[54] Four air divisions and one anti-aircraft artillery division were moved into areas adjacent to Vietnam and were ordered to maintain combat readiness, while eight other air force divisions in nearby regions were designated as second-line units. In the following months, two new airports would be constructed in Guangxi to serve the need of these forces.[55]

In the meantime, Mao used the escalation of the Vietnam War to further radicalize China's political and social life. On 5 August, the PRC government issued a powerful statement, announcing that 'America's aggression against the DRV was also aggression against China, and that China would never fail to come to the aid of the Vietnamese'. The first audience of the statement was virtually the people in China. From 7 to 11 August, over 20 million Chinese, according to the statistics of the Xinhua News Agency, took part in rallies and demonstrations all over China, protesting against 'the US imperialist aggression against Viet-nam,' as well as showing 'solidarity with the Vietnamese people'.[56] Through many such rallies and other similar activities in the following two years, the concept of 'resisting America and assisting Vietnam' would penetrate into every cell of Chinese society, making it a domin-ant national theme that Mao would use to serve the purpose of mobilizing the Chinese population along his 'revolutionary lines'.

Working Out the Specifics of China's Support to Vietnam, Late 1964 to Early 1965

The security commitments Beijing had previously offered Hanoi were given in general terms. It was thus necessary, in late 1964 and early 1965, for Beijing's leaders to define the specifics of China's support to Vietnam in light of both the country's domestic and international needs, as perceived by Mao, and the changing situation in Vietnam. While doing so, their thinking had been influenced by the lessons of the Korean War, as well as by the assumption that the Americans would also learn from their experience in Korea. Consequently, by the spring of 1965, when policy-makers in Washington decided to send more troops to South Vietnam and began Operation Rolling Thunder, Beijing's leaders had decided on three basic principles in formulating China's strategy. First, if the Americans went beyond the bombing of the North and used land forces to invade North Vietnam, China would have to send military forces. Second, China would give clear warnings to the Americans, so that they would not feel free to expand military operations into the North, let alone to bring the war to China. Third, China would avoid direct military confrontation with the United States so long as possible; but if necessary, it would not shrink from a confrontation.

Under the guidance of these principles, Beijing sent a series of warnings to Washington in the spring of 1965. On 25 March, the official *Renmin ribao* (People's Daily) announced in an editorial that China was to offer 'the heroic Vietnamese people any necessary material support, including the supply of weapons and all kinds of military materials', and that, if necessary China was also ready 'to send its personnel to fight together with the Vietnamese people to annihilate the American aggressors'. Four days later, Zhou Enlai made the same open announcement at a mass rally in Tirana, the capital of Albania, where he was making a formal visit.[57] On 2 April, Zhou asked Mohammad Ayub Khan, Pakistan's president, to convey the following messages to Washington: China would not initiate a war with the United States, but China would definitely offer all manner of support to the Vietnamese; if the United States retaliated against China by starting an all-out war, China would meet it; even though the United States might use nuclear weapons against China, China was sure that the Americans would be defeated.[58]

While sending out these warnings, Beijing's leaders were also preparing for a worst-case scenario. On 12 April, the CCP Central Committee issued the 'Instructions for Strengthening the Preparations for Future Wars', a set of directives that would ultimately be relayed to every cell of Chinese society and became one of the most important guiding documents in China's political and social life for the rest of the 1960s. The document points out that the Americans were escalating their military aggression in Vietnam and directly invading the DRV's air space, a move that also represented a serious threat to China's safety. In light of the situation, the Central Committee emphasized that it was necessary for China to further strengthen its preparations for a war with the US and it thus called on the party, the army and the whole nation to be prepared for this worst possibility. To support the Vietnamese people's struggle to resist America and save their country, the document concluded, was to become the top priority in China's political and social life.[59]

In the meantime, Beijing and Hanoi were endeavouring to achieve agreement on the specifics of Chinese–Vietnamese cooperation over the escalating war. In early April 1965, a Vietnamese delegation led by Le Duan and Vo Nguyen Giap visited Beijing. On 8 April, Liu Shaoqi met the delegation. He told the Vietnamese that 'it was the consistent policy of the Chinese Party that China would do its best to satisfy whatever was needed by the Vietnamese'. Duan then stated that the Vietnamese hoped China would send volunteer pilots, troops and other volunteers to North Vietnam, so that Hanoi would send its own troops to the South. He further expressed the hope that the support from China would achieve four main goals: restrict American bombardment to areas south of either the 20th or 19th parallels; defend Hanoi and areas north of it from American air bombardment; defend North Vietnam's main transportation lines; and raise the morale of the Vietnamese people. Following Mao's instructions, Liu agreed to most of Duan's requests.[60]

Considering the need to clarify further the scope and nature of the support from China, Ho Chi Minh secretly visited China in May and June 1965. In a meeting with Mao on 16 May, Ho clarified that Hanoi was determined 'to take the main burden of the war by themselves'. What the Vietnamese needed, he stated, was China's material and military support, so that Hanoi could send its own people to fight in the South. Mao was ready to provide such assistance, and he promised Ho that China would offer 'whatever support was needed by the Vietnamese'. Ho then asked Mao to commit China's resources to building twelve new roads for Vietnam. Mao gave his consent immediately.[61]

On the basis of Ho's trip to China, Van Tien Dung visited Beijing in early June 1965. His meetings with Luo Ruiqing finalized the guiding principles and concrete details of China's support to Vietnam under different circumstances: if the war remained in its current status, that is, if the United States was directly involved in military operations in the South while using only the airforce to bombard the North, the Vietnamese would fight the war by themselves, and China would offer military and material support in ways the Vietnamese had chosen. If the Americans used their naval and air forces to support a South Vietnamese invasion of the North, China would send its air and naval forces to support North Vietnamese operations. If American land forces were directly involved in invading the North, China would use its land forces as the strategic reserves for the Vietnamese, and carry on operational tasks whenever necessary. Dung and Luo also had detailed discussions about the actual form China's military involvement would take in different scenarios. If the Chinese airforce was to enter the war then the first choice would be to use Chinese volunteer pilots and Vietnamese planes in operations; the second choice would be to station Chinese pilots and planes on Vietnamese air fields, and enter operations there; and the third choice would be to adopt the 'Andong model,[62] that is, when engaging in military operations, Chinese pilots and planes would take off from and return to bases in China. If Chinese land forces were to be used in operations in Vietnam, they would basically serve as a reserve force; but, if necessary, Chinese troops would participate in fighting. Luo emphasized that the Chinese would enter operations in any of the above forms in accordance with the actual situation.[63]

In an overall sense, the Chinese–Vietnamese cooperation in the mid-1960s had demonstrated some notable features. First, unlike the First Indo-China War, in which Chinese military and political advisers were directly involved in the Viet Minh's decision-making and Beijing was well aware of every important move, the Vietnamese communists did not let the Chinese interfere in Hanoi's decision-making. If necessary, Beijing would be consulted or informed, but decision-making was now completely in Hanoi's own hands. Second, Beijing and Hanoi appeared to have reached a fundamental agreement in the spring and summer of 1965 that the Vietnamese would fight the war with their own forces; China's main role would be to guarantee logistical support and defend the North, allowing the Vietnamese to send as many troops to the South as possible. Third, although top Chinese and Vietnamese leaders did consider the possibility of large-scale direct Chinese military involvement in Vietnam, the consensus seems to have been that unless the American land forces directly invaded the North, Chinese land forces would not be used in operations in Vietnam.

China's Aid to Vietnam, 1965–9

From 1965 to 1969, China's support to Vietnam took three main forms: the engagement of Chinese engineering troops in the construction and maintenance of defence works, air fields, roads and railways in

North Vietnam; the use of Chinese anti-aircraft artillery troops in the defence of important strategic areas and targets in the northern part of North Vietnam; and the supply of large amounts of military equipment and other military and civil materials.

The Dispatch of Chinese Engineering Troops

On 27 April 1965, the PRC and DRV governments signed an agreement by which China would help Vietnam construct new railways and supply Vietnam with transportation equipment. According to this agreement and a series of supplementary agreements thereafter, China was to offer assistance on a total of a hundred projects. Among the most important projects were: rebuilding the Hanoi–Youyiguan Railway and Hanoi–Thai Nguyen Railway, which involved transforming the original meter-gauge rail to one of standard gauge, and adding dozens of new stations, bridges and tunnels; building a new standard-gauge railway between Kep and Thai Nguyen to serve as a circuitous supplementary line for both the Hanoi–Than Nguyen and Hanoi–Youyiguan lines; constructing a series of bridges, ferries, temporary railway lines and small circuitous lines in the northern part of North Vietnam; and reinforcing eleven important railway bridges to make sure that they had a better chance of surviving air attacks and natural flooding.[64] During his 16 May 1965 meeting with Mao, Ho further asked Mao to commit China's strength to the construction of twelve roads in North Vietnam, to which Mao agreed.[65] On 30 May, Beijing and Hanoi signed a formal agreement stipulating that China would send its engineering troops to build and rebuild twelve roads in North Vietnam and link them to China's road system. During the construction of these roads, China would also be responsible for defending its engineering units against American air attack.[66]

Following the above agreements, from June 1965 to late 1969, seven divisions of Chinese engineering units entered Vietnam during different periods. The first division was composed of six regiments of China's best railway corps (with another two regiments joining after August 1968), one railway prospecting team and around a dozen anti-aircraft artillery battalions. The total strength of the division reached 32 700 at its peak. It began arriving in Vietnam on 23 June 1965, and most of its units were to stay in Vietnam until late 1969. According to Chinese statistics, when the last unit left Vietnam in June 1970, the division had completed 117 kilometres of new railway lines, rebuilt 362 kilometres of old lines, built 39 new rail bridges and 14 tunnels and established 20 new railway stations.[67]

The second division consisted of three engineering regiments, one hydrology brigade, one maritime transportation brigade, one communication engineering brigade, one truck transportation regiment and a few anti-aircraft artillery units, with a total strength of over 12 000. As the first group of Chinese engineering troops to assume responsibilities in Vietnam, it entered Vietnam on 6 June 1965. Its main tasks were to construct permanent defence works and establish communication systems in fifteen offshore islands and eight coastal spots in the Tonkin Gulf area. The division was also assigned the task to fight together with North Vietnamese troops should American troops invade the North. All units of this division would leave Vietnam in several groups between July and October 1966.[68]

The third division was mainly comprised of Chinese air force engineering troops. Its main task was to build in Yen Bay, a large air base complex that would allow the use of jet planes, together with a large underground shelter for planes. The main force of the division entered Vietnam in November 1965. After completing the air base in May 1969 and the underground plane shelter in October 1969, the division left Vietnam.[69]

The fourth, fifth and sixth divisions were all road construction engineering troops, commanded by an independent 'Road Construction Headquarters', and totalled over 80 000 soldiers. The five engineering regiments of the fourth division were from the Guangzhou Military Region. They were given the task of rebuilding the main road linking Pingxiang and Jinxi, both in China's Guangxi Province, to Cao Bang, Thai Nguyen and Hanoi. The five regiments of the fifth division were from the Shenyang Military Region, whose main task was to construct a new road from Lao Cai, a town bordering China's Yunnan Province, to Yen Bay, and link it with the road to Hanoi. The six regiments of the sixth division were from the Kunming Military Region and the Railway Corps. They were responsible for the construction of a new road from Wenshan in Yunnan to link the road construction by the fifth division, as well as a new road along the Vietnamese–Chinese border, so that Vietnam's north–south-bound main roads would be connected. These divisions entered Vietnam in October–November 1965, and returned to China by October 1968.[70] An official Chinese military source shows that they had accomplished the building and rebuilding of seven roads with a total length of 1206 kilometres, 395 bridges with a total length of 6854 metres and 4441 road culverts with a total length of 46 938 metres. The total cubic metres of earth and stone involved in completing these projects was 30.5 million.[71]

The seventh division was to replace the second division and enter Vietnam in December 1966. It was composed of three construction and engineering regiments and several anti-aircraft artillery battalions, and had over 16 000 soldiers. Its main tasks were to construct permanent underground defence works in the Red River delta area and build underground plane shelters for the Hanoi airport. The division completed these tasks and left Vietnam in November 1969.[72]

In short, Beijing's despatch of engineering troops to Vietnam occurred mainly between late 1965 and late 1968. These troops were assigned the tasks of constructing defence works, roads and railways in the northern part of North Vietnam. Most of their projects were located in areas north of Hanoi, and none of them was south of the 20th parallel. The majority of the troops left Vietnam before the end of 1969, and by July 1970 all of them had returned to China.

The Use of Anti-aircraft Artillery Troops in Defending Important North Vietnamese Targets and Covering Chinese Engineering Troops

From early August 1965 to March 1969, a total of 16 divisions (63 regiments) of Chinese anti-aircraft artillery units, with a total strength of over 150 000, engaged in operations in Vietnam. These units, which entered Vietnam in eight separate stages, were mainly from the artillery forces, the airforce, the navy and, in some cases, the Kunming and Guangzhou Military Regions. Following China's experience during the Korean War, the Chinese military leadership adopted a rotation strategy for these troops – usually a unit would stay in Vietnam for around six months and then be replaced by another. Their tasks were to defend strategically important targets such as critical railway bridges in the Hanoi–Youyiguan and Hanoi–Lao Cai lines, and to cover Chinese engineering troops. There is no evidence that any of these units had been engaged in operations south of Hanoi or in the defence of the Ho Chi Minh Trail. The last unit of Chinese anti-aircraft artillery forces left Vietnam in mid-March 1969. The Chinese statistics claimed that these troops had fought a total of 2154 battles and were responsible for shooting down 1707 American planes and damaging another 1608.[73]

Military and Other Material Support to Vietnam

After 1964–5, China's military and other support to Vietnam increased dramatically. Mao issued explicit instructions that supporting Vietnam should be given top priority. On 16 June 1965, Mao made it clear that China's economic structure should be further transformed in order to meet the need of 'preparing for coming wars'.[74]

One Chinese source reveals the contents of an agreement signed on 11 June 1967 by Liao Kaifen, deputy director of the Logistical Department of the Kunming Military Region, and his Vietnamese counterpart, the deputy head of the logistical bureau of the PANV's North-Western Military Region, in which China offered material support to Vietnamese troops stationed in upper Laos in 1967. The total number of Vietnamese troops there, as claimed by the Vietnamese side, was 1870. In addition to weapons and other military equipment, China pledged to equip the Vietnamese forces right down to the level of supplies for personal hygiene: 5500 sets of uniforms, 5500 pairs of shoes, 550 tons of rice, 55 tons of pork meat, 20 tons of salt, 20 tons of fish, 20 tons of sesame and peanuts, 20 tons of white sugar, 6.5 tons of soy sauce, 8000 toothbrushes, 11 000 bottles of toothpaste, 24 000 pieces of regular soap, 10 600 pieces of scented soap and 74 000 cases of cigarettes. Altogether, this agreement covers 687 items, including such minor items as ping-pong balls, volley balls, pens, mouth-organs and sewing needles.[75] This agreement reflects the magnitude of China's support for the Vietnamese.

As far as the general trend of China's military support to Vietnam is concerned, one finds a sharp increase in supply of weapons and other military equipment in 1965. Compared with the level of 1964, the supply of guns increased 1.8 times, from 80 500 to 220 767; gun bullets increased almost 5 times, from 25.2 million to 114 million; pieces of different types of artillery increased by over 3 times, from 1205 to 4439; and artillery shells increased nearly 6 times, from 335 000 to 1.8 million. The amounts of China's military supply fluctuated between 1965 and 1968, but the total value of material supplies remained at roughly the same level. Then, in 1969–70, a sharp drop occurred in

China's military supply to Vietnam, which happened at the same time that all of China's troops were pulled back. Not until 1971–2 would we see another significant increase of China's military delivery to Vietnam, but, as will be discussed later, for reasons very different from the factors behind China's support during the 1965–8 period.[76]

To summarize, China's aid to Vietnam after 1965 was substantial. Beijing provided the Vietnamese with large amounts of military and other material assistance. Over 320 000 Chinese engineering and anti-aircraft artillery forces (the peak year was 1967, when 170 000 Chinese troops were present in Vietnam) were directly engaged in the construction, maintenance and defence of North Vietnam's transportation system and strategically important targets, especially in areas north of the 21st parallel. Such support allowed Hanoi to use its own manpower for more essential tasks, such as participating in battles in the South, and maintaining the transportation and communication lines between the North and the South. Moreover, Beijing's support, as both Allen Whiting and John Garver have pointed out, played a role in deterring further American expansion of war into the North.[77] It is therefore fair to say that, although Beijing's support may have been short of Hanoi's expectations, without the support, the history, even the outcome, of the Vietnam War might have been different.

The Emerging Tension Between Beijing and Hanoi, 1966–9

Any analysis of China's involvement in the Vietnam War must ultimately address a single, crucial question: why did Beijing and Hanoi enter the war as close allies – 'brotherly comrades' in the oft-repeated words of Ho Chi Minh – yet became bitter adversaries a few short years after the war's conclusion?

In retrospect, the foundations of the cooperation between Beijing and Hanoi in the 1960s proved tenuous because the considerations underlying the two's policies were driven by distinct priorities. While how to unify their country by winning the war was for the Vietnamese the overriding aim, the orientation of China's Vietnam strategy, as discussed earlier, had to obey such complicated factors as Mao's desire to use the Vietnam conflict to promote China's 'continuous revolution'. Not surprisingly, when large numbers of Chinese engineering and anti-aircraft artillery troops entered Vietnam in 1965, problems between the two countries began to develop. As the Vietnam War went on, differences of opinion turned into friction, sometimes confrontation. The strife between the communist neighbours continued to escalate until Beijing, offended by Hanoi's decision to begin negotiations with the United States in Paris, recalled all of its troops from Vietnam.

The first sign of disharmony appeared over differences regarding the role that the Chinese troops were to play in Vietnam and the proper relationship between Chinese troops and local Vietnamese. When Chinese troops entered Vietnam, they were exhorted to 'use every opportunity to serve the Vietnamese people'. The underlying assumption was that China's support to Vietnam was not only a military task, but also a political mission. It was therefore important for Chinese soldiers to play a model role while in Vietnam, thus promoting the image of China as a great example of proletarian internationalism. Efforts to put such principles into practice, however, were often thwarted by Vietnamese authorities. The Chinese units found that the service they intended to provide to local Vietnamese people, especially that offered by Chinese medical teams, was intentionally blocked by Vietnamese officials. When the Chinese troops tried to follow orders from their superiors to continue to 'use every opportunity to serve the Vietnamese people', friction emerged between the Chinese troops and local Vietnamese authorities.[78] Several such incidents were reported to Mao in late August 1965, only two months after the first Chinese units had entered Vietnam. Mao then instructed Chinese troops in Vietnam 'not to be too enthusiastic [in offering service to the Vietnamese]'.[79] But such precaution would do little to stop the waning of the emotion of solidarity between Beijing and Hanoi.

The deteriorating relationship between Beijing and Moscow, together with the beginning of the Cultural Revolution in China, further triggered tension and conflict between Beijing and Hanoi. Until the mid-1960s, Beijing assumed that the VWP was on the CCP's side in the struggle against 'Soviet revisionism'.[80] But ties between Hanoi and Moscow increased as the Vietnam War progressed. When Khrushchev was ousted by his colleagues in October 1964, Moscow began to provide Hanoi with more substantial support while at the same time calling on socialist countries to adopt a unified stand in supporting Vietnam. On 11 February 1965, the Soviet Prime Minister, A.N. Kosygin, stopped in Beijing on his way back from Vietnam to meet Mao Zedong and Zhou Enlai. He suggested that China and the Soviet Union should stop the polemic between them, so that they would take joint steps to support the struggle of the Vietnamese people. Mao refused Kosygin's suggestion, claiming that his debates with the Soviets would last for another 9000 years.[81] Hanoi had since become silent in its criticisms of 'revisionism'. The gap between Beijing and Hanoi widened as North Vietnam received more support from Moscow. Beijing would not agree to cooperate with the Soviets in establishing a united transportation system as suggested by Moscow, to handle Soviet materials going through Chinese territory, claiming that this would violate the PRC's sovereignty.[82] China did help to deliver Soviet materials to Vietnam, but only on the condition that the operation be placed under Beijing's direct control and be interpreted as a favour from Beijing to Hanoi.[83] The Vietnamese obviously did not appreciate such an attitude.

Hanoi's deep involvement in other parts of Indo-China, especially in Laos, added another vehicle for suspicion and friction between the Chinese and the Vietnamese. Historically the relationship between communists in Vietnam, Laos and Cambodia had been very close. This was not a problem to the Chinese during the First Indo-China War but the situation became quite different during the second war. When a Chinese working team arriving in Laos in early 1965, they reported to Beijing that the Vietnamese virtually controlled the Laotian People's Revolutionary Party, and viewed the presence of the Chinese team as a threat to Hanoi's interests there.[84] Finally, in September 1968, apparently under pressure from Hanoi, Kaysone Phomvihane suggested that Li Wenzheng, the head of the Chinese team at that time, should take a vacation back in China. Beijing interpreted this suggestion as an indication that the continuous presence of the Chinese team was no longer appreciated and ordered the withdrawal of the team.[85] As a result, the distrust between Beijing and Hanoi deepened.

Consequently, all of the accumulated tensions between Beijing and Hanoi were gathered into one crucial question: whether or not Hanoi should engage in negotiations with the United States for a possible peaceful solution of the war. From the moment Hanoi demonstrated an interest in negotiating with the Americans, Beijing expressed a strong objection. In several conversations with Vietnamese leaders in late 1967 and early 1968, Beijing's top leaders advised Hanoi to stick to the line of military struggle.[86] When Pham Van Dong visited Beijing in April 1968, for example, Mao and other Chinese leaders repeatedly emphasized to him that 'what could not be achieved on the battlefield would not be achieved at the negotiation table'.[87] But Beijing now found that its influence over Hanoi's policy decisions had become so limited that Hanoi would go its own way. Zhou Enlai commented during a talk with a Vietnamese delegation headed by Xuan Thuy in early May that Hanoi's agreement on starting negotiations with the Americans was 'too fast and too hurried'.[88] Not surprisingly, Beijing maintained a displeased silence toward the initial exchanges between Hanoi and Washington in early 1968. At about the same time, Chinese engineering troops and anti-aircraft artillery units began to leave Vietnam.

Towards the Demise of the Chinese–Vietnamese Alliance, 1969–75

The late 1960s and the early 1970s witnessed a major turn in the development of Chinese foreign policy. The continuous deterioration of Sino-Soviet relations throughout the 1960s culminated in March 1969 with the eruption of a bloody border war between the two communist powers. The threat from the Soviet Union, gradually replacing that from the United States, became a primary national security concern for the PRC. In the meantime, the Cultural Revolution had passed its zenith. In the summer of 1968, when the Red Guards at Beijing's Qinghua University opened fire on members of the 'Workers' Mao Zedong Thought Propaganda Team', which was sent there by Mao himself, the CCP chairman felt the urgent need to re-establish the communist state's control over society (which had been dramatically weakened during the period 1966–9). As a result, international tension as a source of domestic mass mobilization became less desirable from Mao's perspective.

It was against this background that subtle changes occurred in Sino-American relations. The first sign of Mao's changing attitude toward the United States came in early 1969, when he personally ordered the highly unusual publication of Richard Nixon's inauguration speech, in which the US president stated that Washington was willing to develop relations with *all* countries in the world, in all major Chinese newspapers.[89] After the CCP's Ninth Congress in April 1969, Mao instructed a group of veteran revolutionaries, all of whom had been criticized during the Cultural Revolution, to form a 'study group' to research the international situation (members of this group included Marshals Chen Yi, Xu Xiangqian and Nie Rongzhen). With Mao's and Zhou's encouragement, this group met seven times in the summer and fall of 1969 to discuss the international situation and China's strategy to deal with it. Finally, the group suggested that in order to counterbalance 'the threat from the Soviet Union', China needed to 'improve its relations with the United States'.[90] Late in 1970, in an interview with the American journalist, Edgar Snow, Mao claimed that he would be willing to meet Nixon in Beijing.[91] All of this, combined with positive initiatives and responses from Washington, resulted in the 'Ping-Pong Diplomacy' in spring 1971 (an American table tennis team visited China for the fist time in PRC–US relations), Henry Kissinger's secret visit to Beijing in July 1971 and, finally, Nixon's visit to China in February 1972. With the signing of the Sino-American Shanghai Communiqué on 28 February 1972, the total confrontation existing for over two decades between the PRC and the United States ended.

The Sino-American rapprochement created a new source of potential tension between Beijing and Hanoi. On 13–14 July 1971, immediately after Kissinger's secret visit to Beijing, Zhou Enlai flew to Hanoi to inform the DRV leaders of Beijing's contacts with the Americans. Within twenty-four hours, Zhou held three meetings with Le Duan and Pham Van Dong. He told the Vietnamese that the CCP Politburo had decided to put 'the withdrawal of American military forces from Indo-China, Taiwan, Japan and various countries in South-East Asia' top on China's agenda in negotiations with the Americans. He also emphasized that it was the CCP leadership's belief that, from a long-term perspective, Beijing's new relations with Washington would enhance Hanoi's bargaining power at the negotiation table *via-à-vis* the Americans, as this would help policy-makers in Washington to realize further that America's global strategic emphasis lay in Europe, rather than in Asia.[92] After Nixon's visit to China, Zhou again flew to Hanoi on 4 March 1972 to meet the Vietnamese leaders. He told his Vietnamese hosts that in discussions with Nixon, the Chinese side had made it clear that 'in order to normalise Sino-American relations and to reduce the tension in the Far East, it was essential to solve the Vietnam and Indo-China problem', and that 'China would not pursue the solution of the Taiwan problem as the first step [toward a Sino-American rapprochement]; [the solution of] the Taiwan problem would wait [until after the solution of the Indo-China problem].[93] The Vietnamese leaders, however, were not convinced by these explanations. They regarded Nixon's visit to Beijing as China 'throwing a life buoy to Nixon, who almost had been drowned', claiming it to be evidence of Beijing's 'betrayal' of the cause of the Vietnamese people.[94]

In order to deal with Hanoi's criticism, as well as to demonstrate continuous solidarity with the revolutionary forces in Indo-China, Beijing increased its military and other material support to Vietnam after 1971. For example, the supply of guns increased from 101 800 in 1970 to 143 100 in 1971, 189 000 in 1972 and 233 500 in 1973; delivery of artillery pieces increased from 2212 in 1970 to 7898 in 1971, 9238 in 1972 and 9912 in 1973, and artillery shells increased from 397 000 in 1970 to 1 899 000 in 1971, 2 210 000 in 1972 and 1973 respectively.[95] In May 1972, when the Nixon administration, for the purpose of strengthening its bargaining position in the peace negotiations ni Paris, started another round of bombardment of key North Vietnamese targets and mined Haiphong Harbour, Hanoi asked for support from Beijing, to which Zhou Enlai agreed immediately. Starting in July 1972, the Chinese navy sent twelve minesweepers and four supply ships in five groups to help the Vietnamese dredge the entrance to the Haiphong Harbour.[96]

These gestures on the part of Beijing, however, were not sufficient to bring the Sino-Vietnamese solidarity back to its golden age. In Beijing's and Hanoi's open propaganda, the assertion that China and Vietnam were 'brotherly comrades' could still be heard from time to time, but the enthusiastic devotion to such discourses disappeared. After the signing of the Paris agreement in January 1973, Chinese–Vietnamese relations cooled down continuously.

It is not surprisingly at all, therefore, that after the Vietnamese communists won their country's unification in 1975, relations between Beijing and Hanoi fell quickly into a series of crises. The hostilities between the two countries escalated over such questions as Hanoi's alleged mistreatment of the ethnic Chinese residing in Vietnam, the two sides' conflicting sovereignty claims over the Xisha (Paracel) Islands and the Chinese opposition to Vietnam's claim of its 'special relations' with Laos and Cambodia. Early in 1979, when Vietnamese troops invaded Cambodia to overthrow the Beijing-backed Pol Pot regime, China responded by using its military forces to attack Vietnam 'to teach Hanoi a lesson'. Consequently, China and Vietnam became bitter enemies during most of the 1980s, and not until the late 1980s and early 1990s were the two countries to begin to normalize their relations. The Vietnam War, as it turned out, was to Beijing also a 'lost war'.

8

AUSTRALIA AND THE VIETNAM WAR[1]

Carl Bridge

Few outside Australia and New Zealand today even realize that Australian troops fought in the Vietnam War in the 1960s. The Australian forces barely rate a mention in the standard works.[2] And the story of the impact of the war on Australian politics and society is little known beyond Australia and often greatly misunderstood by Australians themselves. Here, therefore, is a survey of Australia's Vietnam military commitment and experience, both in theatre and on the 'home front'; an attempt to explain why Australia was involved, how its troops conducted themselves and to what ultimate effect.

Three major, related historical factors combined to take Australia to Vietnam: the aftermath of the Second World War in the Pacific; European decolonization of Indo-China, South-East Asia and the Pacific; and the cold war.[3] Let us briefly examine each in turn. The Second World War had brought Japanese forces to Australia's very doorstep, with New Guinea occupied, Darwin bombed and Sydney Harbour raided. In 1942, once the British base at Singapore had fallen, only the United States navy and some isolated Australian garrisons stood between a rampant Japan and Australia. Since the 1850s, when 'yellow hordes' of Chinese miners had flooded into the Australian goldfields, Australians had feared invasion by the 'teeming millions' to their north.[4] Now the Pacific War made their nightmare real. For many of the peoples of Indo-China, South-East Asia and Melanesia, of course, invasion actually occurred. In a few short months, Japan replaced Britain, France, the Netherlands, Portugal, the United States or

Australia as their colonial overlords. After the war it was clear to Australian defence planners that they had now to focus on the northern approaches to Australia. Their old pattern of providing expeditionary forces for Britain's imperial wars in Europe, Africa and the Middle East would no longer suffice. Moreover, Australia needed not only to develop an independent capability in the region, but, if possible, to involve the United States as an ally, and Britain too.

From an Australian point of view, European decolonization further destabilized the region. The Dutch were forced from Indonesia between 1946 and 1962; the French were kicked out of Vietnam in 1954; and the British left Malaya in 1957. When the European empires ended, the influence of communism grew. Indonesia's new regime had communist links and was expansionist; Vietnam was split between a communist north and a pro-Western south; and Malaya/Malaysia suffered a communist guerrilla emergency followed by a confrontation with Indonesia. For Australians, yellow peril was becoming a red peril. To help counter the perceived instability in the very corridor down which invasion had threatened in 1942, Australia entered into three treaties or understandings – what became known in the alphabet soup of the day as ANZAM (1948), with Britain, New Zealand and Malaya for the defence of Malaya; ANZUS (1951), with New Zealand and the US for mutual defence in the Pacific; and SEATO (1955), with France, Britain, the US, New Zealand, Pakistan, Thailand and the Philippines, and South Vietnam, Laos and Cambodia as protocol states. To help give ANZAM and SEATO teeth, Britain, Australia and New Zealand established a brigade-strength Commonwealth Forces Strategic Reserve in Malaya and deployed several squadrons of aircraft there.

The international march of cold war events exacerbated regional tensions. The Soviet Union replaced Nazi Germany as the main threat to the West; and in Asia its ally, communist China, was seen by Australia's conservative government of the period as a godfather to the communist movements in Indonesia, Malaya, the Philippines and Indo-China. A Chinese communist bogey replaced the Japanese fascist bogey of earlier years, and there was talk of a 'Peking–Jakarta axis' and of China's 'satellites'.[5] A success of crises across the globe gave some credence to these fears – Korea, Vietnam, Hungary, Suez, Cuba, Laos, Vietnam again. It seemed the world was slowly going communist, as nations toppled in succession like 'falling dominoes', to use US President Eisenhower's graphic metaphor.[6]

In Australian domestic politics, the cold war coincided with an un-interrupted series of conservative governments: coalitions of the Liberal and Country Parties led from 1949 to 1966 by the indomitable Robert Menzies, and from 1966 to 1972 by his three successors, respectively Harold Holt, John Gorton and William McMahon. These governments were not loath to 'kick the Red can' in order to smear the Labor opposition with the taint of communism and to frighten the electorate into the conservative fold.[7] Menzies and his colleagues almost succeeded in banning the Communist Party of Australia in 1951. Then they conducted a politically astute, McCarthy-like witch-hunt for 'reds under the bed', or 'nests of traitors', following the defection of Third Secretary Vladimir Petrov from the Soviet Embassy in Canberra in 1954. This so disrupted the Australian Labor Party (ALP) that a considerable faction of its Catholic Right, who were increasingly dissatisfied with what they saw as the ALP's lukewarm criticisms of the Soviet Union and communist China, split from the party in 1955 and formed its own Anti-Communist Labor Party, later the Democratic Labor Party (DLP). More royal than the king, the DLP outdid Menzies's own party in cold war zealotry. Moreover, although only a splinter party, the DLP assumed strength beyond its numbers by giving its voting preferences (under Australia's preferential voting system) to the conservatives in election after election. Its votes actually were crucial in determining the Liberal–Country government's return to office in the 1969 federal elections. In this way, the domestic perception of the cold war kept successive conservative governments in power for over two decades.[8]

In this atmosphere, Australia sought to ally itself even more closely with Britain and the US. Britain was encouraged to test rockets and atomic weapons in Australia between 1952 and 1963; and the US established a number of communications bases on Australian soil under an agreement signed in 1963. An intelligence-sharing agreement had been in place since 1947. Australia was now able to concentrate its defence capability in its own region and shelve older plans to deploy Australian troops to the Middle East should global war break out.[9] But British and American interests and priorities were not necessarily the same, nor were either necessarily the same as those of Australia. What might be called a 'yo-yo' diplomacy developed, with Australian policy being pulled first one way then the other. In 1949 Australia followed the US in refusing to recognize Red China while Britain did recognize it. In 1951 Australia and the US kept the British out of ANZUS. In 1954 Australia favoured the British solution in

Vietnam over the US's. And in 1956 Australia supported the British invasion of Suez against US wishes. It was thought in Australia that one 'great and powerful friend' or the other would step in should Australia need help.[10]

This thesis was tested and found wanting in 1961–2, when Australia called upon both Britain and the US to curb Indonesia's bid to absorb Dutch New Guinea. First, the Americans refused to help, because Indonesia was a potential ally in the 'Free World' and Dutch New Guinea was, in the words of one US adviser, merely 'a few thousand square miles of cannibal land'.[11] The Australian foreign minister, Sir Garfield Barwick, had gone too far when he had stated that the US might come to Australia's aid on the New Guinea border. He was removed from office. Australia's other, less 'powerful' but still significant, 'friend', Britain – still smarting after Suez, about to abandon its independent nuclear weapons programme, and preparing its first effort to join the European Common Market – ducked the issue and supported the US This left Australia, despite ANZUS, SEATO and ANZAM, feeling very vulnerable indeed; and the idea began to form in the Australian official mind that Australia would need to rearm and to demonstrate its value to its allies by direct means. Opportunities to do each of these things came in 1964 and 1965.

Australia's armed forces had been allowed to lapse somewhat throughout the 1950s. In 1964 the regular army consisted of only four battalions, one of which was in Malaya, and there were 20 000 in the Citizen Military Forces (the militia); the air force had outdated Sabre fighters and Canberra bombers; and only the navy, centred on its aircraft carrier, packed any real weight. All of this changed in November 1964, when a new defence scheme was introduced, doubling the defence budget over the next three years. Selective conscription of twenty-year-olds, to begin in 1965, would enable the army to build up to 8 battalions (later extended to 9). This, in turn, would make it possible to deploy battalions, if necessary, to Malaya, New Guinea or Vietnam, while, at the same time, keeping a reasonable force at home. For the army chiefs, too, it provided the first chance since the second world war, to develop an expeditionary force of brigade group proportions – a task force, to use the terminology of the day – and this was the smallest force capable of relatively independent, self-contained action in the sorts of conflicts which characterized the limited wars of the decolonization period.[12] The air force had already begun to modernize, by means of the ordering, off the drawing-board, in October

1963 for delivery in 1967 of one of the US's latest strike bombers, the F-111. This plane would give Australia the capacity to strike deep into Asia, including into China. Of controversial 'swing-wing' design, it was destined not to be delivered until 1973. Similarly, the navy ordered new guided missile destroyers and submarines in 1962 that were not due for delivery for several years. (During the years it took to get its new defences in place, Australia was increasingly concerned about having left a window of vulnerability, particularly in the air.) These moves were made to strengthen Australia's independent defence capacity, because the Australian government could foresee the possibility of having to act regionally without either of its major allies. However, the changes also made Australia potentially a more effective ally of the great powers in cold war conflicts.[13]

Chances to assist the great powers were not long in coming. Australia helped the British in March 1965 by sending an Australian battalion, two Special Air Service squadrons, and associated artillery and engineers to Malaysia. They served alongside some 65 000 British and Malaysian troops checking Indonesian incursions on the Sarawak–Indonesia border which were part of Indonesia's *Konfrontasi* campaign to smash the new state of Malaysia. This undeclared war finished in August 1966. Contemporaneously with these events, Australia supported the US and became embroiled militarily in Vietnam. In 1962, 30 military advisers (100 by 1965) formed the Australian Army Training Team Vietnam (AATTV), which was sent to join the 11 300 US 'advisers' already in Vietnam. The Australians' job essentially was to instruct the South Vietnamese forces in jungle warfare methods; skills in which the Australians were especially proficient given their experience in New Guinea between 1942 and 1945, and in Malaya. Also important were the counter-insurgency techniques devised by the British in Malaya and refined by the Australian army – constant patrolling, search and clear, cordon and search, and search-and-destroy. Then, in March 1965, the US began to commit ground troops to prop up the South by landing marines at Danang. As part of this escalation of the war, Australia sent a battalion of infantry and supporting units in June.[14]

The Menzies government was delighted to see a US ground force on the Asian mainland and more than happy to encourage the move by committing Australian troops. The Minister at the Australian Embassy in Washington, Alan Renouf, summed up Australia's reasoning for going into Vietnam as early as May 1964 when he wrote in one of his official communications that it would allow Australia 'to achieve such an habitual closeness of relations with the United States and a sense of mutual alliance that in our time of need...the United States would have little option but to respond as we would want'.[15] In identical vein, Harold Holt, who succeeded Menzies as Australian Prime Minister in early 1966, told a cabinet colleague the following May: 'The USA are there to stay. We will win there and get protection in the South Pacific for a very small insurance premium.'[16]

In the broader perspective of history, why had Australia committed troops to the war in Vietnam? The reasons were several: fear of Red China and of communist instability in the region of Australia's immediate north; Britain's weakness in the region and its imminent withdrawal from it; Australia's relative defence unpreparedness at a time when Australia was beginning to rearm and would take at least three years to feel safer; the need to draw the US into interposing land forces between Australia and China; treaty obligations under SEATO; domestic political pressure from the DLP to do something more tangible to meet perceived cold war dangers; and, from the Australian army's point of view, a chance to develop and test its new Task Force (ATF) capability.

Many Australian commentators have mistakenly seen the role Australia's troops played in Vietnam as being simply adjuncts to the US forces, with no separately defined mission or doctrine.[17] In fact, the Australian contribution in Vietnam was, for much of the time, quite distinct. It falls into four phases: 1962–5, in which, as seen above, the AATTV operated alone in its advisory role; 1965–6, when the initial battalion operated as part of the US 173rd Airborne Brigade (Separate) at Bien Hoa; 1966–9, when the ATF operated as an independent command in Phouc Tuy province; and 1969–72, when the force was scaled down during the period of 'Vietnamization' and finally withdrawn.[18]

At Bien Hoa the lone Australian battalion had considerable difficulty fitting in with US tactics and procedures and suffered from a lack of up-to-date equipment, an unsatisfactory situation that was remedied in March 1966 when the ATF was formed and allocated its own province, Phouc Tuy, where its principal purpose was to defend the main road, Highway 15, between Saigon and the important port of Vung Tau. This location was chosen carefully to allow the Australians maximum independence. They had their own port for direct supply and for separate troop movements and evacuation if necessary. They did not have the complications of the Cambodian border and were in a position to be responsible for their own area and procedures. Within Phouc Tuy the Australians put into practice their own counterinsurgency and jungle warfare doctrine, which was based on constant patrolling, careful searching and interrogation, separating the enemy from its sources of supply and stopping them from recruiting among the civilian population. This hands-on, down-to-earth style contrasted starkly with the US pattern of large-scale airmobile operations against perceived concentrations of enemy scattered right across the country. The American style was one of high- intensity conflict, profligate with men and technology, which produced relatively high body counts on both sides. The Australian style conserved men and equipment and restricted rather than eliminated the enemy.[19]

Something of the pride – and prejudice – associated with the Australian style comes through in this Australian junior officer's description of an encounter between two patrols, one American and the other Australian, near the Suoi Nhac River in 1971:

They [the American patrol] finally turned up approaching our position from the opposite direction from where I expected them and they were a sight to see. They were wearing a variety of gear. Some were in shirts and flak jackets, some had shirts on with short or no sleeves and some had no shirt on but were wearing a flak jacket. They were all wearing helmets with a cluster of various odds and ends on them, from cigarette packs to chewing gum to plastic C ration spoons, held on by a large rubber band . . . We couldn't believe our eyes. Not one man was capable of firing in the direction his eyes were looking . . . Probably the most striking thing of all was that these soldiers were not wearing camouflage cream on their faces. Because of the tropical heat it was uncomfortable to put on, but it cut down the shine on your face in the jungle immensely. It was one of the things that my platoon prided itself on: we would be constantly re-applying cam during the day as sweat removed it . . . I asked [their platoon commander why] he had taken so long to find me. He answered '. . . The goddam track we were following went all over the place and we got a little lost!' I had heard that the Americans were not as well.trained as we may have been, but to walk along tracks in an area where the enemy was known to be operating was just asking for trouble . . . We were beginning to look like world beaters compared with these men.[20]

The Australians fought their most significant action in Phouc Tuy, the battle of Long Tan, on 18 and 19 August 1966. An Australian company

(119 men), trapped by the 275th Viet Cong Regiment, held their position and called in artillery support. They were eventually rescued by a troop of Australian armoured personnel carriers. In the whole action 245 were killed and about 500 injured for the loss of 18 dead and 21 wounded.[21] This engagement was the turning point in the Australians' securing of the province. By 1971, when the last Australian battalion arrived for its tour of duty, Highway 15 was so free of enemy, at least by day, that Saigon families were driving down it to the coast for picnics without the need for armed escorts.[22]

Certainly there were mistakes and frustrations. ATF commander Brigadier S.C. Graham's decision to lay a minefield of 31 000 mines at Dat Do to restrict the supply routes from the plain to the enemy hideouts in the Long Hai Hills backfired when the South Vietnamese could not guarantee the security of the minefield and the enemy dug up mines and used them against the Australians. Laid in March 1967 the minefield, was recognized as a failure within the year and nicknamed by the men 'Graham's Mistake'. It was not finally removed until May 1970. And pacification programmes among the civilian population were of limited use as they had to be filtered through the local US agency responsible.[23] Nevertheless, the Viet Cong recruitment in the province had so dried up by 1971 that the only enemy present were Northerners and mostly confined to fastnesses deep in the Long Hais.[24] In a strictly military sense, then, the Australian army did its job effectively in Vietnam.

Other Australian military contributions to the war came from the Royal Australian Air Force and from the Royal Australian Navy. The airforce sent three squadrons: Caribou transports from 1964; Iroquois helicopters, which were used for troop deployment and medical evacuation, from 1966; and Canberra bombers from 1967. The RAN provided from 1965 the converted aircraft carrier, HMAS *Sydney*, which functioned as Australia's main troop transport, dubbed 'the Vung Tau ferry'; and from 1967 a destroyer that served with the US 7th Fleet, a clearance diving team and crews for a US assault helicopter flight.

All in all, some 50 000 Australians served in Vietnam, with the highest number in theatre at any one time being 8300 in 1969, and 519 died there. This compares with 2.5 million US military who served there, of whom 57 000 died. Thus the Americans were more than twice as likely to be killed as the Australians. (About 1.1 million enemy died.) While a sixth of the US's armed forces served in Vietnam at any one time, only a tenth of Australia's did; and US defence expenditure per capita was twice Australia's.[25] Such discrepancies caused US Under-Secretary of Air Force Townsend Hoopes to complain:

> In 1940 and 1941 when an imperialist, militarist Japan was on the march, Australia had raised nearly 682 000 men and sent them out not only against the Japs, but half-way across the world to fight for King George and the British Empire... In 1967, they were unprepared to make anything remotely resembling a comparable effort.[26]

No wonder one commentator quipped that Australia was willing to fight in Vietnam 'to the last American'.[27] But the US needed Western allies in Vietnam, and at least Australia and New Zealand had helped by joining the war when no other Western nations had.

Australia's rhetoric did not match reality. In July 1966 Prime Minster Harold Holt visited Washington and, borrowing US President Lyndon B. Johnson's electoral slogan, proclaimed that in Vietnam Australia would go 'All the way with LBJ'. Three months later, LBJ's very popular visit to Australia helped the Holt conservative government, running on a pro-war ticket, win a federal election with a landslide majority. In May 1969, Holt's successor, John Gorton, quoting Australia's unofficial national song, told Johnson's replacement, Richard M. Nixon, that 'we will go Waltzing Matilda with you'. In fact, Holt's new ATF had only two battalions; and Gorton imposed a ceiling of three battalions. Australia's response to the war was carefully graduated, designed primarily to achieve just the right degree of 'insurance' with the US so as to guarantee help in the future, but not be too costly in the present. In the American terms of the time, Australian participation allowed for 'more flags' and 'shared casualties' – fine phrases which, though useful for diplomacy, masked Australia's limited military commitment.

Only two months after Gorton's 'Waltzing Matilda' pledge, Nixon's Guam Doctrine of July 1969 announced that the US would only assist allies in conflicts that involved another superpower. This meant that the US would withdraw from Vietnam, and consequently Australia's 'insurance policy' went out of the window. Australia had no choice but to withdraw its troops too. Nixon's decision had been influenced by American popular protest. In Australia, however, the major anti-war demonstrations, the Moratoriums, did not occur until 1970–1 – that is, after Nixon's announcement of withdrawal. Despite Australian popular myth, the Moratoriums played little role in the Australian government's decision to leave.[28] Ironically for Australia, which had held such high hopes of American military involvement in the region, the US forces left mainland South-East Asia within four years of the hapless British.

In Australian domestic political and social terms, the war was at first very popular. When the troops were committed in 1965 less than a third of Australians were opposed; and a similar proportion objected to conscription.[29] The few middle-class housewives who formed the Save our Sons movement and the students and intellectuals in the leftist peace groups on the fringe of the Australian Labor Party (ALP) were voices in the wilderness. Most people, and particularly the DLP, accepted Menzies' simple logic that the war was necessary to parry a 'thrust by Communist China between the Indian and Pacific Oceans', or were convinced by the statement of his hawkish foreign minister, Paul Hasluck, that China was 'an imperialist aggressor... with the power and the will to extend her empire throughout Southeast Asia until it laps the shores of Australia'. Few heeded Arthur Calwell, the ALP leader, when he warned, presciently, that the conflict was a civil war in which the US and Australian forces would dissipate their energies for little positive result.[30] Even when the first conscripts were sent to Vietnam in April 1966 and twenty-one-year-old Private Errol Noack became the first conscript killed in action a month later, public approval did not waver.

The war's popularity was evident in the streets. A splendid parade welcomed the first contingent of Diggers home in June 1966, and President Johnson's visit in October attracted crowds in Sydney and Melbourne that totalled one-and-a-half million, while only about 20 000 demonstrated against him. There was a huge media buildup for LBJ – over 200 000 free flags, posters and badges were distributed in Sydney; the route from the airport was temporarily renamed Johnson Way; a thousand pigeons were released over the presidential motorcade; for the main reception in the art gallery a bush setting, complete with kangaroos and koalas, was constructed; and the ticker-tape that wafted down on the official cars read 'Hooray for LBJ'. So the razzmatazz of American politics was transplanted to Australia.[31] Little wonder that Holt won his impressive electoral victory soon afterwards. But this degree of pro-war unity did not last.

Disquiet both over the war itself and over the issue of conscription grew gradually. Gough Whitlam, the new ALP leader, who had initially supported the war, for the October 1969 general election ran on a ticket that, on Vietnam, was very carefully nuanced: though the ALP was anti-conscription, it would leave the soldiers in Vietnam, but it would strive to end the war soon by negotiating a peace.[32] With this complicated balancing act, and a range of other policies, the ALP managed to increase its vote so dramatically that the conservatives were literally only returned to office on DLP preferences. Whitlam need not have been so cautious on Vietnam, for, by the end of 1969 (and in the wake of Nixon's Guam Doctrine) opinion polls indicated that those in favour of the war had dipped to below 50 per cent of the population and that opposition to conscription was rising. As the war dragged on, the idea seeped into Australian popular conscious-ness that it was unwinnable. Similarly, as more families faced the pro-spect of having their sons conscripted by birthday ballot, they came to resent its arbitrariness. Student demonstrations against the war now attracted wider community support. In May 1970 the first Anti-Vietnam War Moratorium saw some 200 000 people across the nation attend rallies. Its organizers had learnt from the pro-Johnson extra-vaganza of only a few years before – an impressive array of posters, badges and banners became the livery of a new peace army. Jim Cairns, the deputy leader of the ALP, who had been almost a pariah for his consistent opposition to the war, was now a national hero. The war and conscription had split the Australian body politic down the middle, creating a bitter division reminiscent of the conscription debates that had rent the national fabric during the Great War. The demonstrators chants of 'One, two, three, four! We don't want your bloody war!', and 'Hell no! We won't go!' resonated deeply in the Australian psyche.[33]

In 1966, when Sydney demonstrators prostrated themselves in front of the US presidential limousine, the conservative premier of New South Wales had been able to say 'Run over the bastards' and suffer little electoral backlash. But by 1970, when Billy Snedden, the Liberal minister for labour and national service, accused the Moratorium demonstrators of being 'political bikies who pack rape democracy' he was foolishly out of touch, for half of the community was already opposed to the war. Some of the young demonstrators may have been Che Guevara lookalikes, some 'flower power' hippies keen to 'make love not war', but they were also law-abiding citizens exercising their democratic right to protest, and marching alongside them were bishops, middle-aged public servants and suburban housewives.[34]

Menzies' successors became increasingly at sixes and sevens over policy as the icy certainties of the cold war cracked. When Gorton tried to keep up with Nixon by declaring Australia's first troop withdrawals in early 1970, Vince Gair, the reactionary anti-Communist DLP leader, spoke against him. When William McMahon, who succeeded Gorton as prime minister, denounced Whitlam in 1971 for daring to visit China – 'we must not become pawns of the giant communist power in our region'[35] – just two days later Nixon announced his own visit to communist China. It was painfully obvious that Australia's much-vaunted US ally had not bothered to inform McMahon. When McMahon tried to catch up with the social revolution of the late 1960s by forming a Department of Aborigines, the Environment and the Arts and by relaxing film censorship, his government was seen by its supporters as betraying the values that had sustained it during the cold war. The government could not win and was increasingly hoist with its own cold war petard. All Whitlam's Labor Party had to do for the 1972 elections was to run on the slogan 'It's Time' and the electorate responded to the call, returning Labor to government after twenty-three years in opposition.[36]

One of the first acts of the new Labor government was to abolish conscription. Between 1965 and 1972, 761 854 young men turned twenty years old and had to register for conscription. Selection was by birthday. The dates were drawn out of a lottery barrel, and after medical and psychological examination, the government chose 63 735 conscripts. Of these, 19 450 went to Vietnam, where 1479 became casualties, of whom 200 died. A further 34 940 avoided the draft by joining the militia forces. Then there were 1012 men who were accepted by the courts as conscientious objectors. Further, almost 12 000 young men failed to register for conscription. Between 1965 and 1971 some 202 men a year were prosecuted for various offences in the registration process and in the scheme's last year 723 were prosecuted. Most were fined, some were jailed, but only one – Brian Ross – served the maximum penalty of two year's imprisonment. The government's policy was to jail only a token number of registers in the interests of credibility. Overall, Australia's twenty-year-old men had a one-in-twelve chance of being called up. But, opponents argued, in such a lottery no ratio was just: if the war had been deemed by the young men to be worth fighting then they would have volunteered to fight as Australians had in the two world wars, and, as then, conscription would not have been necessary.[37]

Because the numbers of young men who were conscripted and who went to Vietnam were so vastly outnumbered by those who did not, and because the war became unpopular and was ultimately lost, the traditional Australian reverence for the ANZAC fighting man, so evident in the world wars, underwent a temporary reversal over Vietnam. Now the anti-war protesters became the national heroes; particularly the handful of active draft resisters like Mike Matteson, who led 'Scarlet Pimpernel' existences, appearing at demonstrations and giving radio interviews only to be whisked away when the police arrived. In this war the big battalions were not in the armed forces; they were, at least in the final phases, in the Moratoriums protesting against them.[38]

Many on the left claim that it was the anti-Vietnam War protest movement of the late 1960s that created the critique of society that led to the great wave of social and political reform that broke in the next decade.[38] They instance the women's movement – the Australian feminist Germaine Greer's *The Female Eunuch* was published in 1970; environmental awareness – the first so-called 'Green Bans' against the elimination of the remnants of wilderness in the big cities were in 1970; a new awareness of the need for social justice for Aborigines – the referendum granting the federal government powers over Aborigines was in 1967; and more liberal censorship laws – the American rock musical *Hair* with its overt celebration of nudity was staged in Australia in 1969. But memory is selective.

In fact, some of these 1960s reform movements had notable successes when the Vietnam War was still popular in Australia, well before the anti-war protests climaxed in 1970–1. The first defining moments for Aboriginal reform, for example, were the Freedom Rides to northern New South Wales in 1965 and the Gurindji people's Wave Hill land rights strike in 1966. Censorship laws were under challenge from the time of the first publication of *Oz* magazine in 1963 – few Britons realize that the British *Oz* trial was anticipated in Australia by five years – and D.H. Lawrence's *Lady Chatterley's Lover* and Vladimir Nabokov's *Lolita* were removed from the banned list in 1965. The Catholic Church liberalization of Vatican II was in 1965. The contraceptive pill, the necessary prerequisite for the coming revolution in sexual manners, first went on sale in 1961. Equal pay for equal work for women was legislated in 1969. And the Crown of Thorns starfish devastation of the Great Barrier Reef, which arguably began the new environmental awareness, was in 1966. The anti-Vietnam War protests certainly initiated a new phase of mass radical protest, but they did not, by any means, start the clocks ticking on environmental, Aboriginal, censorship or women's issues; they were ticking already.[40] When considering the social revolution of the 1960s, it is important to remember that the 'swinging sixties' also happened in countries not involved in the Vietnam War, such as in Britain, France and Germany, and would have occurred in Australia too, regardless of Australia's participation in the war.

The depth of the political impact of the anti-war movement is also sometimes exaggerated. The Labor election victory of 1972 was by a narrow margin: 47 per cent of the electorate still voted against change. Although half of the community now wanted to end the war, a sizeable minority did not. Even over conscription, while most were now against sending conscripts to Vietnam, polls showed that the majority were still in favour of the scheme itself as a form of home defence. Similarly, after the war, as during it, public opinion was still firmly in favour of the American alliance.[41]

It is also important not to let memory invest the protesters with a saintliness few of them had. Some intellectuals saw in the demonstrations a new form of direct, participatory democracy, by means of which the young would lead their bigoted, war-mongering, sexist, racist parents into a new Eden where such abuses did not exist. But much of the new dispensation was only skin-deep, and there was another crueller, self-satisfied, self- indulgent face to the new world of surf, sex, drugs, and rock and roll. One university teacher noticed it when he sat in a Perth pub in November 1967 and heard some youngsters sing, to the tune of 'The Nickelodeon Song', 'Put another Buddhist in,/In the Buddhist burning bin,/Light him up with kerosene,/And burn him, burn him, burn him.'[42]

Australia's participation in the Vietnam War arose from Australia's cold war defence and foreign policies. Fear of instability to the North reactivated the invasion nightmares of the Second World War. British decline and US indifference fed the first of this anxiety and led Australia's conservative governments and their DLP familiar spirits straight into the quagmire of Vietnam. Domestically, the war, and the conscription that came with it, divided the community right down the middle, recalling another nightmare, the bitter conscription debates of the first world war. The war also helped radicalize a variety of protest movements already underway in the society and it interacted in complex ways with the revolution in middle-class manners that was at the heart of the phenomenon of the swinging sixties. All of this helped to bring

Labor to power with its enigmatically suggestive 'It's Time' slogan. Clearly the war had produced an array of winners and losers.

Though they had lost the war, the Australian armed forces were also winners, for they were in better condition to enter the new self-reliant world of the post-Vietnam era than they had been in a decade earlier. The Australian defence chiefs and the Australian governments of the 1960s had used the Australian deployment to Vietnam to achieve just this result. But for the Vietnam Diggers themselves, recognition by the war-divided community at home has taken a long time. The later homecomings were without fanfare. Only in 1987, was a mass 'Welcome Home' march held; and Australia's Vietnam Memorial – like its Washington equivalent, 'consciously designed to provide a space for catharsis'[43] – was dedicated only in 1992. Internationally speaking, the US withdrawal from the war following the Guam Doctrine forced Australia to begin a direct dialogue with its neighbours in the region; while domestically, the anti-war protest movement helped make Australians look more sympathetically at accommodating diversity within their society.

9

INTERNATIONAL ASPECTS OF THE VIETNAM WAR

Alastair Parker

In 1954 America succeeded France as the opponent of the Viet Minh and the People's Revolutionary Government. In that year, however, President Eisenhower hesitantly rejected immediate war; thereafter his administration and, more clearly, the Kennedy and Johnson administrations slid slowly into war, intermittently adding one extra effort after another to secure victory over Hanoi and to keep South Vietnam in the 'free world'.[1]

At Geneva in 1954 real international negotiations took place; the Viet Minh could get the French out at last provided they did not provoke the USA, while China could hope for increased security without a repetition of the struggle for Korea. A basis for compromise existed.[2] After the collapse of the Geneva agreements public international discussions of Vietnam were unreal: they were to persuade American opinion to accept steadily greater efforts to defeat Hanoi. By publicly pursuing peace, the American government won support for war. And there was always the very small chance that Hanoi would seize an opportunity to accept defeat. For more than a decade America and North Vietnam fought to win, and the American concern to avoid all-out Chinese or Soviet intervention mattered most in international relations. Hence, though seeking victory, the United States never engaged in all-out war.

In 1954 the British government made its position clear. To American policy they would provide 'all assistance short of help'.[3] Eisenhower, faced with McCarthyism and the consequent need to avoid any

196

appearance of an American surrender to communism exploited the British position to diffuse the responsibility of blocking French demands for rescue. Churchill's government lived up to expectations and vetoed armed intervention. Churchill and Eden assembled small groups of ministers, with the service chiefs, on Sunday 25 April 1954, in the morning and in the afternoon. Eden commented on the plan of the Chairman of the US Joint Chiefs of Staff, Admiral Radford, for attacks on China to check its support of communism in Indo- China. Eden insisted that 'anything like open war with China might well involve the Soviet Union and lead to a third world war'. Churchill observed that 'we are being asked...to aid in misleading Congress into approving a military operation which...might well bring the world to the verge of a major war'.[4] Next day, Churchill gave dinner to Admiral Radford at No. 10. The old hero produced words of wisdom:

> The British people would not be easily influenced by what happened in the distant jungles of S.E. Asia; but they did know that there was a powerful American base in East Anglia and that war with China, who would invoke the Sino-Russian Pact, might mean an assault by Hydrogen bombs on these islands. [Churchill warned Radford of] the dangers of war on the fringes, where the Russians were strong and could mobilize the enthusiasm of nationalist and oppressed peoples.[5]

This was the last time that the British government were required to approve US actions in Vietnam. Often they were informed; sometimes asked to help. They never again influenced policy or its execution. However, British opinion mattered. Britain clearly formed part of the 'free world' that the Americans were supposed to be defending in Vietnam. It was an articulate part of the 'free world', speaking and writing in English. British opposition to American action in Vietnam would embarrassingly tend to strengthen the suspicions of the American public and of congressmen. In Kennedy's time, British views on Vietnam did not matter much; as Johnson presided over escalation of American action in Vietnam they did. McGeorge Bundy, President Johnson's national security adviser, one of the three most important of his counsellors, wrote a memorandum for him on the 'British and Vietnam', while US armed intervention in Vietnam was dramatically increasing. Johnson's relations with Harold Wilson determined the tone of Anglo-American relations during his presidency.

Johnson needed domestic acceptance of his actions in Vietnam; British support could help him to get it, by helping him to seem eager for peace and by British approval of the war. Alec Douglas-Home, as prime minister, and the Conservatives in general were no problem. McGeorge Bundy commented that support for American policy in Vietnam would come 'more or less automatically from a Conservative government'. For Wilson it was harder. British support, Bundy commented, was of 'value in limiting the howls of our own liberals...support from Labour is not only harder to get but somewhat more valuable'.[6] However, active British support in Vietnam was not sought before Johnson took over. The British were asked for armed support in Laos before then and the Conservative government was ready to give it, but they were pleased by the immediate outcome, neutralization, which, left to themselves the British would have been delighted to extend to Vietnam. On that point they were firmly restrained. Of course, the British needed American aid: to maintain British 'independent' nuclear weapons, to help the defence of Europe, to back up the pound and, in South-East Asia, for support against Indonesian threats to Malaysia, this last desire was something that they felt could not be relied on.[7]

In consequence, when South-East Asia was discussed, British governments consistently demanded US support for Malaysia in return for support for US policy in Vietnam. Until 1964 this verbal support was not an embarrassing process for British governments; thereafter it needed evasive slipperiness as an increasing number of people, including Labour MPs, objected to American measures to defend South Vietnam. Even so, from early on, the British tried to avoid publicity. In November 1961, McGeorge Bundy was told that 'the U.K. agreed to increased United States aid [to South Vietnam] and will give full support but asks that we keep to a minimum public statements on what we are doing'.[8] The most open display of British support came in April 1963 with a traditional 'showing of the flag' when the British heavy cruiser *HMS Lion* sailed sixty miles upstream to Saigon. President Diem came on board. North Vietnam protested about 'this approval and encouragement for the US imperialists' frantic acts against the Vietnamese people'. They also denounced the 'illegal activities' of R.G.K. Thompson.[9]

Thompson mattered. He was the main British contribution and he had influence. He had been permanent secretary for defence in Malaya and had been in charge of the ultimately successful British counterinsurgency measures against the communist rebellion in Malaya. He led a mission to Vietnam in 1960. In 1961, he was established in Saigon as head of the British Advisory Mission (BRIAM) with four officers (ex-Malayan civil servants), a clerk and two typists. Apart from backing the USA it was useful in putting right the impression of 'our friends in Australia, New Zealand and Pakistan' who 'feel that we are not sufficiently interested in the problems of South-East Asia and that we are not playing our part as we should', as Duncan Sandys, secretary for commonwealth relations, wrote to the chancellor of the exchequer.[10] In Saigon, Thompson was welcome to the authorities as someone who understood guerrilla movements. In 1961 the South Vietnamese ambassador in London told Alec Douglas-Home, then foreign secretary, that 'the Americans were good people who were doing their best for Vietnam, but they had no feeling at all for the situation that they had consistently misunderstood'.[11] This view, and the welcome for Thompson – the ex-colonial ruler – contrasts with the American assumption that they were specially well equipped to intervene in Vietnam because unlike 'France in 1954' the US was not 'a colonial power seeking to reimpose its overseas rule, out of touch with the Vietnamese nationalism'.[12]

Thompson spoke at length to General Maxwell Taylor, Kennedy's military adviser, when he arrived in Saigon to study the situation in Vietnam in October 1961.[13] When Macmillan, as prime minister, conferred with President Kennedy and his advisers in April 1962, Dean Rusk, secretary of state, went out of the way to 'express appreciation for the job he was doing'.[14] In February 1963 Thompson encouraged Diem, whose brother was putting into effect, hastily, clumsily and brutally, Thompson's suggestion of 'strategic hamlets'.[15] In March and April 1963 Robert Thompson spent ten days in Washington. 'He did so much for us...that he would deserve two months home leave even if he had not spent the previous ten months in Vietnam,' wrote Chalmers Wood, the director of the Washington 'Working Group' on Vietnam to the American ambassador in Saigon. The culmination was his conversation with President Kennedy at which only Wood, the and the British ambassador, David Ormsby Gore, were present: 'the President warmly congratulated Bob on his presentation and on his very fine work in Vietnam'. Thompson was important because people who mattered listened to him and because he encouraged his listeners to believe that everything would soon be all right. Success, for him, was just round the corner. He told Kennedy that 'things were moving in our favour'. Vietnamese morale was rising. He thought it possible that the number of military 'advisers' in Vietnam, whose quality he praised, could be reduced by 1000 at the end of 1963 and victory should be evident by mid-1964.[16]

Later, Thompson encouraged hopefulness and confidence in another president, Richard Nixon, at another decisive moment. Thompson saw Nixon in October 1969 and, in November, having been asked to study the current situation in Vietnam, he reported that Saigon held a 'winning position'.[17]

The British also helped to train the South Vietnamese army in jungle warfare and provided some minor welfare services. Furtively, they supplied lethal weaponry. In June 1965 the British ambassador in Washington told Dean Rusk

> that the UK had received a request through Navy channels for certain bombs to be used in Vietnam. The UK was naturally only too happy to sell the bombs, but preferred that in the future it not be said that they were to be used in Vietnam.

Frustratingly 'sanitized' to keep it away from scholarly scrutiny, is a list the CIA produced of 'British contributions to the South Vietnamese War'. There seem to be at least half a dozen items. In 1966 Walt Rostow tried 'to find out what was discussed during the Wilson–Johnson conversations' (it is surprising that even an adviser so close to the President had to work out a list of questions): 'Did the Prime Minister make clear to the President that the UK has no intention of putting any real restrictions on the sale of war material to the US for use in Vietnam?' Rostow had good reason to worry after what the State Department called the 'fiasco in the House of Commons over the sale of arms to the US and Australia for use in Vietnam'; when Wilson had denied that British arms were being sold to Australia or the US for Vietnam and had then had to 'back off', leaving the issue confused.[18]

True to form, Harold Wilson, after his first meeting with Lyndon Johnson, convinced his cabinet minister Barbara Castle that 'he quickly developed a close friendship with Lyndon Johnson'. Wilson looked on the bright side. The evidence suggests that Johnson thought differently. George Ball, one of the president's closest advisers, until he left over Vietnam, reports that 'Johnson took an almost instant dislike to him'. LBJ was also annoyed, it seems, by Wilson's insisting that his press secretary, Marcia Williams, should be present at 'highly restricted meetings' – a view that was not unknown in London. George Brown, British foreign secretary from 1966 to 1968, agrees that 'Johnson didn't really like the Prime Minister much'.[19]

There is no evidence to suggest that Johnson ever changed his mind, though his close advisers urged him to keep Wilson 'on board'. On Wilson's own account, Johnson lost his temper when Wilson in February 1965 tried to imitate Attlee by flying over to Washington to dissuade the President from considering the use of nuclear weapons (which Johnson was not doing):

> I won't tell you how to run Malaysia, and you don't tell us how to run Vietnam... if you want to help us some in Vietnam, send us some men and send us folks to deal with those guerrillas. And announce to the press that you are going to help us. Now, if you don't feel like doing that, go on with your Malaysian problem.[20]

Johnson 'did not see what was to be gained by flapping around the Atlantic with our coat tails out', he remembered. McGeorge Bundy wrote to him four months later:

> on a number of occasions you have shown your skepticism when one or other of us has remarked that the British have been very solid and helpful on Vietnam. And of course you have recollections... of Harold Wilson's effort to telephone his way into a fancy trip to the White House.[21]

British governments want the British public to believe that they have influence on American presidents. More tangibly, the Wilson government needed American help – to retain the 'independent' nuclear deterrent, in the 'confrontation' in Malaysia, against the Smith regime in Rhodesia, and to prop up the sterling exchange in time of crisis. Wilson's rejection of devaluation in 1964 increased British dependence on the United States. To make sure of that help and of that claim to influence, Wilson and his successive foreign secretaries (Patrick Gordon-Walker, Michael Stewart and George Brown), left to themselves, would have been delighted to supply all affordable support to American policies in Vietnam short of risking a third world war. The State Department presented to LBJ a tribute to Wilson in April 1965: 'British government's support for US policy in Vietnam has been stronger than that of our other major allies. It has been skilfully conducted and stoutly maintained by the Prime Minister.' When Gordon-Walker came to Washington before he was foreign secretary he even pressed for firmer action by the US against North Vietnam. Michael Stewart became a hero to the Americans after his careful defence of American actions in the so-called 'Teach-In' at Oxford University on 16 June 1965. The London Embassy sent a rave review: 'lucidity, moderation, fair mindedness, command of fact, conciseness, logical structure... razor-sharp precision... staunch and unwavering support to US', and even suggested that Washington might 'find its argumentation useful'. As for George Brown, he believed that support in Vietnam for the USA must be given to prevent a return to American isolationism.[22] These ministerial supporters of the United States, however, were not left to themselves. Many of the people who might vote Labour disapproved of American actions in Vietnam and some joined in parades and demonstrations. A high proportion of Labour MPs, growing in number to more than a hundred, wanted protest and denunciation rather than applause for America. The American Embassy in London warned McGeorge Bundy in April 1965 that Labour MPs, 'troubled by Vietnam', included 'left-wing hard core, some left-wing (pacifists, liberal woollies, disarmers) and some moderate centrists'. Signatories of a motion, numbering 104, demanded British dissociation from America in Vietnam.[23] Several cabinet ministers shared their views. So there could be no question of sending British soldiers to Vietnam.

Two excuses were offered for the refusal of British troops. One was that Britain, as co-chairman, with the USSR, of the Geneva conference, which might be revived, should remain detached. The other was that British resources were stretched to the limit by the defence of Malaysia against Indonesian 'confrontation'. The latter excuse wore thin as Indonesian politics evolved, and Wilson was left with what the State Department called the 'fig leaf' of the co-chairmanship. As Rostow, by then his closest adviser, told LBJ in July 1966, with the British 'we are up against an attitude of mind, which, in effect, prefers that we take losses in the free world rather than the risks of sharp confrontation.'[24] Wilson solved his dilemmas by providing verbal support for American campaigns, especially by encouraging his foreign secretaries to do so, while putting himself forward as a tireless toiler for peace and understanding. Another problem could develop. Johnson and his advisers were well content to have *their* design for peace emphasized and supported. However, just as they did not want to be criticized by the British, so too they did not wish it to seem that the British were *more* eager for peace than the president, or that they were pressing peace on reluctant Americans. When J. K. Galbraith talked to Harold Wilson, 'an old friend and fellow economist', in March 1965, he reported to the president Wilson's efforts, 'to give you support and hold things in line'. McGeorge Bundy told LBJ that he would telephone Galbraith and get him to warn Wilson that his next visit to the USA 'will be sharply counterproductive if he should use it to put heat on us for negotiations'. In 1966 a member of the White House staff warned the president that Wilson's July visit 'could result in comments by the prime minister that would be a depressant on the widespread support the President is receiving on the military operations in Vietnam'.[25] In consequence, Wilson claimed in public that he acted as an expression of American desires for peace. Privately, he claimed to be the best and most effective statesman for making the combatants see sense. He once claimed in cabinet to have 'the absolute confidence of LBJ' and also of Kosygin, the Soviet prime minister. At a meeting of Labour MPs, Wilson 'said that one of the difficulties of his job was that he couldn't say exactly what he was doing when he was engaged in confidential negotiations', details of which could not be revealed for fear of spoiling the process.[26]

The President and his advisers wanted some British military presence in Vietnam. When Wilson visited Washington in December 1964 Burke Trend, the cabinet secretary, noted 'an initial suggestion that we should continue a token force of 100 men'. George Ball had written that Johnson might suggest a 'joint venture' in Vietnam and Malaysia. 'Regarding Vietnam, he might be asked to make a substantial contribution.' Nothing came of this. The notion remained in American minds. In July 1965 the State Department informed London that we 'recognize the British problem in providing military manpower' but 'we hope both governments [the UK and New Zealand] can find a way to do more'.[27]

Later in July, McGeorge Bundy, speaking also for McNamara and Rusk, in discussing support for sterling, observed 'we want to make very sure that the British get it into their heads that it makes no sense for us to rescue the pound in a situation in which there is no British flag in Vietnam...a British brigade in Vietnam would be worth a billion dollars at the moment of truth for sterling'. On 17 December 1965, when Johnson talked to five of his closest advisers, Rusk remarked 'I really can't see why the British can't put in men to support the Australians.' LBJ replied, 'Wilson is going to do nothing. He wants a DSC for fending off his enemies in parliament.' In July 1966, in the midst of another and graver sterling crisis, Johnson sent a message to Wilson asking, Wilson reports, 'could we not send even a token force? A platoon of bagpipers would be sufficient; it was the British flag that was wanted.'[28]

New Zealand, by contrast, responded, though hesitantly and reluctantly. The government led by Keith Holyoke, the National Party Prime Minister, sent about 500 men, an artillery battery and an infantry company, which, among some resentment, were absorbed into the larger Australian task force. Casualties were high, at 35 dead and 187 wounded. It was the first time that New Zealand had gone to war except as part of the British Empire. At home, the Labour Party, the churches and students mounted vocal opposition. A new Labour government in New Zealand in 1972 reversed the policy towards Vietnam. Troops were withdrawn and diplomatic relations established with North Vietnam and China.[29]

The role Wilson sought was that of the peacemaker, the mediator between Washington and Hanoi, or between the USSR and the USA, who would get them both to restrain their supposed satellites. Best of all, he wanted to do it prominently, strutting on the world stage to the tumultuous applause of a united Labour party and a secure majority of British voters. He may even have believed he could do it! In April 1965 he sent off Gordon-Walker to discuss peace negotiations with Malaysia, Thailand, Laos, Burma, South Vietnam, Cambodia and India. Then there was the Commonwealth Mission, which even he must have thought to be eyewash.

The Commonwealth Mission, a spectacular Wilson production, distracted some attention from Rhodesia at the Commonwealth Conference in June 1965, and it helped to bamboozle the Cabinet and the House of Commons. Barbara Castle, 'determined to have a showdown about Vietnam', was forestalled by Wilson's reference to 'mysterious negotiations... the coup would be pretty big... a very delicate operation'. Two days later 'he was as excited as a schoolboy... it was "very big"'. The prime ministers of Ghana, Nigeria and Trinidad, under the chairmanship of Wilson, would make contact with those involved in Vietnam to set going a peace conference. Wilson promised the US ambassador in London that he would not agree to anything unsatisfactory to the United States. The American government viewed the Commonwealth Mission with unease, and at once set out to control it. The president was declared to be 'keenly interested in the imaginative proposal', but London was told that the US government preferred it to be limited to discussions, though if pressure for 'an appeal for some form of cease-fire' became strong, it must be directed to both sides.[30] On the other hand, Johnson showed 'considerable concern' about what would happen if the communist governments refused to see the mission, as they did, and said that 'he saw no point in having the Prime Minister come to Washington'. It 'could be counterproductive, would achieve little in the interest of peace, and might turn out to be a further embarrassment to the United States'. In other words, LBJ did not want the United States to be treated as if it were not unconditionally eager for moves to peace. Wilson did not try it, but in another gesture to the Labour left he sent Harold Davies, a junior minister with contacts in Hanoi, to try to persuade North Vietnam to accept the mission. Wilson was 'well satisfied with the gesture' but it met no response.[31]

In January 1966, Wilson crushed a lively challenge to his support for America in Vietnam. A journalist, Richard Gott, stood in the Hull by-election on that single issue. Wilson promised a bridge (subsequently built) across the estuary of the local River, Humber, but relied principally on his domestic act as a peacemaker: 'on Vietnam, no nation, no Government has done more to get the parties to the conference table, and we shall continue our efforts'. Gott was held down to a mere 253 votes and Labour increased its majority by over 4000.[32]

Later in 1966 Wilson advertised all his positions. In February he went to Moscow to meet Kosygin, the Soviet prime minister, and, more briefly, Brezhnev, the party general secretary. Kosygin told him privately of 'the inability of the Soviet government to exert any real pressure on Hanoi in the face of continuing militant Chinese pressure', a fact the British (and American) governments often forgot. But Wilson claimed on Soviet television that Britain and the Soviet Union 'could begin to build a bridge'. In July he was there again. Once more he was told that the Soviet Union was 'not going to move towards a conference, or in any way to seek to influence Hanoi on negotiations'.[33] The month before he had moved to pacify the parliamentary Labour Party. He 'disassociated' the British government from the bombing of targets in Hanoi and Haiphong. The American embassy in London explained 'disassociation':

> Wilson can deal with professional Leftists, as he has many times demonstrated. What must be understood is that opposition to US policy in VN, and UKG [UK government] support of their policy, is not monopoly of those extremists. It was because Wilson went part

of the way through disassociation to dramatize importance of 'independent' British position that he was able to avoid wider pattern or revolt in party ranks.

To support American policy Wilson had to complain about some of it. Johnson, whatever his private irritation, responded by making an inflated toast when Wilson visited the White House soon afterwards:

> Sir Henry Wootton, in his letter to James the First, referred to 'my good associates, by whose light and leading I have walked'. Someone suggested, today, Mr. Prime Minister, that I begin by saying this toast: 'my good disassociates'. But that is not the case at all . . . in World War II, Mr Prime Minister, England [sic] saved herself by fortitude and the world by example . . . I must say that England is blessed now, as it was blessed then, with gallant and hardy leadership.[34]

Earlier in 1967 Wilson thought that his apotheosis might be at hand. Wilson imagined that he could influence both President Johnson on the one side and Brezhnev and Kosygin on the other. In February Kosygin came to London. Anatoly Dobrynin, the long-serving – and well-liked – Soviet ambassador in Washington, sums up the event.

> Hanoi had secretly asked us to use the government of Prime Minister Harold Wilson, one of Johnson's few European supporters on Vietnam, to put pressure on Washington to reach a peaceful solution in Vietnam. The Soviet leadership also attached some importance to this. The Johnson administration, for its part, was anxious to take advantage of Kosygin's good offices in Vietnam.

In other words, Moscow thought Wilson could influence the USA while Washington, less confidently, thought Wilson might cause Moscow to restrain Hanoi. They were all wrong. It is not surprising, however, that Wilson became excited.[35]

Johnson ordered a 'pause' in the bombing of North Vietnam to begin on 8 February 1967. As before, this 'pause' was intended at least to justify continued war to the American people and to quieten foreign resentment against bombing. The North Vietnamese government habitually claimed that an end to bombing might permit 'talks'. Once again, an American effort for 'talks' might win support for a continued war or even offer a small chance that Hanoi would give in at last. The US authorities insisted that there should be no increase in 'infiltration', that is the passage of supplies and men from North to South Vietnam during a bombing pause. This equation was persistently put to Hanoi. The British, imagining some special power as peacemakers, thought this plan was best put by them. They seemed to think, naïvely, that they could bring 'talks' that would somehow lead to peace. Wilson did not know what he was talking about; Johnson's criticism 'that the British government's general approach to the war and to finding a peaceful solution would have been considerably different if a brigade of Her Majesty's Forces had been stationed just north of the demilitarized zone in Vietnam' had something to be said for it.[36]

Wilson became very angry over American neglect of the British but covered it up in public. George Brown, Foreign Secretary, went to Moscow in November 1966. He raised, in addition to the routine British suggestion that the co-chairmen should act and revive the Geneva conference of 1954, the latest version of the bombing pause – no infiltration equivalents. He, and Wilson, were put out to discover that the Americans had already passed it through other intermediaries, the latest being the Polish representative on the International Control Commission, a body that futilely overlooked the application of the 1954 Geneva accords. When Kosygin came to London, Brown and Wilson tried out the same formula and then found the Americans had changed it to make the cessation of bombing conditional on a pause in 'infiltration' rather than the other way round.

Wilson complained to Johnson that this put him in 'a hell of a situation'. Next, it appeared, the White House would extend the bombing pause only for six hours. This gave no time, Wilson claimed, for Kosygin to press the new formula on Hanoi: 'a historic opportunity had been missed'. When Chester Cooper, a member of the National Security Council staff, who was in London at Wilson's request, to communicate with Washington, asked Rostow not to change the negotiating formula and so to help Wilson's 'peace-making', Rostow replied firmly. 'We don't give a goddamn about Wilson.'[37] Walt Rostow was not at all anti-British. He had been a visiting professor at Oxford and a fellow of a distinguished Oxford college. He had written an important and widely read study of the British Industrial Revolution. However, he found Wilson a nuisance and an irrelevance when he, and the president, were worrying about increasing volumes of men and supplies moving from North to South Vietnam.

Eric Heffer, a prominent left-wing Labour MP, was nearly right when he told the Commons, after Wilson reported on Kosygin's visit, that the Americans 'do not give a fig for the opinions of this Government', and Edward Heath, for the Conservatives, was entirely right when he explained American worries about 'infiltration'. Wilson, master of fraud, fudge and flannel, was unabashed. He continued to proclaim himself as the great peacemaker and continued to justify his verbal support for American activities. He was the man of magic and mystery: 'there is an initiative, there is a plan that I cannot tell the House, which could bring peace tomorrow and requires a very small move to activate all the very complicated machinery that could give us peace'. In September 1967, Wilson apparently told the cabinet that the British had tried to intervene for peace thirty-seven times. The government's mediating capacity, he claimed, was the reason for its increasingly unpopular refusal to denounce the Americans.[38] How little this amounted to is shown in the conversation in Washington in April 1967 between Averell Harriman 'ambassador at large' for Vietnam contacts, and George Brown, British foreign secretary, before Brown visited Moscow. Harriman 'felt strongly that Moscow, because of its position in the Communist world and its influence on Hanoi, could play a major role in working out a settlement in Vietnam ... somehow the Soviets had to be induced to assume responsibility for bringing Hanoi to negotiations'. Several months later, on 11 January 1968, the same people had a similar conversation before Brown and Wilson went to Moscow again. Harriman thought 'it was most important to find out whether the Russians really wanted to have peace in Vietnam ... The only hope for a peaceful settlement was if the Russians would use their influence.' Such to Washington was the role of the British, to nag the Kremlin; there is no sign that it had any effect. Bill Bundy, the leading State Department expert on Vietnam, came to London to brief Brown and Wilson. He recognized 'that part of Wilson's purpose is to indicate in general terms that the British are in the act'. However, the Americans should 'avoid any implication that we are asking the British to act for us in any way'. For the 'President's Evening Reading' of 23 January Bill Bundy passed on this news of Wilson's visit to Moscow: 'nothing of real note or significance'.[39]

On 8 November 1967 Dean Rusk sent a note to the president asking him to telephone back to him after he had read a telegram from Bruce in London. An informant, whose name has been 'sanitized', told Bruce about a meeting of the parliamentary Labour party when 'for the first time' opposition to Wilson's support for US policy came 'from all sections of the party, ranging through the centre to the right'. Within the cabinet, Barbara Castle, Tony Benn and Richard Crossman led opposition.[40] Bombings, troop deployments and the search for 'talks' were accompanied by demonstrations, especially by students, against American action in Vietnam. In February 1967 Rostow himself gave a lecture at Leeds University, which the American Embassy in London thought had a 'reputation for attracting students who particularly rejoice in left-wing causes'. Rostow met 'vocal outbursts' and 'intense jeering'. The Vice-Chancellor, Sir Roger Stevens, thought 'the majority of students not opposed to US policy with the exception of bombing North Vietnam, which virtually all oppose'. On 16 November 1967 Bruce sent a long and gloomy telegram to Washington. Two days before, he went to Cambridge 'to address the Socratic Society of Churchill College. A student mob, reinforced by ruffians from London, surrounded the hall where the meeting was held and tried to prevent me from entering and leaving. Had it not been for the authorities sending for police reinforcements, I doubt whether I would have emerged from the occasion without serious bodily harm'. On Sunday, 22 October, the US embassy had been attacked 'by some three thousand or more people'. When Harold Wilson was in Cambridge on Sunday, 29 October 'eggs and tomatoes were thrown at him and cries of "Right-Wing Bastard" and "Vietnam murderer" were uttered. His car was kicked, thumped and beaten upon, its roof dented, the radio aerial smashed, and he was only extricated by the efforts of the police'. In consequence, Bruce suggested that Vice-President Hubert Humphrey should abandon his visit to London at the end of November, and last-minute apologies and excuses ('Congressional business') were despatched.[41]

Bruce later recorded that he was besieged in the American Embassy in London 'practically every Sunday for about six months. I am sorry to say that some of the most effective demonstrators in the way of resorting to violence were Americans'. He was asked if he thought 'British students might not have been so vehement if it had not been for American student leadership' and replied 'I think British students would have been vehement. I think the American students carried a little more weight ... because they were, as Americans, attacking American policy in a British context.'[42]

In October 1968 students 'occupied' the London School of Economics. The demonstrations, in Britain and elsewhere combined a bulky swathe of grievances, encouraged and organized, as was often thought, by

'Che Guevarists', 'Trotskyists', anarchists and 'workers revolutionaries'. They attacked the 'authorities' in universities and polytechnics; the Vietnam War was just the most prominent subject. On Sunday, 27 October, 30 000 demonstrators marched and rallied in Hyde Park while about 5000 besieged the American Embassy.

When peace talks opened in Paris between Americans and various Vietnamese, pressure on Wilson lessened. He no longer needed somehow to intervene to bring peace talks. The Conservative government of 1970 to 1974 took in its stride renewed protests against continued violence in Vietnam. In May 1972 when the Labour Left called for protest to Nixon, it replied, in familiar manner, that it was repeatedly trying to get Gromyko, as 'co-chairman' to join in seeking peace. Only Enoch Powell saw clearly that the United States needed, rather than protests, help 'in healing the deep blow to American pride' involved in inescapable defeat. In 1973, Alec Douglas-Home, reporting the Paris settlement, claimed, as usual, that 'the United States has kept in close touch with us during the negotiations'. The Labour government of 1974 had other worries than Vietnam.

The CIA, in a study for the president of 'International Connections of the US Peace Movements' found 'little or no information on the financing of the principal peace movement groups'. Nor could it find 'evidence of any contact between the most prominent peace movement leaders and foreign embassies'. Coordination of the 'peace movement' on an international scale was 'handled by a small group of dedicated men' who 'do not appear to be under communist direction... Their relations are with foreign, private institutions such as Bertrand Russell Peace Foundation.' This Foundation appeared in 1963, when Russell was over ninety, organized and influenced by an American, Ralph Schoenman, 'a helpful, interesting and delightful companion' in Russell's words: not everyone shared this view. In June 1966, they and other leftists set up the 'Vietnam Solidarity Campaign, in which 'the exotic maverick figure of the Pakistani' Tariq Ali was to become prominent.[43] Soon, Russell invited prominent progressives such as Sartre to joint an International War Crimes Tribunal. The National Liberation Front and the Democratic Republic of Vietnam cooperated; the US government did not. After hearings in Sweden, the tribunal found the US government guilty of a grisly list of atrocities. The State Department thought it worth while to circulate US missions abroad with material to counter the tribunal.[44] The CIA reported that under the peace umbrella one finds pacifists and fighters, idealists and materialists, internationalists and isolationists, democrats and totalitarians, conservatives and revolutionaries, capitalists and socialists, patriots and subversives, lawyers and anarchists, Stalinists and Trotskyites, Muscovites and Pekingese, racists and universalists, zealots and non-believers, puritans and hippies, do-gooders and evildoers, non-violent and very violent

– no wonder President Johnson became steadily more gloomy![45]

In Western Europe, 1968 was a year of disorder and discontent. Distinctive grievances surfaced in different countries but Vietnam was everywhere prominent. Students (and sometimes workers) denounced imperialist capitalism, allegedly exemplified by American conduct in Vietnam. In Italy, Germany and France undergraduate students complained of their universities – so too, with less reason, did students in the UK. West Berlin had a high proportion of young people escaping military service who naturally sympathized with American students' hostility to the Vietnam draft. Demonstrations there tended to violence. In Paris, though de Gaulle always made clear his contempt for the Vietnam War, he avoided a compete break with the USA so that, too, became part of local grievances, which in traditional Paris manner brought barricades and set-piece street fighting. Student leaders, Rudi Dutschke and Daniel Cohn-Bendit, became internationally celebrated for their Franco-German agitations. Tariq Ali, in London, was comparatively mild and gentle.[46]

Governments, except Australia and New Zealand, who sent soldiers to Vietnam, disappointed President Johnson. Thailand, South Korea and the Philippines really were 'satellites' as Hanoi called them. Otherwise, no 'third country' troops served in Vietnam. In July 1965 the State Department sent telegrams to twenty-five countries that were 'contributing assistance'. This meant a few medical men, an ambulance or two, advice on irrigation and so forth. The telegrams ordered the delivery of a 'personal letter' from the president asked for 'increased assistance'. The replies showed 'sympathy' for 'resistance to aggression while working for peace'. But they yielded 'little tangible evidence of prospects of substantially increased assistance'. An one time or another, the US government hoped for troops from Greece, Turkey, Brazil, Canada and the Netherlands.[47] Earlier William Bundy in the State Department set out a 'score card' of 'reactions by key countries to our actions in Vietnam'. Among those 'with us pretty strongly' were the usual list plus Germany; George

Ball commented that Chancellor Erhard of West Germany 'was telling us what he believed we would like to hear'. Then 'with us, but wobbly on negotiations' were the UK, Canada and India (which had good reason to fear Chinese expansion). 'With us tepidly' were Japan, Malaysia, Latin America, Italy and other NATO allies. 'Skeptical or opposed' were France and Pakistan, while Africa was 'mixed'.[48]

The attitude of German politicians was complicated. Some thought the division between North and South Vietnam similar to that between East and West Germany and therefore something to be defended against communists. However, American intervention in South-East Asia threatened to reduce support for NATO. Indeed, in the late 1960s the US withdrew 15 000 soldiers from West Germany. Worse still, increased American eagerness for *détente* with the USSR might mean bargains at the expense of West German aspirations. Thus, *Ostpolitik*, West German efforts to improve the Federal Republic's relations with the East, partly came from a German wish to make their own bargains.[49] In Europe, more hostility to American conduct in Vietnam was expressed by the Swedish government than anywhere else. It permitted the Bertrand Russell War Crimes Tribunal to function in Sweden, while de Gaulle cautiously rejected it. The Swedish government expressed 'active neutrality' notably through its leading politician, Olaf Palme. Unusually among European countries, the Swedish government publicly denounced American policy in Vietnam.[50] Most European governments, like the Italian, hoped the Americans would somehow stop and thus remove one of the most successful complaints of their left-wing opposition.[51]

In President Johnson's time, escalation of the war went with variegated attempts at peace. Some were public and publicized to win domestic support for further military effort; some were private to give North Vietnam a chance to surrender. Outside the United States, other powers and personalities tried, as the Chinese foreign minister was reported as saying, 'to get into the act'. In August 1965, for instance, President Tito and Shastri, the Indian prime minister, called for a suspension of bombing and a conference on Vietnam.[52] One of the most spectacular American initiatives was LBJ's venture in December 1967. After attending the funeral of his best free-world ally, the Australian prime minister, Harold Holt, he flew to visit the Pope in Rome. Secret initiatives sometimes came from outside, as when Richard Davis, American ambassador to Romania, 'returning by train from the "annual hunt"' was called in to talk to the Romanian president of the council of state and the foreign minister on 23 January 1967 and told that Hanoi might talk after a cessation of bombing.[53]

In the autumn of 1967, another academic of the first quality made his initial appearance in the Vietnam drama: Henry Kissinger. Two of his French friends used their acquaintance with Ho Chi Minh to visit Hanoi and talk to him and the North Vietnamese foreign minister, Pham Van Dong. Back in Paris they acted as intermediaries between Kissinger and Mai Van Bo, without even managing to arrange a meeting.[54]

Consistently, the government of North Vietnam demanded, as a prerequisite of talks, discussions, etc., that bombing of North Vietnam should be stopped. The United States and North Vietnam both insisted that negotiations should give them control over the future of South Vietnam; both aimed for victory. Usually attempts at talks led only to restatements by each side of its determination to win. The United States government had to demonstrate its pre-eminence in the search for peace. Thus, North Vietnam could be blamed. Foreigners might applaud the pacific nature of American policy. A sufficient number of Americans might be persuaded to accept more and more violence. In these years, 1965–8, Johnson records eight complete bombing pauses over North Vietnam and five partial pauses, that is, no bombs near Hanoi.[55]

The largest complete pause before the end of 1968 was for five weeks starting at the end of December 1965. That pause had been brooded about, agonized over, by Johnson and his advisers for weeks. It marked the climax of the most energetic American attempt at peace talks. Already, in November 1965 Rusk talked to 'more than 70 foreign ministers', a marathon of conversation designed to show that Hanoi was to blame. President Johnson talked over and over again about the bombing pause and the 'peace offensive'. On 28 December 1965, for instance, he spoke from the LBJ ranch in Texas to Averell Harriman, now 'ambassador at large', with his characteristic combination of relaxed jocularity and worried tension. Since there were

all these people thinking there could be peace, if we were only willing to have peace, we ought to give it the old college try... if you don't mind packing up your old kit bags, going to visit your old friend Tito, tell him how we feel and how I feel, sit down and talk to him... then probably get in to see that Hungarian foreign minister, you can go to Hungary, Poland, Yugoslavia, any place you drop in or out.

'What about seeing Bo in Paris?' asked Harriman. 'That would be good. He ought to be talked to.' Soon after LBJ explained it all when he said he would soon ask Congress for $25 billion for Vietnam and send an extra 500 000 men,

> then I can say the day before Christmas no bombing, and then we sent Harriman to Poland and Yugoslavia and we sent Goldberg [US Ambassador to the UN] and Rusk here and Wilson [Mennen Wilson, in charge of Africa in the State Department] there. We have walked the last mile.

On 5 January 1966 Dean Rusk explained to the National Security Council that 113 countries 'have been contacted since the offensive was launched December 28 . . . special emissaries have been sent to 34 foreign governments'. The president commented 'we have a better basis to call on the US people, not only for their sons, but also for their treasure. Americans feel better if they know we have gone the last mile.'[56]

The United Nations did not become prominent. The administration suspected the Security Council. A reference to it might lead to 'a debate which would lead to such things as recommendations for a cessation of bombing and recommendations for including the Viet Cong [the rebels in South Vietnam] in any negotiations as an equal negotiating party'. The UN had to be taken into account, however. One solution was to win the friendship of U Thant, the secretary-general. In mid-January 1966 McGeorge Bundy drafted an obsequious letter for the president to send to him:

> I remain eager to exhaust every possible means of bringing the parties to the negotiating table. I want to be certain that every possible opportunity is afforded the other side to hear, comprehend and answer our pleas for peace. I continue to hope you will do whatever you can to help bring an end to the tragic conflict in Vietnam. I want to express also my continuing appreciation for your untiring efforts in the cause of peace in Vietnam.

In practice, the UN played no part.[57]

In 1968 came change. In consequence, the only countries who mattered were the USSR, China, the US and North and South Vietnam. 'Satellites' of the United States, South Korea, the Philippines, Thailand,

Australia and New Zealand, like the United Kingdom, had never affected American decisions over Vietnam. The 'puppet' government of Saigon, with its 'puppet army' mattered more, after United States policy began to change. Instead of America's making sure that South Vietnam could be independent, South Vietnam was to defend its own independence. American policy became simply to get out. It should be done on America's terms, 'honorably', leaving South Vietnam safe. However, United States policy, executed by President Nixon and Henry Kissinger, became reminiscent of the negotiating position attributed, perhaps apocryphally, to Bismarck when trying to bully Andrassy. 'If you will not accept my terms' he thundered, and then struck the table with ferocious emphasis, and went on, 'I shall have to accept yours.'[58] Nixon and Kissinger struck at Laos, Cambodia, Hanoi and Haiphong, to weaken North Vietnam. At the same time, they tried to persuade the USSR and, more of a novelty, China to abandon North Vietnam.

On 31 March 1968 Lyndon Johnson surprised the world by announcing that he would not stand for re-election as president. In February, the American army asked for over 200 000 reinforcements to be added to the half-million Americans already serving in Vietnam. A hesitant president eventually refused, and on the contrary, began to tell the South Vietnamese that they must increasingly look after themselves: 'Vietnamization' of the war must begin; America had reached the limit. It was not surrender, but to avoid it he felt he must make yet another gesture towards peace. Hence, he announced a partial halt to bombing of North Vietnam. 'My biggest worry', the president recorded, 'was the divisiveness and pessimism at home. I knew the American people were deeply worried.' As usual, American international policy was domestic policy. The year 1968 brought this novelty: tranquillizing the Americans now involved direct, sustained American contacts with Hanoi. On 13 May 1968, Averell Harriman and Cyrus Vance met North Vietnamese representatives in Paris. On 30 October Johnson made possible what he hoped would be serious discussions of peace terms by ordering the total end to the bombing of North Vietnam. Both sides of South Vietnam, the government and the National Liberation Front would be there: in January 1969 agreement on the shape of the negotiating table brought this about. The new president, Richard Nixon, soon reduced the formal Paris contacts to futility. Henry Cabot Lodge was substituted for Harriman as a reliably loyal exponent of White House instructions. Kissinger explains of the Paris talks 'we had to convince the American public that we were eager to settle the war, and Hanoi that we were not so anxious that it could afford to outwit us'. The formal Paris talks at the Majestic Hotel lost any point other than to show willing; the real talks were between Americans (Kissinger) and North Vietnamese (Xuan Thuy or Le Duc Tho). These talks were secret, even furtive. The secretary of state and his department were not told. Henry Kissinger became Harold Kirschman and the talks went on in a humble house in a Paris suburb. Only after two years and ten meetings did Nixon reveal the secret talks. Meanwhile, Nixon tried to bomb and blast Hanoi into submission, that is to say to force North Vietnam to accept conditions under which the existing South Vietnamese military leaders, Thieu and Ky, or some approved substitutes, could securely run South Vietnam. A well-informed and scholarly article suggests that 'the Nixon administration had turned aside from the viable opportunity left to it by the Johnson administration in 1969, thereby extending the nation's involvement in this costly war for four more years'.[59] However, given continued insistence on America's terms, it is unlikely that anything could have come out of the formal talks.

The United States would have to accept Hanoi's plan before peace could be made. The People's Republic and the National Liberation Front wanted a good chance to unite Vietnam under communism. In 1969–72 Nixon tried repeated acts of violence to escape. However, he soon made a critical retreat. In June 1969 Clark Clifford, the defence secretary under Johnson, suggested that 100 000 American troops should be withdrawn in 1969 and all the rest in 1970. In public, Nixon replied 'I would hope that we could beat Mr Clifford's timetable.'[60] Nixon had just announced the withdrawal of 25 000 men. In September he promised 35 000 more and in December 50 000. In April 1970 he added the prospect of another 150 000, and in April 1971 100 000 more were to leave by December. In November 45 000 were announced. By August 1972 all ground combat troops had left, and only 27 000 service personnel remained at the end of the year. All this was to quieten American opinion and to forestall the breakdown of discipline in the armed forces.

The eighteen, mostly secret talks in Paris between Kissinger and the North Vietnamese spread over three and a half years; they were usually futile, repetitious and time-wasting. Moves towards peace went with further American retreats. In September 1970 Nixon accepted a cease-fire 'in place' – that is to say, the US agreed that the North Vietnamese army could remain in South Vietnam. In April 1972 they accepted that areas in which units of the North Vietnamese army remained would be regarded as territory run by the People's Revolutionary Government and not by Saigon. In October 1972 Kissinger agreed to the setting up of a 'National Council of National Reconciliation and Concord': this meant, in plain language, that the National Liberation Front (Viet Cong) in South Vietnam would be accepted as a force equal to the Saigon government. The only concession made by North Vietnam was that it ceased to insist that the Americans should turn out President Thieu of South Vietnam before their departure. The North Vietnamese were left to do it themselves. Nixon tried to avoid concessions to Hanoi. He tried at the same time to make South Vietnam capable of self-defence, and to persuade Thieu that he had succeeded. Elaborate and expensive military actions struck South Vietnam's neighbours. Cambodia was secretly bombed, heavily, in 1969 and then invaded in 1970 – to destroy North Vietnamese 'sanctuaries' over the border from South Vietnam and to track down and put out of action the supposed headquarters (COSVN) of North Vietnamese and Viet Cong activity in South Vietnam. In 1972 they mined Haiphong Harbour to cut off seaborne supplies to North Vietnam. Then, at the end of 1972, came the 'Christmas bombing': heavy attacks on Hanoi and Haiphong.[61]

Nixon and Kissinger were less worried than Johnson had been about full-scale Chinese or Soviet Russian intervention in support of Hanoi. In 1970 relations between America and China began to improve, and in June 1971 China agreed that Nixon should visit Beijing. In October 1971 improving relations with China's rival, the USSR, led to an announcement that Nixon would go to Moscow in May 1972. Early in 1966, when Johnson was discussing the resumption of bombing of North Vietnam, Dean Rusk declared that 'bombing policy' should 'be kept under firm control' to avoid 'the dangers of the Chinese coming in' and the president remarked, 'I don't want war with Russia or China.'[62] Nixon was more aggressive.

Nixon promised President Thieu that the United States would keep South Vietnam going after peace was agreed (eventually in January 1973). The United States would continue, even increase, its provision of munitions, and should North Vietnam attack, would bomb critical targets into obliteration. However, the displays of ferocity put on by Nixon in 1969–72 made it steadily less likely that US opinion would tolerate continued intervention in support of Saigon. This reaction was reinforced by the Kent State killings and My Lai massacre.

In June 1973 Congress blocked all American military action in Vietnam. Military aid was drastically curtailed and the supply of weapons and ammunition to South Vietnam checked.[63] High inflation, bringing corruption and looting, helped to destroy morale. On 1 May 1975 Saigon became Ho Chi Minh City.

Acknowledgements

I am grateful for the help of everyone at the Lyndon B. Johnson Library and particularly Regina Greenwell, Charlaine Burgess, Jacqueline Demsky, and Irene Parra. Roger Louis and Dagmar made visits to Austin, Texas, exceptionally enjoyable.

Robert Dallek generously supplied valuable documentary evidence.

My warm thanks go to Janette Swaine for indispensable help.

NOTES AND REFERENCES

Introduction

1. R. S. McNamara (with B. Van De Mark), *In Retrospect: The Tragedy and Lessons of Vietnam* (New York, 1995), p. 212.

1 Origins And Alternatives: Comments, Counter-facts and Commitments

1. David G. Marr, *Vietnam 1945. The Quest for Power* (Berkeley, 1995) pp. 280–281.
2. Stein Tønnesson, *The Vietnamese Revolution of 1945: Roosevelt, Ho Chi Minh and de Gaulle in a World at War* (Oslo–London, 1991) p. 405, fn. 193.
3. Robert S. McNamara, *In Retrospect: The Tragedy and Lessons of Vietnam* (New York, 1995); reviewed in *Asian Affairs*, February 1996.
4. A. J. Stockwell (ed.), *British Documents on the End of Empire Malaya Part II: The Communist Insurrection 1948–1953* (London, 1995).
5. Tønnesson, op. cit., p. 364.
6. Tønnesson, 'Did FDR provoke the Japanese Coup of 9 March 1945 in French Indochina?', paper presented to the Society of Historians of American Foreign Relations, June 1992.
7. S. Tønnesson, *1946: Déclenchement de la guerre d'Indochine* (Paris, 1987).
8. A. Short, *The Communist Insurrection in Malaya* (London, 1975) p. 60.
9. William J. Duiker, *The Communist Road to Power in Vietnam* (2nd edn) (Boulder, Colorado 1996).
10. Ronald H. Spector, *United States Army in Vietnam. Advice and Support: The Early Years 1941–1960* (Washington, DC, 1983).
11. *Foreign Relations of the United States – 1953*, vol XII, p. 433.
12. *Ibid.* p. 1305.
13. Jacques Dalloz, *The War in Indo-China 1945–54* (Dublin, 1990), p. 169.
14. Francois Joyaux, *La Chine et le Réglement du Premier Conflit d'Indochine* (Paris 1979) p. 297,
15. William Conrad Gibbons, *The US Government and the Vietnam War Part: I 1945–1961* (Washington, DC 1984) p. 261.
16. *Foreign Relations of the United States – 1954*, vol. XIII, p. 2154.
17. Gibbons, op. cit., p. 260.
18. Robert Buzzanco, *Masters of War: Military Dissent and Politics in the Vietnam Era* (Cambridge 1996), p. 55.

19.	*United States-Vietnam Relations 1945–1967* (The 'Pentagon Papers'), bk 2, IV, A5, p. 90.
20.	*Ibid*. p. 92.
21.	Gibbons, op. cit., *part II: 1961–1964*, p. 15.
22.	Quoted in A. Short, *The Origins of the Vietnam War* (London, 1989), p. l239.
23.	McNamara, op. cit., p. 39.
Other quotations may be found in Short, *The Origins of the Vietnam War*.

## 2	Coping With The United States: Hanoi's Search for an Effective Strategy

1.	T. Hoopes, as cited in Leslie H. Gelb and Richard K. Betts, *The Irony of Vietnam: The System Worked* (Washington, 1979) p. 22.
2.	For further accounts, see Marilyn B. Young, *The Vietnam Wars, 1945–1990* (New York 1991) p. 103; and Neil Sheehan, *A Bright Shining Lie: John Paul Vann and America in Vietnam* (London 1990).
3.	See Mark Bradley, in Jayne Werner and Luu Doan Huynh (eds), *The Vietnam War: Vietnamese and American Perspectives* (New York, 1993) ch. 1.
4.	'Resolution of the Enlarged Plenum Conference of the ICP Central Committee, 15–17 January 1948', *Party Documents* (Hanoi, vol. 6, 1964) p. 5.
5.	See Chen Jian, 'China and the First Indochina War', *China Quarterly*, no. 133 (March 1993) pp. 93–5.
6.	Ho Chi Minh, *Selected Writings*, vol. 5 (Hanoi 1985) p. 122.
7.	*Party Documents* (vol. 9) p. 60.
8.	As Andrew Rotter pointed out, the DRV was the last communist regime to recognise the PRC. In a memorandum to Secretary of State Acheson, American ambassador to Thailand, Edwin Stanton, quoted a reliable source who reports that the decision on whether to accept Chinese aid remained a 'tremendous problem for the Ho Chi Minh government'. See A. Rotter, *The Path to Vietnam: Origins of the American Commitment to Southeast Asia* (Ithaca, 1987) pp. 100, 171.
9.	It might well be the reason why American officials called the DRV's offers for bilateral cooperation with the US during this period 'naïve'. Interview by the author with Nordic historian Stein Tønnesson, February 1995.
10.	For more debate, see Robert Garson, *The United States and China Since 1949*, (London, 1994) p. 41.
11.	*Party Documents*, vol. 8, p. 260; Tran Buoi, *The Anti-American Resistance of the Vietnamese People* (Hanoi, 1985) p. 33; Institute of Party History, *Party Events, vol. 3: 1954–1975* (Hanoi 1985) pp. 34–5.
12.	For further accounts, see Institute of International Relations, *President Ho Chi Minh and Diplomatic Activities* (Hanoi, 1990) pp. 163–4. See also 'Diplomatic Initiatives and Foreign Relations of the DRV' in Carlyle A. Thayer, *War by Other Means: National Liberation and Revolution in Vietnam, 1954–1960* (Sydney, 1989) pp. 33–7, 73–9, 159–67.
13.	Quang Loi, *On the Last 8 Years of Implementing the Geneva Accords in Vietnam* (Hanoi, 1962) pp. 10–11.

14. Bui Dinh Thanh, *Vietnam: 45 Years of Combating, Constructing and Renovating* (Hanoi 1990) p. 49.
15. Geir Lundestad, *East, West, North, South: Major Developments in International Politics, 1945–1990* (Oslo 1994) ch. 4, pp. 101–21.
16. Nguyen Khac Vien, *Contemporary Vietnam* (Hanoi 1981) p. 173.
17. Nguyen Huu Tho, 'The National Liberation Front: A Founding Part of the Vietnamese History', in Vietnamese Father Front, *Under the Same Banner* (Hanoi, 1993) p. 16.
18. Le Duan, *On the Vietnamese People's War* (Hanoi, 1994) p. 103.
19. Institute of International Relations, *President Ho Chi Minh and Diplomatic Activities*, p. 170.
20. Nhuyen Huu Tho, 'The National Liberation Front', p. 20.
21. Tran Bach Dang, 'The Armed Struggle in the South', *Under the Same Banner*, p. 835.
22. *Ibid.* p. 835.
23. *Ibid.* p. 836.
24. The Institute of Army History, *A History of the Anti-American War*, vol. 11 (Hanoi, 1990) pp. 45–6.
25. Phan Minh Thao, 'The Truong Son Route', *Under the Same Banner*, p. 599.
26. Interview of researchers in Hanoi by the author, December 1994.
27. See George Herring, *America's Longest War: United States and Vietnam, 1950–1975*, 1st ed. (New York 1979) pp. 73–5.
28. *The Third VWP National Congress Documents*, vol. 1 (Hanoi, 1960) p. 23; see also US Department of Defense, *United States–Vietnam Relations 1945–1967 Pentagon Papers* (Washington, 1971) IV. A. 5, pp. 65–6.
29. 'Nguy' is the Vietnamese term for the US-nurtured Saigon regimes.
30. Le Duan, 'Letter to Muoi Cuc [Nguyen Van Linh]', *Letters to the South* (Hanoi, 1985) p. 60.
31. *Ibid.* p. 60.
32. Le Duan, *On the Vietnamese People's War*, p. 160.
33. Interviews of researchers in Hanoi by the author, December 1994.
34. For more accounts on Laos, see Ralph Smith, 'Laos: The Limits of Détente', in *An International History of the Vietnam War*, vol. I (New York, 1983) pt II, ch. 7, pp. 115–34. See also, Kaysone Phomvihane, *On the Main Experience and Questions of the Lao Revolution* (Hanoi, 1979).
35. Le Duan, *On the Vietnamese People's War*, pp. 157–8.
36. *Ibid.* p. 186.
37. For example, see Thomas McCormick, *America's Half- Century: United States Foreign Policy in the cold war* (Baltimore, MD, 1989) p. 150.
38. Geir Lundestad, *East, West, North, South: Major Developments in International Politics, 1945–1990* p. 123; George McT. Kahin, *Intervention: How America Became Involved in Vietnam* (New York, 1987) p. 397.
39. See Jeffrey Kimball, 'How Wars End: The Vietnam War', *Peace & Change*, 20 (January 1995) p. 191.
40. Le Duan's speech 'On the Vietnamese Revolution's Methods', given in the Journal of People's Army Editorial Board's Meeting in March 1967, first published in Le Duan, *On the Vietnamese People's War*, pp. 293–4.

41. Le Duan, 'Letter to the COSVN November 1965', *On the Vietnamese People's War*, pp. 240–293.

42. Le Duan, 'Letter to Xuan [Nguyen Chi Thanh], May 1965', *On the Vietnamese People's War*, p. 205.

43. Le Duan, 'Letter to the COSVN, November 1965', *On the Vietnamese People's War*, p. 241.

44. *Events in Party's History*, p. 392. This timing coincides with Ngo Vinh Long's estimation that Hanoi made its decision for the general offensive–general uprisings by the end of December 1966. See Ngo Vinh Long, 'The Tet Offensive and Its Aftermath', *Indochina Newsletter*, no. 49 (January–February 1988) p. 3. James J. Wirtz, however, argued that the decision was made in July 1967 at a party conference following the funeral of Nguyen Chi Thanh. See James J. Wirtz, *The Tet Offensive: Intelligence Failure in War* (Ithaca, 1981) p. 66.

45. Le Duan, 'Letter of 18 January 1968 to COSVN', *On the Vietnamese People's War*, pp. 338–9.

46. In the American historiography of the Vietnam War, the Vietnamese general offensive and general uprisings has been known as the Tet offensive. For more American accounts of the Tet offensive, see 'A Very Near Thing: Tet offensive and After, 1968', in George Herring, *America's Longest War: United States and Vietnam, 1950–1975* (New York 1979) ch. 6, pp. 183–216; Wirtz, *The Tet Offensive: Intelligence Failure in War*; and 'Tet', in Stanley Karnow, *Vietnam: A History* (London 1994) ch. 14.

47. Quoted in Tran Van Tra, 'Tet: The 1968 General Offensive and General Uprisings', in *The Vietnam War: Vietnamese and American Perspectives*, p. 40.

48. *Ibid.* pp. 52–3.

49. Tran Bach Dang, 'Tet: A Strategic Repertoire', in *Under the Same Banner*, p. 317.

50. Nguyen Co Thach, 'Interview', given to the SRV's MOFA, *Journal of International Relations* (September 1990) Hanoi.

51. Chester Cooper, *The Lost Crusade: America in Vietnam* (New York, 1970) p. 517; and George Ball, 'A Dissenter in the Government', in Andrew Rotter (ed.), *Light at the End of the Tunnel: A Vietnam War Anthology* (New York, 1971) ch. 10, p. 174.

52. *Ibid.* pp. 173–4.

53. The DRV's Foreign Ministry File of Public Statements, Hanoi.

54. Interview with researchers and senior diplomats by the author, November–December 1994, Hanoi.

55. Recalling the 1968 events, General Westmoreland wrote that the Vietnamese, in fact, forced the US to the negotiating table, when many Americans thought that the US administration initiated the talks without pressure to do so. He wrote: 'The enemy had already achieved the goal of unilateral de-escalation on the American side, stopping the bombing, halting reinforcements, and denying an aggressive strategy and in the process had brought the Americans to the conference table while many Americans thought instead that they were bringing them there. He was free at that point to pursue a new strategy of talk and fight and, in the process, drag

out the war.' See General William C. Westmoreland, *A Soldier Reports* (New York, 1976) p. 361.

56. The number was given by the PLAVN High Command Statistics Department in Tran Buoi, *A History of the Anti-American War*, p. 311. See also Marilyn B. Young, *The Vietnam Wars*, pp. 223–4.

57. The DRV's Foreign Ministry File on Public Statements, Hanoi.

58. Ho Chi Minh, *Selected Writings* (Hanoi 1989) p. 347.

59. *Ibid.* p. 351.

60. The DRV's Foreign Ministry files on the Paris negotiations, Hanoi.

61. *Party Documents* (vol. 11) p. 237.

62. *Ibid.* vol. 12, p. 35.

63. For further discussion see, for example, Institute of International Relations, *An Epoch-Making Victory and the Diplomatic Struggle*, pp. 35–40.

64. Nguyen Viet, 'The Bertrand Russell International Court on American War Crimes, *The Journal of Army History*, no. 28 (Hanoi, April 1988) pp. 27–9.

65. See 'Ho Chi Minh and the Forming of the World People's Front Supporting the Vietnamese People against American Aggressors', Institute of International Relations, *President Ho Chi Minh and Diplomatic Activities*, pp. 188–217.

66. *Ibid.* p. 217.

67. Richard H. Shultz Jr, *The Soviet Union and Revolutionary Warfare: Principles, Practices and Regional Comparison* (Stanford, 1988) pp. 46–76.

68. *Ibid.* p. 184.

69. *Ibid.* p. 217. Ho Chi Minh himself tried to influence the US peace movement by continuously making statements and sending open letters 'to the American people'. For example, in his Appeal to the Nation on 16 July 1966 he said: 'President Johnson, answer these questions publicly before the American people and the peoples of the world: Who has sabotaged the Geneva Agreements which guarantee the sovereignty, independence, unity and territorial integrity of Vietnam? Have the Vietnamese troops invaded the United States and massacred Americans? Or isn't it the US government which, on the contrary, has sent US troops to invade Vietnam and massacre the Vietnamese people?' See Ho Chi Minh, *Selected Writings*, pp. 308–9.

70. For the latest account on the issue, see Robert Dallek, 'Lyndon Johnson and Vietnam: The Making of a Tragedy', *Diplomatic History*, vol. 20, no. 2 (Spring 1990) pp. 147–62.

71. See, for example, 'The First American Journalist to Visit Hanoi', in Luu Van Loi and Nguyen Anh Vu, *Diplomatic Offensives and Secret Contacts Before the Paris Negotiations* (Hanoi, 1990) ch. 15, pp. 175–93.

72. Quoted in Nguyen Thi Binh's 'My Years of International Activities', *Under the Same Banner*, pp. 373–4.

73. Henry Kissinger, *Diplomacy* (New York, 1994) p. 685.

74. Institute of International Relations, *President Ho Chi Minh and Diplomatic Activities*, p. 218.

75. The thirteenth resolution of the VWP Central Committee, 26 January 1967. Quoted in *Events in Party History* (Hanoi, 1970) p. 390.

76. Interviews with Hanoi's senior diplomats by the author, September 1995, Hanoi.
77. Chester Cooper, *The Lost Crusade*, p. 517; and George Ball, 'A Dissenter in the Government', p. 174.
78. Kissinger, *Diplomacy*, p. 684.
79. Pham Van Dong commented in a speech to DRV diplomats at their sixth Conference in June 1969: 'Because of the military and diplomatic struggles, the political situation in South Vietnam is greatly changing in our favour. The influence and image of the revolutionary forces have been greatly strengthened.' The DRV's Foreign Ministry files on the Paris negotiations, Hanoi.
80. George Herring, *LBJ and Vietnam: A Different Kind of War* (Austin, 1994) p. 177.
81. Institute of International Relations, *An Epoch-Making Victory and the Diplomatic Struggle* (Hanoi, 1985) p. 71.
82. See Robert S. McNamara, *In Retrospect: The Tragedy and Lessons of Vietnam* (New York, 1995).
83. William Shawcross, *Sideshow: Nixon, Kissinger and the Destruction of Cambodia* (New York 1979) p. 87.
84. Le Duan, 'Speech at the VWP Central Committee Conference, Hanoi, November 1964', *On the Vietnamese People's War*, p. 179.

3   South Vietnam

1. See the Senator Gravel Edition of *The Pentagon Papers* (Boston, 1971) vol. I, p. 214. This will be referred to hereinafter as the *Pentagon Papers*. Officially the 'History of the US Decision Making Process on Vietnam Policy', this 47–volume, top-secret inquiry into US involvement in Indochina was commissioned by Robert McNamara and headed by Leslie Gelb. It was completed in January 1969, and 43 volumes of it were made public in June and July 1971 by the *New York Times*.
2. *Ibid.* p. 177.
3. James Gavin (General), *Crisis Now* (New York, 1968) pp. 57–9.
4. Fore details see: Truong Nhu Tang, *A Viet Cong Memoir: An Inside Account of the War and Its Aftermath* (New York, 1986) pp. 234–90.
5. In the two official papers General Van Tien Dung was also given as the co-author, since he was General Giap's aide at the time. The August–September issue of *Vietnam Courier* in both the French and English editions contained an edited translation of this article. But according to Dr Nguyen Khac Vien, who was the editor of this journal at the time and who was one of the best-known Vietnamese intellectuals internationally, the translation was already in the press in July. Dr Vien first confirmed the reasons for the withdrawal of General Giap's article and his subsequent travails to this writer in January 1980. The *Vietnam Courier's* English translation was later published in book form in 1976 by RECON Publications (Philadelphia, Pennsylvania) under the title: *How We Won the War*, by General Vo Nguyen Giap.

6. 'Dong Chi Le Duc Tho noi ve mot so van de tong ket chien tranh va bien soan lich su quan su' (Comrade Le Duc Tho discusses a number of questions on the General Assessment of the War and the Writing of Military History), *Tap Chi Lich Su Quan Su* [Journal of Military] History) (March 1988) pp. 1–10.
7. Van Tien Dung, *Our Great Spring Victory: An Account of the Liberation of South Vietnam* (New York, 1977).
8. Tran Van Tra, *Vietnam: History of the Bulwark B2 Theatre*, vol. 5: *Concluding the 30 Years War* (Washington, DC: Foreign Broadcast Information Service, South East Asia Report no. 1247, Joint Publication Research Services (JPRS) 82783, 2 February 1983).
9. *Pentagon Papers*, I, p. 214.
10. *Ibid.* p. 226.
11. *Ibid.* p. 218–19.
12. George McT. Kahin, *Intervention: How America Became Involved in Vietnam* (New York, 1987), pp. 96–8 (hereafter *Intervention*); Marilyn B. Young *The Vietnam Wars, 1945–1990* (New York, 1991), pp. 55–7 (hereafter *Vietnam Wars*); Gabriel Kolko, *Anatomy of a War: Vietnam, the United States and the Modern Historical Experience* (New York, 1994) pp. 92–6 (hereafter *Anatomy*).
13. Quynh Cu, *Dong Khoi o Ben Tre* (General Uprisings in Ben Tre) (Hanoi, 1985) (hereafter *Dong Khoi*), pp. 24–6.
14. Ban Chi Dao Tong Ket Chien Tranh Truc Thuoc Bo Chinh Tri (The Central Command on Overall Assessment of the War Directly under the Supervision of the Politburo), *Tong Ket Cuoc Khang Chien Chong My, Cuu Nuoc: Thang Loi va Bai Hoc* (Overall Assessment of the Resistance against the Americans to Save the Country: Victory and Lessons), Luu Hanh Noi Bo (For Internal Circulation Only) (Hanoi 1995), pp. 39–40, 310. General Doan Khue, member of the Politburo and Defence Minister, General Van Tien Dung and Lieutenant General Tran Van Quang were the principal directors of this official assessment. Hereafter *Tong Ket*.
15. *Ibid.* p. 39.
16. Jayne S. Werner and Luu Duan Huynh (eds), *The Vietnam War: Vietnamese and American Perspectives* (New York, 1993) p. xxii (hereinafter *Vietnamese and American Perspectives*).
17. *Ibid.* pp. 41–2; for excerpts of Resolution Fifteen, see *Dong Khoi*, pp. 60–2.
18. *Dong Khoi*, p. 188.
19. Nguyen Khac Nhan, 'Policy of Key Rural Agrovilles', *Asian Culture*, vol. 3, nos. 3 and 4 (July-December 1969) p. 32; Milton E. Osborne, *Strategic Hamlets in South Vietnam* (Ithaca, New York 1965), p. 22; William A. Nighswonger *Rural Pacification in Vietnam* (New York, 1966) p. 46 (hereafter *Rural Pacification*). Colonel Nighswonger was a senior AID (Agency for International Development, a CIA front) officer for the Pacification Programme.
20. *Rural Pacification*, pp. 61–3.
21. *Tong Ket*, p. 42. In the endnote to this statement on p. 311, it is stated that, in varying degrees, the control of local administration was returned to the people in 1100 of the total of 1296 villages in the Southern region and in

4440 of 4700 hamlets in the central provinces. In Ben Tre, in 1960 two-thirds of all the land that had been confiscated by the Diem regime was returned to the peasants (*Dong Khoi*, p. 195).

22. *Tong Ket*, p. 43.
23. Quoted in *Dong Khoi*, p. 194. General Hoang Van Thai died suddenly under suspicious circumstances in June 1986. He had incurred the displeasure of both General Secretary Le Duan and Chief Party Organizer Le Duc Tho for his frankness. General Thai had been a trusted friend and confidant of General Giap. They were also in-laws. For details see Thanh Tin, *Mat That: Hoi Ky Chinh Tri cua Bui Tin* (True Face: The Political Memoirs of Bui Tin) (California 1994), pp. 193–4 (hereafter, *Mat That*). Colonel Bui Tin was the person who received the surrender of General Duong Van (Big) Minh on 30 April 1975 in Saigon. He later became the deputy editor of the party daily, *Nhan Dan*. Since 1989 he has lived in exile in France because of disagreement with party leadership and party lines.
24. Truong Nhu Tan, *A Viet Cong Memoir: An Inside Account of the Vietnam War and its Aftermath* (New York, 1985) pp. 70–80 (hereinafter *Viet Cong Memoir*). Also see the appendix on pp. 319–28 for complete transcripts of the manifesto and programme of the Front.
25. *Ibid.* p. 80.
26. *Vietnam Wars*, p. 72; *Anatomy*, p. 128.
27. *Bao Cao Dien Bien 21 Nam Khang Chien Chong My va Nhung Bai Hoc ve Toan Dan Danh Giac cua Long An* (Report on Developments in the 21 Years of Resistance against the Americans and the Lessons of the Entire Population Fighting the Enemy in Long An) (Long An: Ban Tong Ket Chien Tranh Tinh Long An (Committee on Assessment of the War in Long An Province) pp. 106–23 (hereafter *Bao Cao . . . Long An*).
28. *Vietnam Wars*, pp. 82–4; for the use of chemicals to destroy crops, also see Seymour M. Hersh, 'Our Chemical War', *The New York Review of Books*, 25 April 1968; Ngo Vinh Long, 'Leaf Abscission?' in Barry Weisberg (ed.), *Ecocide in Indochina* (New York, 1970) pp. 54–63.
29. *Vietnam Wars*, pp. 89–90.
30. *Rural Pacification*, p. 64.
31. *Intervention*, pp. 178–285; *Vietnam Wars*, pp. 91–104.
32. *Pentagon Papers*, vol. II, p. 460.
33. *Tong ket*, pp. 54–5, 311–2.
34. *Vietnamese and American Perspectives*, p. xxii.
35. *Pentagon Papers*, vol. II, pp. 472–3.
36. For details see William C. Westmoreland, *A Soldier Reports* (New York, 1976).
37. *Pentagon Papers*, vol. IV, p. 442.
38. *Ibid.* pp. 433–5.
39. Pro-war American intellectuals were excited by the prospects as they reprinted the whole study introduced by McNamara in the May 1996 issue of the pro-war journal *Vietnam Perspectives*.
40. *Pentagon Papers*, vol. IV, p. 376.
41. *New York Review of Books*, 25 April 1968.
42. *Pentagon Papers*, vol. II, p. 569.

43. *Ibid.* vol. IV, p. 441.
44. R.W. Apple Jr, 'Vietnam Signs of Stalemate, *New York Times*, 7 August 1967, pp. 1, 14.
45. *Pentagon Papers* vol. II, p. 507.
46. 'South Vietnam Situation Today', Reuters News Agency, 11 March 1967.
47. *Pentagon Papers*, vol. IV, pp. 339–51.
48. For an account of the election, see Francis H. Craighill III and Robert C. Zelnick, 'Ballots or Bullets: What the 1967 Elections Could Mean', in *Vietnam: Matter for the Agenda* (Los Angeles, 1968). For reports in the Saigon press, see *Than Chung* 16 August 1967; *Chanh Dao*, 3 October 1967.
49. Tran Bach Dang, 'Mau Than: Cuoc Tong Dien Tap Chien Luoc' (Mau Than (Tet Offensive): A Strategic General Rehearsal), *Tap Chi Lich Su Quan Su* (Journal of Military History), February 1988, pp. 57–64.
50. *Mau Than Saigon* (The Tet Offensive in Saigon) (Ho Chi Minh City, 1988) p. 4. *Tap Chi Lich Su Quan Su* reprinted most of Resolution 14 in its February 1988 issue on pp. 2–3, but says that the document (Emperor Quang Trung Resolution) was issued by the Central Committee on 1 January 1968. One can only surmise that there must have been internal disagreements for this long delay.
51. The latest and most comprehensive treatment from many perspectives is in Marc Jason Gilbert and William Head (eds), *The Tet Offensive* (Westport, Connecticut, 1996).
52. See my 'The Tet Offensive and Its Aftermath' in the above volume, pp. 89–123, for details.
53. W. Averell Harriman, *America and Russia in a Changing World* (New York, 1971) pp. 136–40.
54. For the Pentagon admission, see Richard McCarthy, *The Ultimate Folly* (New York, 1969) pp. 49–50. For official Vietnamese documents and accounts of ecological damage and hunger, see 12 November, 17 November, 20 November, 26 November and 8 December 1970 issues of *Tin Sang*, a Catholic Saigon daily. Also see the 2 December 1970 issue of *Xay Dung* the most pro-Thieu Catholic daily in Saigon.
55. *Tin Sang*, 3 August 1971. According to United States Information Service statistics released on 3 January 1972, the Nixon administration had supplied the ARVN with 910 000 sub-machine-guns and machine-guns, 775 airplanes, 2100 pieces of artillery and tanks, 940 naval boats and 45 000 military vehicles.
56. For details, see my study in *The Tet Offensive*, pp. 115–18; also see *Vietnamese and American Perspectives*, pp. 120–1.
57. *Tin Sang*, 15 February 1971.
58. Wilfred Burchett, *Grasshoppers and Elephants: Why Viet Nam Fell* (New York, 1977) pp. 144–5.
59. *Vietnamese and American Perspectives*, pp. 121, 128.
60. Tran Vu, '1971: Nam Phan Cong Thang Loi Gianh Quyen Chu Dong Chien Truong' (1971: A Year of Successful Counter-offensives that Regained Initiatives on the Battlefronts'), *Lich Su Quan Su*, April 1991, pp. 4–5.

61. *Chinh Luan*, 14 November 1974.
62. *The Vietnam Wars*, pp. 286–9.
63. Dong Chi 'Le Duc Tho noi ve mot so van de tong ket chien tranh va bien soan lich su quan su' (Comrade Le Duc Tho discusses a number of questions on the General Assessment of the War and the Writing of Military History) *Tap Chi Lich Su Quan Su* (March 1988) pp. 1–10.
64. *Fiscal year 1974 Authorization for Military Procurement, Research and Development, Construction Authorization for Safeguard ABM, and Active Duty and Selected Reserve Strengths*, hearings before the Committee on Armed Services, United States Senate, 93rd Congress, pt 3, Authorizations (Washington, DC, 1973) p. 1383.
65. *Vietnam: May 1974*, Staff Report Prepared for the Use of the Committee on Foreign Relations, United States Senate (Washington, DC, 5 August 1974) p. 22.
66. *Bao Cao ... Long An*, pp. 127–30.
67. Economic aid to the Thieu regime during the same period was also increased and channelled through various programmes such as the Foreign Assistance Act and 'Food for Peace'. For example, on 17 and 18 December 1974, Congress passed Foreign Assistance Act, authorizing $450 million in economic aid to Saigon. This was $100 million more than the amount authorized by Congress in fiscal year 1974. According to the 16 February 1975 issue of *Dien Tin*, 90 per cent of US economic aid to the Thieu regime had been used to maintain the war. For detailed reports on the economic blockade and its impact, see the *Congressional Record*, 20 May 1974 and 4 June 1974.
68. *Dai Dan Toc* (The Greater National Community, a Saigon daily run by a group of deputies in the Lower House) 8 August 1974.
69. *Dai Dan Toc*, 30 August 1974.
70. *Chinh Luan* (Official Discussion, a very conservative Saigon daily newspaper which was accused by others as having a CIA connection at the time) 5 November 1974.
71. *Dien Tin*, 6, 20, 22 and 24 September 1974; *Dai Dan Toc*, 30 September 1974.
72. *Dien Tin*, 20 September 1974.
73. *But Thep* (Iron Pen, an extremely conservative Saigon daily) 7 October 1974.
74. This was reported frequently in the Saigon press. For examples see *Dai Dan Toc*, 19 November 1974; *Dien Tin*, 22 November and 16 December 1974.
75. *Chinh Luan, Dong Phuong, Song Than* (Divine Waves) 2 November 1974.
76. *Dien Tin*, 3 November 1974.
77. *Song Than, Dong Phuong Chinh Luan*, 7 November 1974.
78. *Chinh Luan*, 25 September 1974.
79. *Bao Cao ... Long An*, pp. 131–2.
80. *Washington Post*, 2 November 1974.
81. *Hoa Binh*, 27 September 1974.
82. *Washington Post*, 7 October 1974.
83. *A Viet Cong Memoir*, pp. 258–90. General Tran Van Tra said at the Columbia University conference that in most cases, cities and towns were taken

over before the arrival of Northern troops. In Saigon there were already 10 000 sappers and 10 000 guerrilla commandos prior to the final North Vietnamese assault. See *Vietnamese and American Perspectives*, pp. 121–2.

4 The United States and Vietnam

1. *Public Papers of the Presidents of the United States: Harry S. Truman, 1947* (Washington, DC, 1963) pp. 176–80.
2. William J. Duiker, *U.S. Containment Policy and the Conflict in Indochina* (Stanford, California, 1994) pp. 128–31, 364–69.
3. David L. Anderson, 'Dwight D. Eisenhower and Wholehearted Support of Ngo Dinh Diem', in David L. Anderson (ed.), *Shadow on the White House: Presidents and the Vietnam War, 1945–1975* (Lawrence, Kansas, 1993) pp. 42–47.
4. David L. Anderson, *Trapped by Success: The Eisenhower Administration and Vietnam, 1953–1961* (New York, 1991) pp. 53, 72–3, 116–17, 128–9.
5. *Ibid.* 151–8, 177.
6. William J. Duiker, *The Communist Road to Power in Vietnam* (Boulder, Colorado, 1981) pp. 187–9.
7. Gary R. Hess, 'Commitment in the Age of Counterinsurgency', in Anderson, *Shadow on the White House*, p. 69.
8. National Security Action Memorandum no. 52, 11 May 1961, US Department of State, *FRUS 1961–1963*, vol. 1, *Vietnam, 1961*, p. 133; see also 'A Program of Action to Prevent Communist Domination of South Vietnam', 1 May 1961, ibid, pp. 93–115.
9. Maxwell Taylor to Kennedy, 3 November 1961 *FRUS, 1961–63*, 1:479–503; National Security Action Memorandum no. 111, 22 November 1961, *ibid*, 656–7; Chester Bowles, *Promises to Keep: My Years in Public Life, 1949–1969* (New York, 1971) pp. 408–9.
10. Statistics on US military personnel in South Vietnam are from US Department of Defense, OASD (Comptroller), Directorate for Information, Washington, DC.
11. Gary R. Hess, *Vietnam and the United States: Origins and Legacy of War* (Boston, 1990), 73–5; Neil Sheehan, *A Bright Shining Lie: John Paul Vann and America in Vietnam* (New York, 1988) pp. 203–65.
12. George McT. Kahin, *Intervention: How America Became Involved in Vietnam* (Garden City, NY, 1987) pp. 146–68; Ellen J. Hammer, *A Death in November: America in Vietnam, 1963* (New York, 1987) pp. 177–80.
13. Kahin, *Intervention*, pp. 168–82; Hammer, *A Death in November*, pp. 280–310.
14. Hess, 'Commitment in the Age of Counterinsurgency', pp. 81–3; Hammer, *A Death in November*, p. 211; Jeffrey J. Clarke, *Advice and Support: The Final Years* (Washington, DC, 1988) p. 275.
15. National Security Action Memorandum no. 273, 26 November 1963, *FRUS, 1961–63*, vol. 4, *Vietnam, August–December 1963*, pp. 637–40.

16. Quoted in George C. Herring, *America's Longest War: the United States in Vietnam, 1950–1975*, 3rd edn (New York, 1996) p. 122.
17. Quoted in George C. Herring, 'The Reluctant Warrior: Lyndon Johnson as Commander in Chief', in Anderson, *Shadow on the White House*, p. 96.
18. On Johnson's leadership style see George C. Herring, *LBJ and Vietnam: A Different Kind of War* (Austin 1994); Lloyd C. Gardner, *Pay Any Price: Lyndon Johnson and the Wars for Vietnam* (Chicago, 1995).
19. Herring, *America's Longest War*, pp. 130–3.
20. Quoted in Robert S. McNamara (with Brian Van De Mark), *In Retrospect: The Tragedy and Lessons of Vietnam* (New York, 1995) p. 134.
21. US Department of State, *Bulletin* (24 August 1964) p. 268.
22. Brian Van De Mark, *Into the Quagmire: Lyndon Johnson and the Escalation of the Vietnam War* (New York, 1991) pp. 23–6; William J. Duiker, *Sacred War: Nationalism and Revolution in a Divided Vietnam* (New York, 1995) pp. 166–75.
23. McGeorge Bundy to Johnson, 7 February 1965, *FRUS 1964–1968*, vol. 2, *Vietnam, January–June 1965*, pp. 174–85; Lyndon Baines Johnson, *Vantage Point: Perspectives of the Presidency, 1963–1969* (New York, 1971) pp. 121–32; Herring, *America's Longest War*, p. 161.
24. Quoted in Herring, *America's Longest War*, p. 151.
25. Bui Diem with David Chanoff, *In the Jaws of History* (Boston, 1987), p. 127.
26. Robert McNamara to Johnson, 1 July 1965, *FRUS, 1964–1968*, vol. 3, *Vietnam, June–December 1965*, pp. 97–104.
27. Herring, *America's Longest War*, pp. 150–5; Larry Berman, *Planning a Tragedy* (New York, 1982) pp. 105–53.
28. *Public Papers of the Presidents of the United States: Lyndon B. Johnson, 1965* (Washington, DC, 1967) pp. 394–9.
29. Intelligence Memorandum, 15 April 1965, *FRUS, 1964–68*, vol. 2: pp. 558–60; Allen E. Goodman, *The Lost Peace: America's Search for a Negotiated Settlement of the Vietnam War* (Stanford, California, 1978), pp. 23–8.
30. William C. Westmoreland, *A Soldier Reports* (New York, 1976) pp. 198–9.
31. George Donelson Moss, *Vietnam: An American Ordeal*, 2nd edn (Englewood Cliffs, New Jessey, 1994), pp. 201–3.
32. Herring, *America's Longest War*, pp. 156, 170–1.
33. Hess, *Vietnam*, pp. 97–8; Moss, *Vietnam*, pp. 207–13.
34. Stanley Karnow, *Vietnam: A History* (New York, 1983) p. 514.
35. Ibid. 491–8; Hess, *Vietnam*, pp. 99–102.
36. William S. Turley, *The Second Indochina War: A Short Political and Military History, 1954–1975* (Boulder, Colorado, 1986) pp. 99–117; Herring, *America's Longest War*, pp. 203–11.
37. Robert Buzzanco, *Masters of War: Military Dissent and Politics in the Vietnam Era* (Cambridge, 1996) pp. 311–40 (quote on p. 311).
38. Johnson, *Vantage Point*, p. 435; Clark Clifford with Richard Holbrooke, *Counsel to the President: A Memoir* (New York, 1991) pp. 511–19.
39. Ronald H. Spector, *After Tet: The Bloodiest Year of the War* (New York, 1993) pp. 24–5; Herring, *America's Longest War*, pp. 228–34.
40. Johnson, *Vantage Point*, pp. 513–29.

41. Richard M. Nixon, 'Asia after Vietnam', *Foreign Affairs*, 46 (October 1967) p. 111; Jeffrey P. Kimball, '"Peace with Honour": Richard Nixon and the Diplomacy of Threat and Symbolism', in Anderson, *Shadow on the White House*, pp. 152–4.

42. Kimball, '"Peace with Honor"', pp. 158–62.

43. Quoted in Eric M. Bergerud, *The Dynamics of Defeat: The Vietnam War in Hau Nghia Province* (Boulder, Colorado, 1991) p. 234; Moss, *Vietnam*, pp. 327–8.

44. William Shawcross, *Sideshow: Kissinger, Nixon and the Destruction of Cambodia* (New York, 1979) pp. 146–54; Henry Kissinger, *White House Years* (Boston 1979) pp. 483–505.

45. Hess, *Vietnam*, pp. 124–7.

46. Kissinger, *White House Years*, pp. 1016–31.

47. Kimball '"Peace with Honor"', pp. 167–9; Hess, *Vietnam*, pp. 127–30.

48. Kimball '"Peace with Honor"', pp. 170–7; Hess, *Vietnam*, pp. 130–5; Nixon to Thieu, 5 January 1973, in Nguyen Tien Hung and Jerrold L. Schecter, *The Palace File* (New York, 1986) p. 392.

49. Arnold R. Isaacs, *Without Honor: Defeat in Vietnam and Cambodia* (New York, 1984) pp. 69–70, 447–77.

5 The Anti-Vietnam War Movement in the United States

1. For events of the anti-war movement described in this essay see Tom Wells, *The War Within: America's Battle Over Vietnam* (Berkeley, 1994). Among the many other books worth consulting on the movement are Charles De Benedetti, *An American Ordeal: The Antiwar Movement of the Vietnam Era* (Syracuse, NY, 1990); Fred Halstead, *Out Now! A Participant's Account of the American Movement Against the Vietnam War* (New York, 1978); Nancy Zaroulis and Gerald Sullivan, *Who Spoke Up? American Protest Against the War in Vietnam, 1963–1975* (Garden City, NY, 1984); Kirkpatrick Sale, *SDS* (New York, 1973).

2. Chester Cooper memo 23 August 1965, meeting of Public Affairs Policy Committee for Vietnam, National Security File, Country File, Vietnam, box 197, Lyndon Baines Johnson Library (hereafter LBJL).

3. *Washington Post*, 10 May 1984.

4. See, for example, Wells, *The War Within*, p. 137.

5. Don Oberdorfer, 'The "Wobble" on the War on Capitol Hill', *New York Times Magazine*, 17 December 1967, pp. 30–1 and 98–197.

6. Personal interview with Eugene McCarthy; McCarthy, *The Year of the People* (Garden City, NY, 1969) p. 45.

7. Philip E. Converse and Howard Schuman, '"Silent Majorities" and the Vietnam War', *Scientific American*, 222 (June 1970) p. 20 (see graph).

8. McGeorge Bundy to President Johnson, 10 November 1967, Vietnam Reference File, box 1, LBJL.

9. Sidney Verba and Richard A. Brody, 'Participation, Policy Preferences, and the War in Vietnam', *Public Opinion Quarterly*, 34 (Fall 1970) p. 329; Sidney

Verba, Richard A. Brody, Edwin B. Parker, Norman H. Nie, Nelson W. Polsby, Paul Ekman and Gordon S. Black, 'Public Opinion and the War in Vietnam', *American Political Science Review* 61 (June 1967) pp. 325–6.

10. Harlan Hahn, 'Correlates of Public Sentiments about War: Local Referenda on the Vietnam Issue', *American Political Science Review*, 64 (December 1970) pp. 1190–2.
11. *Washington Post*, 18 December 1967.
12. Daniel Hallin, *The 'Uncensored War': The Media and Vietnam* (Berkeley, 1989) pp. 188, 198; Todd Gitlin, *The Whole World is Watching: Mass Media in the Making and Unmaking of the New Left* (Berkeley, 1980) pp. 219–21.
13. On GI dissent, see David Cortright, *Soldiers in Revolt: The American Military Today* (Garden City, NY 1975).
14. On labour's attitudes towards the war, see Wells, *The War Within*, pp. 63, 138, 143, 219, 366, 427, 447, 496, 563, 642. On the Nixon White House's involvement in pro-war activity by labour, see ibid, pp. 426, 447, 478, 509; various documents in White House Special Files, Colson, boxes 20, 95, Nixon Project (hereafter NP).
15. Col. Robert D. Heinl Jr, 'The Collapse of the Armed Forces', *Armed Forces Journal*, 7 June 1971 (reprint) p. 3.
16. *Washington Post*, 3 May 1971.
17. Wells, *The War Within*, pp. 247, 254–7, 306.
18. Personal interview with H.R. Haldeman.
19. Personal interview with Lawrence Eagleburger.
20. Personal interview with Richard Helms.
21. See, for example, documents in the White House Central Files, Confidential File, HU,box 57, LBJL; Personal Papers of Warren Christopher, box 8, LBJL; White House Central Files, HU, boxes 59, 60, LBJL; White House Central Files, Aides Files, Nimetz, box 14, LBJL; White House Special Files, Dean, boxes 80, 81, 82, 83, 84, 85, 86, NP; White House Special Files, Haldeman, boxes 40, 41, 43, 121, 130, NP; White House Special Files, Ehrlichman, boxes 3, 20, NP; White House Central Files, HU, box 24, NP.
22. Wells, *The War Within*, pp. 375, 492, 496–7, 499, 504, 506–7, 509–10, 540, 543, 546.
23. Action Memorandum to John Ehrlichman, 24 June 1969, White House Special Files, Krogh, box 57, NP.
24. President Johnson to Ramsey Clark, 3 October 1967, Diary Backup, box 80, LBJL; Wells, *The War Within*, Joseph Califano to President Johnson, 21 October 1967, 11:20 a.m., 11:55 a.m., 1:55 p.m., 3:00 p.m., White House Central Files, Aides Files, Nimetz, box 14, LBJL.
25. On the Johnson and Nixon administrations' efforts to counter the movement, including those efforts discussed here, see Wells, *The War Within*, passim.
26. Wells, *The War Within*, pp. 439–41.
27. *Ibid*. p. 4, 5, 33, 69, 135, 183, 190, 204–11, 252, 312–15, 415, 448, 514, 517, 617.
28. Personal interview with George Christian.
29. Personal interview with Thomas Moorer.

30. Personal interview with Richard Helms.
31. CIA, 'International Connections of the U.S. Peace Movement', 15 November 1967 National Security File, Intelligence File, box 3, LBJL.
32. Wells, *The War Within*, pp. 4, 211–12, 315–18.
33. *ibid.* p.102.
34. George Christian, *The President Steps Down: A Personal Memoir of the Transfer of Power* (New York, 1970), p. 159.
35. Personal interview with Craig McNamara.
36. Wells, *The War Within*, pp. 106–12, 197, 198, 366, 373–74, 422, 430, 432, 605.
37. Personal interview with Craig McNamara.
38. Personal interview with Paul Nitze.
39. Personal interview with William Watts; Seymour Hersch, *The Price of Power: Kissinger in the Nixon White House* (New York, 1983) p.131.
40. Personal interview with Paul Warnke.
41. On the movement's impact on US politics in Vietnam during the Johnson and Nixon administrations, see Wells, *The War Within*, pp. 4–5, 105, 151, 152–3, 154, 155–7, 158, 252, 254–7, 288, 289, 290, 308, 326, 345, 377–9, 397, 415, 434–5, 463, 470, 512–13, 535, 541, 562–3, 579–80.
42. Phone interview with Clark Clifford; Clifford, 'A Vietnam Reappraisal: The Personal History of One Man's View and How It Evolved', *Foreign Affairs*, 47 (July 1969) p. 612.
43. Townsend Hoopes, *The Limits of Intervention: An Inside Account of How the Johnson Policy of Escalation in Vietnam Was Reversed* (New York: 1973), p. 216.
44. Thomas Powers, *Vietnam: The War at Home* (New York: 1) p. 72.
45. Personal interview with Morton Halperin.
46. Henry Kissinger, *White House Years* (Boston: 1979) pp. 507 and 516.
47. On the movement's impact on public opinion, elites, Congress and the media, see Wells, *The War Within*, pp. 37–38, 76–7, 85–6, 120–1, 123, 136–7, 192, 219, 250–1, 257–61, 299, 300–3, 365, 427, 513, 568, 573, 574, 575, 576–7.
48. Personal interview with John Oakes.
49. Personal interview with Tom Wicker.
50. Personal interview with Theodore Hesburgh.
51. Personal interview with John Oakes.
52. Personal interview with Arthur Schlesinger.
53. Personal interview with Richard Helms.
54. Haldeman's notes of 4 May 1971, meeting with Nixon, White House Special Files, Haldeman, box 43, NP.
55. Personal interviews with Eric Sevareid, James Reston, John Sherman Cooper, Eugene McCarthy, John Oakes, Theodore Hesburgh, Arthur Schlesinger and Tom Wicker.
56. Personal interview with H.R. Haldeman.
57. Personal interview with Richard Helms.
58. Among the many books worth consulting on the Watergate scandal itself are Fred Emery, *Watergate: The Corruption of American Politics and the Fall of Richard Nixon* (New York, 1994); J. Anthony Lukas, *Nightmare: The*

Underside of the Nixon Years (New York, 1976); Stanley I. Kutler, *The Wars of Watergate: The Last Crisis of Richard Nixon* (New York, 1990).
59. Wells, *The War Within*, pp. 290–2, 548, 570, 571.
60. *Ibid*. pp. 412–15, 448–9, 548, 570.
61. *Ibid*. pp. 359–64, 515–21, 541–2, 548, 569, 570, 574.
62. *Ibid*. pp. 517, 518–19, 548.
63. *Ibid*. pp. 309–10, 521, 549, 569–71, 573; Hersh, *Price of Power*, pp. 637–38.
64. On the harmful effects of infighting and protesters' failure to appreciate their power, see Wells, *The War Within, passim*.
65. Personal interview with Bettina Aptheker.
66. Personal interview with Doug Dowd.

6   Developing an Alliance: The Soviet Union and Vietnam, 1954–75

1. For the details on the 1954 Geneva conference on Indo-China and for an analysis of its final documents see Robert F. Randle, *Geneva 1954: The Settlement of the Indochinese War* (Princeton, 1969).
2. David L. Anderson, *Trapped by Success: The Eisenhower Administration and Vietnam, 1953–1961* (New York, 1991) p. 63.
3. See, for example, Anthony Eden, *Full Circle: The Memoirs of Anthony Eden* (Boston, 1960); James Cable, *The Geneva Conference of 1954 on Indochina* (London, 1986); Francois Joyaux, *La Chine et le réglement du premier conflict d'Indochine (Genève 1954)* (Paris, 1979); Randle, op. cit.
4. Memorandum of Conversation, Molotov–Eden, 21 July 1954. Arkhiv vneshnei politiki Rossiiskoi Federatzii (Archive of the Foreign Policy of the Russian Federation, hereafter AVPRF), fond 06, opis' 13a, papka 25, delo 8, list 120.
5. Verbatim Record of the Final Plenary Session, 21 July 1954. AVPRF, f. 0445, op. 1., p. 6, d. 27, l. 108.
6. Addendum 1 to the draft of the Resolution of the CPSU CC, 'Instructions for the Talks with the Governmental Delegation of the Democratic Republic of Vietnam'. AVPRF, f. 022, op. 8, p. 177, d.30, ll. 12, 14. See also the same document, AVPRF, f. 06, op. 14, p. 12, d. 171, ll. 15–24.
7. Anderson, *Trapped by Success*, p. 126.
8. Final Declaration on Indochina, 21 July 1954. Lloyd C. Gardner, *Approaching Vietnam. From World War II Through Dienbienphu* (New York, 1988) appendix, p. 416.
9. Memorandum of Conversation, Pham Van Dong–K.V. Novikov, the head of the Foreign Ministry South-East Asia Department, 27 July 1954. AVPRF, f. 06, op. 13a, p. 35, d. 158, ll. 45–46.
10. K. V. Novikov to Vyacheslav Molotov, 29 July 1954. ibid. ll. 1–2.
11. Draft of the 'Joint Communique of the Soviet Government and the Government of the Democratic Republic of Vietnam', undated. ibid. f. 06, op. 14, p. 12, d. 172, ll. 52–56.

12. USSR Foreign Ministry Memorandum 'On Economic and Technical Assistance Rendered by the Soviet Union to the DRV', 3 December 1955, AVPRF, f. 079, op. 10, p. 10, d. 15, ll. 61–62.
13. Memorandum of conversation, K.V. Novikov–Nguyen Long Bang, 9 August 1954. ibid. op. 9, p. 6, d. 5, l. 63.
14. AVPRF, f. 079, op. 9, p. 6, d. 5, ll. 68, 75.
15. 'Instructions for the Talks with the Governmental Delegation of the Democratic Republic of Vietnam', l. 19.
16. General Antonov to Deputy Foreign Minister Valerian Zorin, 10 June 1955, AVPRF, f. 079, op. 10, p. 9, d. 8, l. 32.
17. Memorandum of Conversation, Mikhail Zimianin–Ho Chi Minh, Pham Van Dong, Vo Nguyen Giap, 17 March 1956. ibid. op. 11, p. 13, d. 5, l. 15.
18. Political letter of the Soviet embassy in the DRV, 'Some Questions of Coordination of Economic and Scientific-Technical Aid by the Countries of the Socialist Camp', 28 April 1960. ibid. op. 15, p. 28, d. 3, l. 2.
19. James R. Arnold, *The First Domino: Eisenhower, the Military, and America's Intervention in Vietnam* (New York, 1991) pp. 307–8.
20. *Ibid.* p. 310.
21. Molotov to the CPSU CC, top secret, 19 May 1955. AVPRF, f. 06,op. 14, p. 12, d. 170, l. 1; Draft of the telegram to Paris. ibid. f. 079, op. 10, p. 9, d. 8, l. 14.
22. Lloyd C. Gardner, *Approaching Vietnam*, p. 314.
23. Memorandum of conversation, Truong Chinh–L. Sokolov, chargé d'affaires ad interim, September 1955. AVPRF, f. 079, op. 10, p. 9, d. 5, l. 133.
24. *Boevoi Avangard V'etnamskogo Naroda. Istoriia Kommunisticheshoi Partii V'etnama* (Militant Vanguard of the Vietnamese People. History of the Communist Party of Vietnam). Trans. from the Vietnamese (Moscow, 1981) p. 114–16.
25. Suren Mkhitarian, T. Mkhitarian, *V'etnamskaia Revolutziia: Voprosy Teorii i Praktiki* (The Vietnamese Revolution: Problems of Theory and Practice) (Moscow, 1986) p. 212.
26. *Ibid.* p. 213.
27. Political Letter of the Soviet embassy in the DRV, 'The IIIrd Congress of the Workers' Party of Vietnam'. 26 September 1960. AVPRF, f. 079, op. 15, p. 28, d. 3, l. 13.
28. In a telegram to the Soviet ambassador in Paris that contains Moscow's evaluation of the 1964 visit, the CPSU Central Committee reached a conclusion: 'In general, the meeting of the representatives of the CPSU and WPV showed that the WPV leadership occupied obviously pro-Chinese attitude toward a number of the most important issues of our times. However, the behaviour of the Vietnamese delegates, the tone of their presentations led us to conclude that the CPSU and other fraternal parties have the possibility to maintain and develop contacts with the WPV, while patiently explaining to the Vietnamese comrades the general course of the world communist movement as it was defined by the Moscow conferences of 1957 and 1960 and demonstrating the disastrous effect of the present course of the Chinese splitters and those who support them'. Tzentre Khraneniia Sovremennoi

Docimentatzii (Storage Center for Contemporary Documentation, here-after SCCD), fond 4, optis' 18, delo 582, St-95/462g, March 15, 1964.

29. Robert S. McNamara with Brian Van De Mark, *In Retrospect: The Tragedy and Lessons of Vietnam* (New York, 1995) pp. 131–8.

30. SCCD, f. 5, op. 59, d. 332, l. 26; op. 60, d. 375, l. 48; National Security Archive, V-23–24, Westmoreland vs. CBS, col. IV, box 2.

31. Memorandum 'Value of Soviet Military Aid to North Vietnam', 26 October 1965, Library of Congress, Manuscript Division, W. Averell Harriman papers, Special Files, Subject File: Vietnam, General, box 520.

32. Political report of the Soviet embassy in the DRV for 1966. SCCD, f. 5, op. 58, d. 263, l. 148; Political report for 1967. ibid. op. 59, d. 332, l. 26; Political report for 1968. ibid. op. 609, d. 375, l. 48.

33. Political report for 1967, SCCD, f. 5, op. 59, d. 332, l. 27.

34. Political report for 1966, *ibid*, op. 58, d. 263, l. 150.

35. Main Intelligence Directorate of the General Staff (GRU) to the CPSU CC International Department, 1 December 1966. SCCD, f. 5, op. 598, d. 254, l. 172.

36. Douglas Pike, *Vietnam and the Soviet Union: Anatomy of an Alliance* (London, 1987) pp. 56–7.

37. Political report of the Soviet embassy in Hanoi for 1966. SCCD, f. 5, op. 58, d. 263, l. 130.

38. Political letter 'On the Political Situation in South Vietnam and the DRV Position', 19 November 1964. SCCD, f. 5, op. 50, d. 631, l. 253.

39. Memorandum of Conversation, Harriman-Zorin, 18 January 1969. Harri-man papers, Special Files: Public Service, Subject File: Paris Peace Talks, box 559.

40. Political report of the Soviet embassy in the DRV for 1969. SCCD, f. 5, op. 61, d. 459, l. 126; 'List of the Principal Agreements Between the USSR and the DRV', undated. ibid. op. 66, d. 71, ll. 120–2.

41. Political letter of the Soviet embassy in the DRV 'On the Possibilities and Specifics of Coordination of the DRV Foreign Policy with the Soviet Union and Other Socialist Countries', 25 June 1970. SCCD, f. 5, op. 62, d. 492, l. 149.

42. Political letter of the Soviet embassy in the DRV 'On the Policy of the Workers' Party of Vietnam Toward Resolution of the Problems of Indo-china and On Our Tasks Followed from the Decisions of the XXIV CPSU Congress', 21 May 1971. ibid. f. 5, op. 63, d. 516, l. 1.

43. CPSU CC Secretariat to the Soviet ambassadors in Hanoi and Vientiane, 30 November 1972. SCCD, f. 4, op. 22, d. 1015, St- 64/15g.

44. Memorandum of Conversation, Soviet ambassador Ilia Scherbakov–Le Thanh Nghi, deputy prime minister, 20 March 1973. SCCD, f. 5, op. 66, d. 782, ll. 40, 44.

45. USSR Ministry of Foreign Affairs South-East Asia Department's memor-andum 'Soviet-Vietnamese Relations at the Present Stage', 4 July 1973. SCCD, f. 5, op. 66, d. 71, ll. 74–5.

46. USSR Ministry of Foreign Affairs South-East Asian Department's memor-andum 'Soviet–Vietnamese Relations at the Present Stage', top secret, 4 December 1973. ibid. d. 779, l. 153.

47. USSR Ministry of Foreign Affairs South-East Asian Department's memor-
    andum 'Toward the Situation in the Workers' Party of Vietnam', 4 July
    1973. SCCD, f. 5, op. 66, d. 71, l. 83.
48. Boris Ponomarev to the CPSU CC 'On the Proposal to the Vietnamese
    Friends', 12 February 1974. SCCD, f. 4, op. 22, d. 1240, St-113/10g.

7   China and the Vietnam Wars

1. For a Chinese account, see Huang Zhen, *Ho Chiming he zhongguo* (Ho Chi
   Minh and China, Beijing, 1987) chapters 1–4.
2. Luo Guibo, 'The Inside Story of China's Support to Vietnam', *Shiji* (Cen-
   tury) no. 2, 1993, pp. 11–12; interview with Luo Guibo, August 1992.
3. For a more detailed account of the Liu–Stalin meeting, see Shi Zhe, 'With
   Mao and Stalin: The Reminiscences of a Chinese Interpreter, Part II: Liu
   Shaoqi in Moscow' (trans. by Chen Jian), *Chinese Historians*, vol. 6, no. 1
   (Spring 1993) pp. 1–24 (Shi Zhe was Mao Zedong's Russian language
   interpreter). For the Mao–Stalin meeting, see Pei Jianzhang (chief ed.),
   Zhonghua renmin gongheguo waijiaoshi (A Diplomatic History of the People's
   Republic of China, Beijing, 1993) p. 18.
4. Luo Guibo, 'The Inside Story of China's Support to Vietnam', pp. 11–12;
   interview with Luo Guibo, August 1992.
5. Pei Jianzhang (chief ed.), *Zhonghua renmin gongheguo waijiaoshi*, p. 89.
6. Luo Guibo, 'The Inside Story of China's Support to Vietnam', pp. 13–14.
7. Li Ke, 'Chinese Military Advisers in the War to Assist Vietnam and Resist
   France', *Junshi lishi* (Military History) no. 3, 1989, p. 27; Luo Guibo, 'The
   Inside Story of China's Support to Vietnam', p. 14; Han Huanzhi *et al.*,
   Dangdai zhongguo jundui de junshi gongzuo (The Military Affairs of Contemporary Chinese Army, Beijing, 1988) vol. 1, pp. 520, 576.
8. Han, *Dangdai zhongguo jundui de junshi gongzuo*, vol. 1, pp. 518–20; Editorial Group for the History of Chinese Military Advisers in Vietnam (eds),
   Zhonguo junshi guwentuan yuanyue kangfa douzheng shishi (A Factual Account
   of the Participation of Chinese Military Advisory Group in Vietnam, Beijing, 1990) pp. 3–4.
9. Editorial Group, *Zhonguo junshi guwentuan yuanyue kangfa douzheng shishi*,
   pp. 5–7.
10. Xu Peilai and Zheng Pengfei, *Chen Geng jiangjun zhuan* (A Biography of
    General Chen Geng, Beijing, 1988) pp. 580–1.
11. Han, *Dangdai zhongguo jundui de junshi gongzuo*, vol. 1, pp. 521–2; Chen
    Gen, *Chen Geng riji* (Chen Geng's Diaries, Beijing, 1984) vol. 2,
    pp. 9, 11.
12. Editorial Group, *Zhonguo junshi guwentuan yuanyue kangfa douzheng shishi*,
    pp. 44–6.
13. Chen, *Chen Geng riji*, vol. 2, 39–42; Hani, *Dangdai zhongguo jundui de junshi
    gongzuo*, vol. 1, pp. 524–7; Editorial Group, *Zhonguo junshi guwentuan
    yuanyue kangfa douzheng shishi*, p. 25.

14. For a more detailed discussion, see Chen Jian, 'China and the First Indo-China War', *China Quarterly*, no. 133 (March 1993) pp. 94–6.
15. Editorial Group, *Zhonguo junshi guwentuan yuanyue kangfa douzheng shishi*, p. 30.
16. *Ibid.* pp. 52, 56.
17. Han, *Dangdai zhongguo jundui de junshi gongzuo*, vol. 1.
18. Editorial Group, *Zhonguo junshi guwentuan yuanyue kangfa douzheng shishi*, p. 87.
19. Han, *Dangdai zhongguo jundui de junshi gongzuo*, vol. 1, p. 529; Editorial Group, *Zhonguo junshi guwentuan yuanyue kangfa douzheng shishi*, pp. 88–9.
20. Editorial Group, *Zhonguo junshi guwentuan yuanyue kangfa douzheng shishi*, pp. 89–90.
21. Han, *Dangdai zhongguo jundui de junshi gongzuo*, vol. 1, p. 530.
22. Mao Zedong to Peng Dehuai, 3 April 1954, and Mao Zedong to Peng Dehuai and Huang Kecheng, 28 April 1954, *Jianguo yilai Mao Zedong wengao* (Mao Zedong's Manuscripts since the Founding of the People's Republic, Beijing, 1987–) vol. 4, pp. 474–5, vol. 5, p. 91.
23. Han, *Dangdai zhongguo jundui de junshi gongzuo*, vol. 1, p. 532; Editorial Group, *Zhonguo junshi guwentuan yuanyue kangfa douzheng shishi*, p. 114.
24. Chen Geng, *Chen Geng riji*, vol. 2, pp. 22, 31.
25. Xue Mouhong *et al.*, *Dangdai zhongguo waijiao* (Contemporary Chinese Diplomacy, Beijing, 1988) p. 65.
26. Wang Bingnan, *Zhongmei huitan jiunian* (Recollections of the Nine Year Sino-American Talks, Beijing, 1985) pp. 5–6.
27. Shi Zhe, 'Random Recollections of the Geneva Conference', *Renwu* (Biological Journal) no. 1, 1989, pp. 37–8; Li Lianqing, *Da waijiaojia Zhou Enlai: shezhan rineiwa* (The Great Diplomat Zhou Enlai: The Geneva Debate, Hong Kong, 1994) pp. 85–6.
28. Li Haiwen, 'The Role Zhou Enlai Played at the Geneva Conference for Restoring Peace in Indo-China', unpublished paper (cited with author's permission), pp. 1–2; Li, *Da waijiaojia Zhou Enlai: shezhan rineiwa*, p. 86.
29. Guo Ming *et al.*, *Zhongyue guanxi yanbian sishinian* (Forty-Year Evolution of Sino-Vietnamese Relations, Nanning, 1992) p. 100.
30. Qu Xing, 'On Zhou Enlai's Diplomacy at the Geneva Conference of 1954', in Pei Jianzhang *et al.*, *Yanjiu Zhou Enlai – waijiao sixiang yu shijian* (Studying Zhou Enlai's Diplomatic Thought and Practices, Beijing, 1989) pp. 255–6; Guo, *Zhongyue guanxi yanbian sishinian*, pp. 100–1.
31. Qu, 'On Zhou Enlai's Diplomacy at the Geneva Conference of 1954', p. 257; and Li, *Da waifiaojia Zhou Enlai: shezhan rineiwa*, p. 276.
32. Qu, 'On Zhou Enlai's Diplomacy at the Geneva Conference of 1954', pp. 257–8; Wang, *Zhongmei huitan jiunian*, p. 13.
33. Qu, 'On Zhou Enlai's Diplomacy at the Geneva Conference of 1954', p. 257.
34. Ho Chi Minh, 'Report to the Sixth Meeting of the VWP Central Committee', 15 July 1954, *Selected Works of Ho Chi Minh* (Hanoi, 1963) vol. 2, pp. 290–8.
35. Li, *Da waijiaojia Zhou Enlai: shezhan rineiwa*, pp. 352–8; Qu, 'On Zhou Enlai's Diplomacy at the Geneva Conference of 1954', p. 258.

36. Shi Zhongquan, *Zhou Enlai de zhuoyue fengxian* (Zhou Enlai's Outstanding Contributions, Beijing, 1993) p. 286; Guo, *Zhongyue guanxi yanbian sishinian*, pp. 65–6.

37. Editorial Group, *Zhongguo junshi guwentuan yuanyue kangfa douzheng shishi*, pp. 142–3.

38. Guo, *Zhongyue guanxi yanbian sishinian*, p. 66; for a Vietnamese version of the story, see *The Truth about Vietnamo-Chinese Relations over the Past Thirty Years* (Hanoi, 1979) pp. 29–33.

39. Guo, *Zhongyue guanxi yanbian sishinian*, p. 67; and the Institute of Diplomatic History under Chinese Foreign Ministry (eds), *Zhou Enlai waijiao huodong dashiji, 1949–1975* (A Chronicle of Zhou Enlai's Important Diplomatic Activities, Beijing 1993), pp. 279–80.

40. Li Ke and Hao Shengzhang, *Wenhua dageming zhong de renmin jiefangjun* (The People's Liberation Army during the Cultural Revolution, Beijing 1989), pp. 408–9.

41. Guo, *Zhongyue guanxi yanbian sishinian*, p. 69; Wang Xiangen, *Kangmei yuanyue shilu* (A Factual Account of Resisting America and Assisting Vietnam, Beijing 1990), pp. 25–6.

42. Qu Aiguo, 'Chinese Supporters in the Operations to Assist Vietnam and Resist America', *Junshi shilin* (The Circle of Military History) no. 6, 1989, p. 40.

43. *ibid.* p. 40.

44. Tong Xiaopeng, *Fengyu sishi nian* (Forty Years of Storms, Beijing, 1996) vol. 2, pp. 219–20. Tong was the long- time head of Zhou Enlai's administrative office.

45. Li and Hao, *Wenhua dageming zhong de jiefangjun*, p. 418.

46. Qu, 'Chinese Supporters in the Operations to Assist Vietnam and Resist America', p. 40.

47. See *Zhou Enlai waijiao huodong dashi ji*, p. 413.

48. Li Ke, 'Chinese People's Support in Assisting Vietnam and Resisting America Will be Remembered by History', *Junshi ziliao* (Military History Materials) no. 4, 1989, p. 30; and Tong Xiaopeng, *Fengyu sishi nian*, vol. 2, pp. 220–1.

49. Cong Jin, *Quzhe quianjin de shinian* (The Decade of Tortuous Advance, Zhengzhou, 1989) pp. 505–24; Zheng Qian, 'The Nationwide War Preparations Before and After the CCP's Ninth Congress', *Zonggong dangshi ziliao* (CCP History Materials) no. 41 (April 1992) p. 205.

50. See Wang Jiaxiang's report to the CCP Central Committee, 29 June 1962; the original of the document is kept at Chinese Central Archives. An abridged version of the report is published in *Wang Jiaxiang xuanji* (Selected Works of Wang Jiaxiang, Beijing, 1989) pp. 446–60, which, however, omits the part on Chinese policy towards Vietnam.

51. Cong, *Quzhe qianjin de shinian*, pp. 576–7, 579.

52. Li and Hao, *Wenhua dageming zhong de jiefangjun*, p. 408; Qu, 'Chinese Supporters in the Operations to Assist Vietnam and Resist America', p. 40; and *Beijing Review*, 30 November 1979, p. 14.

53. Wang Dinglie *et al.*, *Dangdai zhongguo kongjun* (Contemporary Chinese Air Force, Beijing, 1989) p. 384.

54. Liu Yuti and Jiao Hongguang, 'The Operations Against Invading American Planes in the Chinese–Vietnamese Border Area in Guangxi' in Wang Renshen *et al.*, *Kongjun: huiyi shiliao* (The Air Force: Memoirs and Reminiscences, Beijing, 1992) pp. 559–60. Liu was then the Seventh Army's deputy commander and Jiao was deputy political commissar.

55. Wang, *Dangdai zhongguo kongjun*, p. 384.

56. *Renmin ribao*, 7 and 12 August 1965.

57. *Renmin ribao*, 25 and 30 March 1965.

58. Zhou Enlai's conversation with Ayub Khan, 2 April 1965, *Zhou Enlai waijiao wenxuan* (Selected Diplomatic Papers of Zhou Enlai, Beijing, 1990) pp. 436–43.

59. Zheng, 'The Nationwide War Preparations Before and After the CCP's Ninth Congress', p. 205; Qu, 'Chinese Supporters in the Operations to Assist Vietnam and Resist America', p. 41.

60. Li and Hao, *Wenhua dageming zhong de jiefangjun*, p. 415; Wang, *Kangmei yuanyue shilu*, p. 44; Han, *Dangdai zhongguo jundui de junshi gongzuo*, vol. 1, 539–40; Shi Yingfu, *Mimi chubing yare conglin* (Sending Troops Secretly to the Sub-Tropical Jungles, Beijing, 1990) pp. 14–16.

61. Wang, *Kangmei yuanyue shilu*, pp. 39–44; Li and Hao, *Wenhua dageming zhong de jiefangjun*, p. 422.

62. Andong is a border city on the Yalu. During the Korean War, Chinese and Soviet air forces used bases on the China side of the Sino-Korean border to fight the American air force over northern Korea. This was known as the 'Andong model'.

63. Li and Hao, *Wenhua dageming zhong de jiefangjun*, p. 417.

64. Han, *Dangdai zhongguo jundui de junshi gongzuo*, vol. 1, p. 545; Li and Hao, *Wenhua dageming zhong de jiefangjun*, p. 421; Wang, *Kangmei yuanyue shilu*, pp. 100–1.

65. Wang, *Kangmei yuanyue shilu*, p. 46; and Li and Hao, *Wenhua dageming zhong de jiefangjun*, p. 422.

66. Han, *Dangdai zhongguo jundui de junshi gongzuo*, vol. 1, p. 548.

67. Qu, 'Chinese Supporters in the Operations to Assist Vietnam and Resist America', pp. 41–2; Han, *Dangdai zhongguo jundui de junshi gongzuo*, vol. 1, pp. 545–7.

68. Li and Hao, *Wenhua dageming zhong de jiefangjun*, pp. 418–9; Han, *Dangdai zhongguo jundui de junshi gongzuo*, vol. 1, pp. 540–1.

69. Li and Hao, *Wenhua dageming zhong de jiefangjun*, pp. 420; Han, *Dangdai zhongguo jundui de junshi gongzuo*, vol. 1, pp. 543.

70. Han, *Dangdai zhongguo jundui de junshi gongzuo*, vol. 1, p. 548; Qu, 'Chinese Supporters in the Operations to Assist Vietnam and Resist America', pp. 41–2.

71. Han, *Dangdai zhongguo jundui de junshi gongzuo*, vol. 1, p. 550.

72. Qu, 'Chinese Supporters in the Operations to Assist Vietnam and Resist America', p. 42; Han, *Dangdai zhongguo jundui de junshi gongzuo*, vol. 1, pp. 540–1.

73. This summary of the operations of Chinese anti-aircraft artillery forces in Vietnam is based on the following sources: Han, *Dangdai zhongguo jundui*

de junshi gongzuo, vol. 1, pp. 550–3; Qu, 'Chinese Supporters in the Operations to Assist Vietnam and Resist America', p. 43; Wang, *Dangdai zhongguo kongjun*, chapter 17.

74. Cong, *Quzhe qianjin de shinian*, p. 467.
75. Li and Hao, *Wenhua dageming zhong de jiefangjun*, pp. 410–11.
76. For a detailed discussion, see John W. Garver, 'Sino- Vietnamese Conflict and the Sino-American Rapprochement', *Political Science Quarterly*, vol. 96, no. 3 (Fall 1981) pp. 445–64.
77. Allen Whiting, *The Chinese Calculus of Deterrence: India and Vietnam* (Ann Arbor, 1975) pp. 194–5; and Garver, 'Sino-Vietnamese Conflict and the Sino-American Rapprochement', *Political Science Quarterly*, vol. 96, no. 3 (Fall 1981) pp. 447–8.
78. Wang, *Kangmei yuanyue shilu*, pp. 61–72.
79. *Ibid.* p. 74.
80. For a discussion, see R.B. Smith, *An International History of the Vietnam War* (London, 1983–91) vol. 2, chapter 12; vol. 3, chapter 9.
81. For a more detailed description of Mao's conversation with Kosygin, see Cong, *Quzhe qianjin de shinian*, pp. 607–8.
82. Wang, *Kangmei yuanyue shilu*, p. 226.
83. According to official Chinese sources, during the entire period of the Vietnam War, China 'helped transfer 5750 train trucks of materials in aid from other socialist countries to Vietnam, including materials from the Soviet Union'. ibid. p. 226.
84. Quan Yanchi and Du Weidong, *Gongheguo mishi* (The Secret Envoys from the [Peoples] Republic, Beijing, 1990) pp. 249–51; and Hu Zhengqing, *Yige waijiaoguan de riji* (A Diplomat's Diary, Jinan, 1991), pp. 161–6.
85. Quan and Du, *Gongheguo mishi*, pp. 250–1.
86. Guo, *Zhongyue guanxi yanbian sishinian*, p. 68; see also Garver, 'Sino-Vietnamese Conflict and the Sino-American Rapprochement', pp. 448–50.
87. The Institute of Diplomatic History under Chinese Foreign Ministry, *Zhou Enlai waijiao huodong dashiji, 1949–1975*, p. 524.
88. *Ibid.* pp. 524–5.
89. See Gong Li, *Kuayue honggou: zhongmei guanxi de yanbian, 1969–1979* (Bridging the Chasm: The Evolution of Sino-American Relations, 1969–1979, Zhengzhou, 1992) p. 40.
90. For a detailed account of the activities of this group, see Xiong Xianghui, 'The Prelude to the Opening of Sino-American Relations', *Zhonggong dangshi ziliao* (CCP History Materials) no. 42 (June 1992) pp. 56–96.
91. See *Mao Zuxi 1970nian yu sinuo de tanhua* (Chairman Mao's Talks with [Edgar] Snow in 1970, Beijing, 1970).
92. For the Indo-China part of the CCP Politburo's resolution on improving relations with the United States, see Gong, *Kuayue honggou*, pp. 105–6; on Zhou's visit to Hanoi and meetings with Duan and Dong, see The Institute of Diplomatic History under Chinese Foreign Ministry, *Zhou Enlai waijiao huodong dashiji*, pp. 596–7.
93. Guo, *Zhongyue guanxi yanbian sishinian*, pp. 102–3.
94. Guo, *Zhongyue guanxi yanbian sishinian*, p. 103.

95. Li and Hao, *Wenhua dageming zhong de renmin jiefangjun*, p. 416.
96. Qu, 'Chinese Supporters in the Operations to Assist Vietnam and Resist America', p. 43; Yang Guoyu *et al.*, *Dangdai zhongguo haijun* (Contemporary Chinese Navy, Beijing, 1988) pp. 421–9; and Ma Faxiang, 'Zhou Enlai Directs the Operations of Helping Vietnam Sweep Mines', *Junshi lishi* (Military History) no. 5, 1989, pp. 35–7.

8   Australia and the Vietnam War

1. A version of this Chapter was read as a paper to the 14th Conference of the International Association of Historians of Asia, Chulalongkorn University, Bangkok, May 1996.
2. For example, Gabriel Kolko, *Vietnam: Anatomy of A War, 1940–75* (New York, 1986) ignores them altogether, and Michael Maclear, *Vietnam: The Ten Thousand Day War* (London, 1981) has five short mentions.
3. For good accounts see Peter Edwards, *Crises and Commitments: The Politics and Diplomacy of Australia's Involvement in South East Asian Conflicts, 1948–1965* (Canberra, 1992), and Gregory Pemberton, *All the Way: Australia's Road to Vietnam* (Sydney, 1987).
4. See Eric Andrews, *Australia and China. An Ambiguous Relationship* (Melbourne, 1987).
5. See Gregory Clark, *Fear of China* (Melbourne, 1967).
6. In a press conference in April 1954, probably quoting US political columnist Joseph Alsop; see Nigel Rees, *Sayings of the Century* (London, 1987) p. 212.
7. For example, 'With the black cloud of Communist China hanging to the north, we must make sure that our children do not end up pulling rickshaws with hammer and sickle signs on their sides,' R.G. Casey, Menzies' foreign minister, told a party gathering in 1954; *The Age*, 13 May 1954, cited in John Murphy, *Harvest of Fear: A History of Australia's Vietnam War* (Sydney 1993) pp. xvii–xviii.
8. For accounts, see Ann Curthoys and John Merritt (eds.), *Australia's First cold war*, 2 vols (Sydney 1985–6); Robert Manne, *The Petrov Affair* (Sydney, 1987); Robert Murray, *The Split* (Melbourne, 1970).
9. See Ritchie Ovendale, 'The cold war, 1949–51', in Carl Bridge (ed.), *Munich to Vietnam* (Melbourne, 1991) p.58.
10. The term is R.G. Menzies's: *Commonwealth* [of Australia] *Parliamentary Debates*, 29 March 1962.
11. Robert Korner's term in a memorandum of 1961 for the US National Security Council, cited in Pemberton, *All the Way*, p. 86.
12. On task force thinking, see Ian McNeill, 'The Australian Army and the Vietnam War', in Peter Pierce *et al.* (eds.), *Vietnam Days* (Melbourne, 1991) ch. 1.
13. For a contemporary analysis of Australia's new defence policies, see T.B. Millar, *Australia's Defence*, 2nd edn (Melbourne, 1968).
14. McNeill, 'The Australian Army and the Vietnam War', pp. 17–18.

15. Renouf to Canberra, 11 May 1964, cited in Michael Sexton, *War for the Asking: Australia's Vietnam Secrets* (Melbourne 1981), p. 44.

16. Entry for 19 May 1966 in Don Aitkin (ed.), *The Howson Diaries. The Life of Politics* (Melbourne, 1987) p.223. Howson was Minister for Air.

17. For example, Frank Frost, *Australia's War in Vietnam* (Sydney, 1987) and Terry Burstall, *Vietnam, The Australian Dilemma*, (Brisbane, 1993).

18. The best short account is McNeill, 'The Australian Army and the Vietnam War'; see also Jeffrey Grey, *A Military History of Australia* (Melbourne, 1990) ch. 10.

19. McNeill, 'The Australian Army and the Vietnam War', pp.41–61; General Sir Phillip Bennett, 'Foreword' to J. M. Church, *Second to None. 2RAR as the ANZAC Battalion in Vietnam, 1970–71* (Sydney 1995) p. i.

20. Gary McKay, *In Good Company: One Man's War in Vietnam* (Sydney, 1987) pp. 80–2.

21. The best account is in Ian McNeill, *To Long Tan: The Australian Army and the Vietnam War, 1950–1966* (Canberra, 1993) pt 4.

22. McNeill, 'The Australian Army and the Vietnam War', p. 59.

23. Frost, op. cit., pp. 95–8 and chs 6–8.

24. McNeill, 'The Australian Army and the Vietnam War', p. 59.

25. Grey, op. cit., p. 238; Kolko, op. cit., p. 200; *Daily Telegraph* (London), 4 April 1995. There were also about 1000 Australian women in Vietnam during the war, nearly all of whom were civilians, and three women were killed; Siobhan McHugh, *Minefields and Miniskirts: Australian Women and the Vietnam War* (Sydney, 1993), pp. 50, 76.

26. Cited in Pemberton, *All the Way*, p. 327.

27. Peter King, 'Introduction' to Peter King (ed.), *Australia's Vietnam: Australia in the Second Indo-China War* (Sydney, 1983) p. 10.

28. For a comparative discussion see Ann Curthoys, 'The Anti-War Movements', in J. Grey and J. Doyle (eds), *Vietnam: War, Myth and Memory* (Sydney, 1992) ch. 6.

29. See the graphs in Murphy, op. cit., pp. 279–80.

30. *Commonwealth* [of Australia] *Parliamentary Debates*, 29 April 1965, 29 March 1966, and 4 May 1965. For a contemporary insider's perspective on the obsession with the China threat within Australian official circles at this time see Clark, op. cit. Clark points out that Hasluck, rather bizarrely, even sought to ally Australia with the Soviet Union against China, pp. 176–7. See also Clark, 'Vietnam, China and the Foreign Affairs Debate in Australia: A Personal Account', ch. 2 in King (ed.), *Australia's Vietnam*, pp. 18–21.

31. Patrick Lawnham, 'How LBJ Won Our Election', *The Australian*, 18 October 1966; Curthoys, op. cit., p. 93, and Curthoys, 'Mobilising Dissent' in Gregory Pemberton (ed.), *Vietnam Remembered* (Sydney, 1990), p. 146.

32. For an example of Whitlam's masterly fence-sitting in 1969, see Graham Freudenberg, *A Certain Grandeur: Gough Whitlam in Politics* (Ringwood, 1987), pp.166–9. See also Kim C. Beasley, 'Federal Labor and the Vietnam commitment', in King (ed.), *Australia's Vietnam* ch. 3.

33. Curthoys, 'Anti-War Movements', p. 96; personal experience.

34. *Sydney Morning Herald*, 24 July 1968, *Commonwealth* [of Australia] *Parliamentary Debates*, 7 May 1970; 'bikies' is Australian slang for 'Hell's Angels'.
35. *The Australian*, 13 July 1971.
36. Freudenberg, op. cit., ch. 15.
37. The figures are from Ann Marie Jordens, 'Conscription and Dissent' in Pemberton (ed.), *Vietnam Remembered*, pp. 67–70. For accounts of resistance to the draft see Michael E. Hamel-Green, 'The Resisters', ch. 6 in P. King (ed.), *Australia's Vietnam*; Bob Scates, *Draftmen Go Free: A History of the Anti-Conscription Movement in Australia* (Melbourne, 1988). There was, of course, conscription for home defence during the world wars, and conscripts were sent to New Guinea at a crucial stage of the Second World War.
38. Ken Inglis, 'ANZAC and the Australian military tradition', *Current Affairs Bulletin*, vol. 54, no. 11, 1988. For Matteson and his colleagues in the 'underground resistance' see Hamel-Green, op. cit., pp. 123–5.
39. See, for example, Margaret Reynolds' remarks in McHugh, op. cit., p. 252, and, more cautiously, Curthoys, 'Anti-War Movements', p.107, footnote 25.
40. Some of these issues are explored in Donald Home, *Time of Hope: Australia 1966–72* (Sydney, 1980) and Robin Gerster and Jan Bassett, *Seizures of Youth: 'The Sixties' and Australia* (Melbourne, 1991).
41. See the tables in Murphy, op. cit., pp. 279–80, and Murray Goot and Rodney Tiffen, 'Public Opinion and the Politics of the Polls', ch. 7 in P. King (ed.), *Australia's Vietnam*.
42. See G. Bolton, *Oxford History of Australia*, vol. 5 (Melbourne, 1990) p.172.
43. Jeff Doyle, 'Short-Timers' Endless Monuments' in Grey and Doyle (eds), op. cit., p.112.

9   International Aspects of the Vietnam War

1. Stephen E. Ambrose, *Eisenhower the President* (London, 1984) pp. 176–85.
2. James Cable, *The Geneva Conference of 1954 on Indochina* (Basingstoke and London, 1986).
3. *Ibid*. p. 141.
4. Public Record Office, Kew [PRO] CAB 129/68, c155(54).
5. PRO. PREM 11/645 folios 69–71.
6. *Foreign Relations of the United States* [FRUS] 1964–1968, vol. II, Vietnam January-June 1965 (Washington, 1996) pp. 716–17.
7. John F. Kennedy Library, Boston, Mass, Presidential Office Files, box 127, file 10, no.136.
8. *Ibid*. box 128, file 2, no.11.
9. PRO. FO371/170138,DV1212/1–2.
10. PRO. PREM 11/3736, 25 July 1961.
11. *Ibid*. 1 November 1961.
12. Lyndon B. Johnson Library, Austin Texas [LBJ Lib] National Security File [NSF], Memos to the President, box 3, file June 1965 (1 of 2), no. 10, p. 8.

13. Walt Rostow, *The Diffusion of Power* (New York, 1972) p. 280.
14. FRUS 1961–3, vol. XXIV, Laos Crisis (Washington, 1994) p. 708.
15. PRO FO371/170100, DV1017/14.
16. FRUS 1961–1963, vol. III (Washington, 1991) pp. 198–205.
17. Stephen E. Ambrose, *Nixon, The Triumph of a Politician 1962–72* (New York, 1989) p. 306; Henry A. Kissinger, *The White House Years* (London, 1979) p. 436.
18. LBJ Lib NSF, Country File UK, box 208, Memos vol. VI, 7/65–9/65 (2 of 2) no. 243; box 210, Memos vol. IX, no. 138; box 216, Wilson Briefing Book (1 of 2) Memo for President no. 32, and Wilson Briefing Book (2 of 2) no. 57.
19. Barbara Castle *The Castle Diaries 1964–70* (London, 1984), intro. p. xiv; George W. Ball *The Past Has Another Pattern* (New York, 1982) p. 336; George Brown, *In My Way* (London 1971) p. 146.
20. Harold Wilson, *The Labour Government 1964–70: A Personal Record* (London, 1971) p. 80.
21. *FRUS 1964–68*, II, pp. 230, 716–17.
22. LBJ Lib, NSF Country File UK, box 212, vol. 15, no. 55/b; NSF, Memos to the President, box 3, June 1965 (2 of 2); George Brown, *In My Way*, pp. 141–2.
23. LBJ Lib, NSF Country File UK, box 207, UK Cables vol. 3, 2/65–4/65, no. 35.
24. LBJ Lib, NSF Country File UK, box 216, Wilson Briefing Book (2 of 2), no. 57; (1 of 2), no. 2.
25. LBJ Lib, President's Confidential File box 12, CO35 UK 1965, letter from Galbraith 9 March 1965; UK 1966, Memo for the President from R.E. Kintner, 7 July 1966.
26. R.H.S. Crossman, *The Diaries of a Cabinet Minister, Vol. II, 1966–8* (London, 1976) p. 237; Tony Benn, *Out of the Wilderness, Diaries 1963–67* (London, 1987) p. 446.
27. PRO. PREM 13/104 fol. 67; LBJ Lib, NSF Country File UK, box 213, PM Wilson visit December 64, no. 5; box 208, UK Cables 7/65–9/65, no. 146.
28. LBJ Lib, NSF Country File UK, box 215, Memo for President , 28 July 1965; *FRUS 1964–68*, III, p. 644; Wilson, *The Labour Government*, p. 264.
29. Steve Hoadley, *The New Zealand Foreign Affairs Handbook*, 2nd edn (Auckland, 1992), pp. 19, 95–7; G.W. Rice (ed.), *The Oxford History of New Zealand*.
30. *The Castle Diaries*, pp. 37, 40; *FRUS 1964–68*, III, pp. 15, 11; LBJ Lib NSF box 207, UK Cables, vol. 5, 6/65, no. 30.
31. *FRUS 1964–68*, III, p. 40; *The Castle Diaries*, p. 46.
32. *The Times*, 1966, 5 January p. 6, 22 January p. 6, 28 January p. 12.
33. Wilson, *The Labour Government*, pp. 214, 254.
34. LBJ Lib, NSF Country File box 209, UK Cables, vol. VIII, 1/66–7/66, Doc 8; ibid, box 216, PM Wilson Briefing Book (1 of 2) Doc 21.
35. Anatoly Dobrynin, *In Confidence, Moscow's Ambassador to America's Six cold war Presidents 1962–1968* (New York, 1995) p. 155.
36. Lyndon B. Johnson, *The Vantage Point, Perspectives of the Presidency, 1963–1969* (London, 1972) p. 255.

37. Harold Wilson, *The Labour Government*, p. 365; LBJ Lib, Oral Histories. Chester L. Cooper, AC74–200, interview 3, p. 19.
38. *The Times*, 15 February 1967, p. 18; Crossman, *Diaries Vol. II*, p. 499.
39. LBJ Lib, NSF UK box 211, vol IX, no. 109; ibid, box 212, Memos vol. XIII, nos. 231, 334.
40. LBJ Lib, NSF UK box 211, UK Cables XII no. 94; Crossman, *Diaries Vol. II*, p. 499; *The Castle Diaries*, p. 300.
41. LBJ Lib, NSF UK box 210, UK Memos X, no. 143a; ibid., boxes 211–2, UK Cables XII, nos. 27a, 103.
42. LBJ Oral Histories, David K.E. Bruce AC73–39, part 2, pp. 6–7.
43. Crossman, *Diaries Vol. III*, p. 240; Kenneth Morgan, *The People's Peace, British History 1945–89* (Oxford, 1990), p. 293; *Parliamentary Debates*, House of Commons, Series V, vol. 837, cols. 60, 98 and vol. 849, col. 461.
44. Bertrand Russell, *Autobiography, Vol. 3 1944–67* (London, 1969), pp. 158–64, 169–71; Tom Wells, *The War Within, America's Battle over Vietnam* (Berkeley and London, 1994), pp. 141–3.
45. LBJ Lib, NSF Intelligence File Boxes 2, 3, 5; 8, 9 no. 1a, 15 November 1967.
46. Tariq Ali, *Streetfighting Years* (London, 1987) *passim*.
47. *FRUS 1964–68*, III, pp. 269–70, 617, 686.
48. *Ibid*. II, p. 292; III p. 112.
49. Dennis L. Bark and David R. Green, *A History of West Germany*, vol. 2, *Democracy and its Discontents 1963–80* (Oxford 1989) pp. 24, 41, 46, 54, 164–5.
50. Tariq Ali, pp. 122–3; Franklin D. Scott, *Sweden, The Nation's History* (Minneapolis, 1971), p. 511; George C. Herring (ed.), *The Secret Diplomacy of the Vietnam War. The Negotiating Volumes of the Pentagon Papers* (Austin, Texas, 1983), p. 531.
51. Henry A. Kissinger, *White House Years* (London, 1979), p. 104.
52. PRO. FO 371/180527 DV103110/3/G; *FRUS 1964–8*, III, p. 289.
53. Johnson, *The Vantage Point*, pp. 378–80; Herring, *Secret Diplomacy*, p. 775.
54. Herring, *Secret Diplomacy*, p. 522.
55. Johnson, p. 578.
56. *FRUS 1964–8*, III, pp. 560, 720, LBJ Lib, NSF, NSC meetings file, box 2, no. 3.
57. Johnson, pp. 579–91; *FRUS 1964–8*, III, p. 239; LBJ Lib NSF Memos to the President, box 6, McGeorge Bundy, 1–18 January 1966, no. 19.
58. Johnson, pp. 422, 502–5, 531.
59. Kissinger, pp. 266, 439, 1043–4; Kent Sieg, 'The Lodge Peace Mission of 1969 and Nixon's Vietnam Policy', *Diplomacy and Statecraft*, 7(1) (March 1996) pp. 175–96.
60. Stephen E. Ambrose, *Nixon*, vol. 2, *The Triumph of a Politician 1962–72* (New York, 1989) pp. 278–9.
61. Allen E. Goodman, *The Lost Peace: America's Search for a Negotiated Settlement of the Vietnam War* (Stanford, California, 1978), pp. 60, 70–2, 76–7; Kissinger, p. 1353.
62. George C. Herring, *America's Longest War. The United States and Vietnam 1950–75* (New York, 1979), pp. 222–44; Kissinger, pp. 698, 762; LBJ Lib NSC Meeting Notes File box 1, 27 January 1966.
63. Herring, *America's Longest War*, pp. 254–61.

INDEX